Lake Baikal
Siberia's Great Lake

the Bradt Travel Guide

Marc Di Duca

www.bradtguides.com

Bradt Travel Guides Ltd, UK
The Globe Pequot Press Inc, USA

edition
1

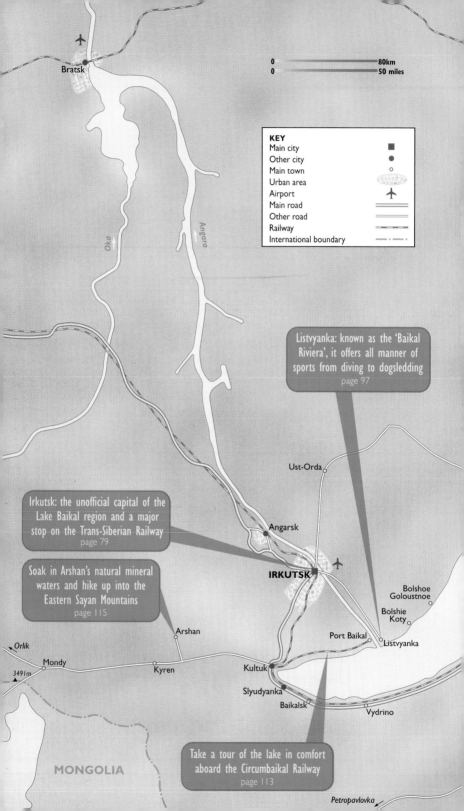

Bratsk

0 | 80km
0 | 50 miles

KEY
Main city ■
Other city ●
Main town ○
Urban area
Airport ✈
Main road
Other road
Railway
International boundary

Oka

Angara

Listvyanka: known as the 'Baikal Riviera', it offers all manner of sports from diving to dogsledding
page 97

Ust-Orda

Irkutsk: the unofficial capital of the Lake Baikal region and a major stop on the Trans-Siberian Railway
page 79

Angarsk

IRKUTSK

Soak in Arshan's natural mineral waters and hike up into the Eastern Sayan Mountains
page 115

Bolshoe Goloustnoe

Bolshie Koty

Orlik

Arshan

3491m

Mondy

Kyren

Port Baikal

Listvyanka

Kultuk

Slyudyanka

Baikalsk

Vydrino

MONGOLIA

Take a tour of the lake in comfort aboard the Circumbaikal Railway
page 113

Petropavlovka

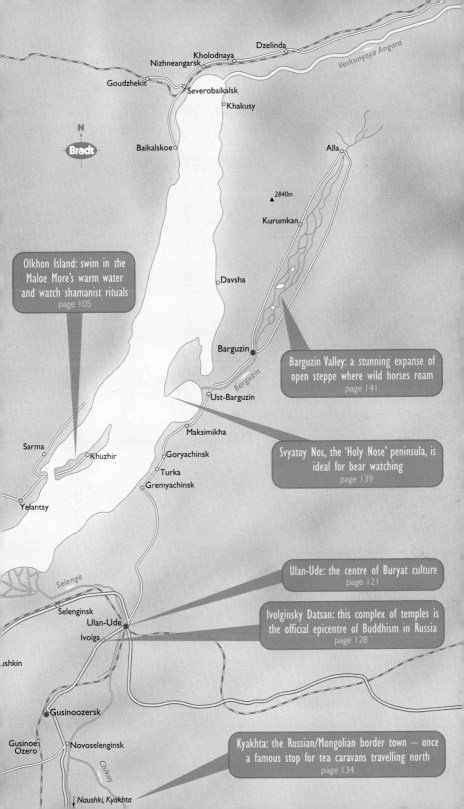

N

Bradt

Kholodnaya
Dzelinda
Nizhneangarsk
Verkunyaya Angara
Goudzhekit
Severobaikalsk
Khakusy
Baikalskoe

Alla

▲ 2840m

Kurumkan

Olkhon Island: swim in the Maloe More's warm water and watch shamanist rituals
page 105

Davsha

Barguzin

Barguzin Valley: a stunning expanse of open steppe where wild horses roam
page 141

Barguzin

Ust-Barguzin

Maksimikha

Svyatoy Nos, the 'Holy Nose' peninsula, is ideal for bear watching
page 139

Sarma
Khuzhir
Goryachinsk
Turka
Gremyachinsk

Yelantsy

LAKE BAIKAL

Selenga

Ulan-Ude: the centre of Buryat culture
page 121

Selenginsk
Ulan-Ude
Ivolga

Ivolginsky Datsan: this complex of temples is the official epicentre of Buddhism in Russia
page 128

ushkin

Gusinoozersk

Gusinoe Ozero
Novoselenginsk

Chikoy

Kyakhta: the Russian/Mongolian border town — once a famous stop for tea caravans travelling north
page 134

↓ Naushki, Kyakhta

Lake Baikal

Don't miss...

Trans-Mongolian/Trans-Siberian railways
Experience the world's most legendary rail journeys
(MDD) pages 120 and 43

Lake Baikal in winter
The lake contains enough water to cover the entire earth in a 20cm puddle (JTBPC/Alamy) page 5

Buddhist temples
Ivolginsky Datsan,
near Ulan-Ude
(P/D) page 128

**Nerpa seals on the
Ushkanie Islands**
One of only two species
of freshwater seal
in the world
(I/FLPA) page 140

Olkhon Island
Shaman Rock — one of
the lake's most
photogenic shorelines
(MDD) page 110

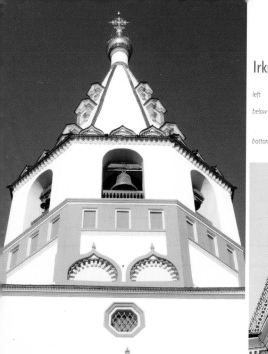

Irkutsk

left Bogoyavlensky cathedral (T/D) page 89

below Elaborately carved eaves of a traditional wooden house (MDD) page 79

bottom Food market (WK/Alamy) page 87

above left   **Typical Siberian block of flats** (MDD) page 79

above right   **Irkutsk's Lenin statue — just one of thousands still standing across the Russian Federation** (MDD) page 90

below   **Singers in traditional costume** (BB/Alamy)

Olkhon Island

AUTHOR

Born in the UK, **Marc Di Duca** (*www.marcdiduca.com*) became enthralled by all things Slavic during almost two decades of living, working and travelling in post-Communist eastern Europe. Fifteen trips to Russia and Ukraine have provided him with a deep insight into life in those countries, an admiration for their peoples and an appreciation of their cultures and ways of life. His Ukrainian wife and in-laws have armed him with a sound knowledge of Russian to add to his fluent Czech.

A respected travel author, Marc has written guidebooks to destinations as diverse as Madeira, Britain and Siberia for most mainstream travel publishers. He unashamedly admits that it was the trainspotter's travel dream of riding the Trans-Siberian Railway that first drew his gaze across the map of Russia to rest on Siberia's own watery eye – Lake Baikal.

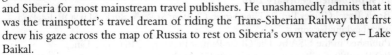

AUTHOR'S STORY

Colin Thubron's definitive Siberian travelogue *In Siberia* has given many a traveller itchy feet, usually followed by a rummage on the internet for 'Trans-Siberian Railway timetables' and daydreams of a slow journey east. So when Bradt approached me to write the first English-language guide to Siberia's Lake Baikal, I jumped at the chance, as even after two decades of life, work and travel in the former communist world, the idea of following, at least partially, in Thubron's footsteps was a tantalising prospect.

Inspired by tales of Siberia, armed with my kitchen-table Russian and enthused by the idea of putting this enticing destination on high-street bookstore shelves, I headed east across the Eurasian steppe. Though intrigued back home by the mind-boggling wilderness and the weird-and-wonderful life forms inhabiting the depths of the world's deepest lake, on the ground it was the human story and diverse cultures of this remote corner of the globe that made my trips to Lake Baikal so absorbing. But research in Eastern Siberia is definitely a case of taking the rough with the smooth. Despite its obvious attraction for tourists and potential as a popular destination, Lake Baikal's infrastructure is threadbare, its people often grumpy and Russian bureaucracy inept and Byzantine. But a smile and a little perseverance are usually enough to see you through, and months of travel in the region allowed me to scratch the surface and discover the Russians' (and Buryats') love of this Sacred Sea, and their overwhelming and genuine hospitality towards those who come to explore its shores.

Of course all credit must go to Bradt for commissioning this ground-breaking guide, the first in English dedicated solely to Lake Baikal. Most mainstream travel guide publishers would shy away from a guide to any Russian region, most hardly venturing beyond the cultural highlights of Moscow and St Petersburg. This has left the endless expanses of the vast Russian Federation, its cities, cultures, languages and people, virtually unchartered and ripe for the Bradt treatment. In commissioning this guide, Hilary Bradt, Adrian Phillips and Donald Greig have remained true to the Bradt philosophy of publishing books to places straddling the road less travelled, thus opening up another very special part of the globe to intrepid travellers.

PUBLISHER'S FOREWORD   *Adrian Phillips, Publishing Director*

I must confess that there was much 'umming' and 'ahhing' at several Publishing Meetings before we confirmed that we'd proceed with a guide to Lake Baikal. Despite our own enthusiasm, a wholly unscientific straw poll of friends and contacts suggested that few had even heard of the deepest lake on earth. I'm so pleased that we decided to take the plunge (if you'll excuse the pun…). It's extraordinary to think of a single lake holding 20% of the world's freshwater, and its attractions are clearly beginning to garner wider attention – it even featured recently in a BBC travel programme. Marc di Duca is one of the leading writers on eastern Europe, and we're delighted that he has added this exciting, unique title to his Bradt portfolio.

First published February 2010

Bradt Travel Guides Ltd, 23 High Street, Chalfont St Peter, Bucks SL9 9QE, England
www.bradtguides.com
Published in the USA by The Globe Pequot Press Inc, 246 Goose Lane,
PO Box 480, Guilford, Connecticut 06475-0480

Text copyright © 2009 Marc Di Duca
Maps copyright © 2009 Bradt Travel Guides Ltd
Photographs copyright © 2009 Individual photographers
Editorial Project Manager: Emma Thomson

ISBN-13: 978 1 84162 294 1

British Library Cataloguing in Publication Data
A catalogue record for this book is available from the British Library

Photographs Alexkar08/Dreamstime (A/D), Aurora Photos/Alamy (AP/Alamy), Bill Bachmann/Alamy (BB/Alamy), Blickwinkel/Alamy (B/Alamy), Chelovek/Dreamstime (C/D), Dickie Duckett/FLPA (DD/FLPA), Donald M Jones/Minden Pictures/FLPA (DMJ/MP/FLPA), Franz Faltermaier/Westend 61 GmbH/Alamy (FF/W/Alamy), Iain Masterton/Alamy (IM/Alamy), Imagebroker/FLPA (I/FLPA), JTB Photo Communications/Alamy (JTBPC/Alamy), Kalervo Ojutkangas/Nordicphotos/Alamy (KO/N/Alamy), Konrad Wothe/Minden Pictures/FLPA (KW/MP/FLPA), Marc Di Duca (MDD), NASA/Alamy (N/Alamy), Oleg Moiseyenko/Alamy (OM/Alamy), Olivier Renck/Aurora Photos/Alamy (OR/AP/Alamy), Peter Shmelev (PS), Pimenova/Dreamstime (P/D), TKV/Dreamstime (T/D), Neil Bowman/FLPA (NB/FLPA), Terry Whittaker/FLPA (TW/FLPA), Winfried Wisniewski/FLPA (WW/FLPA), Wolfgang Kaehler/Alamy (WK/Alamy)
Front cover Shaman rock on Olkhon Island (PS)
Back cover Circumbaikal railway (OM/Alamy), Buryat woman in traditional wedding attire, Olkhon Island (OR/AP/Alamy)
Title page Old Believer, Tarbagatay (MDD), Tearoom sign at Taltsy Museum (MDD), Sacred tree, Olkhon Island (MDD)
Maps Maria Randall, Malcolm Barnes (colour map)

Typeset from the author's disc by Wakewing, High Wycombe
Printed and bound in India by Nutech Print Services

Acknowledgements

A huge спасибо (thank you) goes to: Adrian Phillips of Bradt Guides for having the pluck to commission the first English-language travel guide to a region of Russia; Hilary Bradt for coming up with the original idea; Jack (Yevgeny) Sheremetoff for his amazing support, kindness and hospitality throughout my time in Irkutsk; Sesegma (Svetlana) Rabdanova of Baikal Naran Tour for showing me the wonders of Buryatiya and for use of her apartment in Ulan-Ude; all the staff at Baikal Naran Tour for the tours and for answering my incessant questions; Valera Semeykin for the free bed and delicious breakfast in Listvyanka; Evgeny Maryasov for his enthusiasm, hospitality and the unforgettable hike from Baikalskoe; the Beketovs of Ust-Barguzin for their hospitality and great food; Alyona Maryasova for opening a hostel in Severobaikalsk (and letting me stay there); Nikita Bencharov for the log cabin on Olkhon Island; Tanya Kalinina for her advice and moral support throughout, and for her work on the language section; Rachel Mikos in Prague for sharing her deep knowledge of the Mongolian world; Sue in Eastbourne for her steady supply of Siberia-related newspaper articles; Sheryl Mera for the Trans-Siberian guide and useful advice; Heike Mall and Roger Just, authors of the *Baikal See und Region* guide; all at Meridian109 in Nizhneangarsk; the staff of Real Russia in London for sorting out my Russian visa; post-Soviet connoisseur René Fischer for the nights out 'researching' in Irkutsk and his amusing website; Tom Umbreit at Baikalplan in Dresden; and everyone else I met in eastern Siberia who drove me, fed me, suffered my Russian and welcomed me into their homes.

DEDICATION

To my grandmothers: Elsie Clark and Bertha Di Duca

Contents

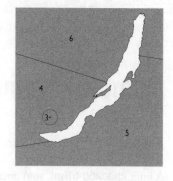

UPDATES WEBSITE

For the latest travel news about Lake Baikal, please visit the new interactive Bradt update website: http://updates.bradtguides.com.

This update website is a free service for readers and for anybody else who cares to drop by and browse, so if you have any comments, queries, grumbles, insights, news or other feedback, you're invited to post them on the website.

LIST OF MAPS

Introduction

For many, Siberia is the last blank space in the atlas, a vast and meaningless void too immense to even imagine, a gigantic chunk of steppe and nameless forest bound in eternal ice and snow, where nothing has ever happened. But one feature breaks the monotony, one stretch of blue interrupts the sea of anonymous earth, like a tear in Siberia's cloth – the curve of Lake Baikal, Siberia's watery eye, its pearl, its focus.

As you are about to discover in the pages of this book, Lake Baikal is a truly astonishing place. It is the world's deepest lake, holding a fifth of the world's fresh water, and one of the most ancient geographical features on the planet, estimated to be 25–30 million years old. Away from mind-bending numbers and superlatives, Baikal's normally mild-mannered and drinkably pure waters are backed by a wall of mountain peaks, creating some seriously jaw-dropping vistas even in populated areas. Long isolated from their original ancestors, some of Baikal's species of flora and fauna have performed almost Australasian transformations, with many weird and wonderful fish and animals inhabiting dry land and chilly water. Summer sees the lake's beaches and campsites swarm with Russians on once-a-year warm-weather get-aways from Siberia's superheated mega-cities. And yet, despite Lake Baikal's significance, beauty and popularity within Russia, surprisingly few in the West know much about it.

Of course a guide to a lake could never be just about the water itself, and must focus on what defines the lake – the surrounding land and its people. A trip to the Baikal region is a journey into a little-known corner of Asia inhabited by a fascinating jumble of cultures, from the indigenous semi-nomadic Evenk in his wooden tepee to the city-dwelling Buryat, from the Catholic descendant of Polish exiles to the mobile-phone-toting Russian businessman whose lifestyle differs little from his European counterparts. Baikal is also a place where Buddhism, shamanism and Orthodox Christianity clash and merge, the lines between them often blurred in superstition and by fear of a fickle environment. The flayed eaves of Buddhist temples, onion-domed Orthodox churches and shaggily adorned shamanistic sites dot land- and cityscape, all working places of worship where travellers can witness religion in the raw. When temple fatigue kicks in, few places are better than eastern Siberia for flits into untamed backcountry and unpeopled landscapes. New trails are being marked out, countless peaks await the hiker's boot and even the lake itself becomes traversable when subzero temperatures from January through to May freeze its surface hard as steel.

Most travellers call at Lake Baikal's pebbly shores via the Trans-Siberian Railway, swapping the snug confines of four-bunk compartments for outings into the boundless wilderness, before re-boarding for onward journeys to Moscow, Beijing or Ulaanbaatar. However, an increasing number of Europeans are choosing to visit Baikal as a destination in its own right, taking two or more weeks to explore further than Irkutsk and Listvyanka and access less-beaten tracks. An ever-growing number of tour companies now offer tours to the region, though most who make it to this neck of the taiga normally approach travel from an independent point of view. A fascinatingly hands-on way of experiencing Baikal is as a volunteer on one of the trail construction projects organised by the Great Baikal Trail (see page 105).

Lake Baikal and the surrounding region is certainly not a classic come-for-the-weather holiday destination, and eastern Siberia's cities, towns and resorts are pretty rough-hewn and unpolished. Away from the railway lines, transport infrastructure is skeletal and ad hoc, with some outlying locations virtually unconnected to the outside world. Accommodation in the cities can range from Western luxury to Asian crash pad, and eateries are, for the most part, portion-miserly but price-flamboyant. Customer service is still largely an alien notion in eastern Siberia, as is the provision of unbiased tourist information and the need for staff to speak foreign languages. But for many travellers it is precisely this unrefined character that makes Baikal such a fascinating place to visit, and one where an authentic travel experience can still be had, a world away from the world's mainstream holiday industry. So master a few Russian phrases, embrace the post-Soviet disarray, soak up Baikal's incredible wide-screen views and feel the timelessness of this mythical wilderness all around you, and your time around Siberia's sacred sea will have been well spent.

FEEDBACK REQUEST

Russia is a country in transition where things are in a constant state of flux. Parts of the Baikal region have been declared a 'tourist zone' by the Russian authorities, meaning big changes can be expected in the coming years, with major developments in the pipeline and some controversial projects set to get under way. If on your travels you discover something you think deserves attention in future editions, such as a new hotel, museum, restaurant or method of transport, especially in the more remote parts of the region, please get in touch with me at e info@bradtguides.com. I'd also be interested in hearing about your travel experiences around Lake Baikal, and about anything you think should be included in future editions of this book.

Part One

GENERAL INFORMATION

LAKE BAIKAL AND THE REGION AT A GLANCE

Location Eastern Siberia, on the border between Russia and Mongolia, at 51°27'N–55°46'N and 103°43'E–109°56'E

Area of the lake 31,500km²

Geography Deep lake contained by cliffs, hills and mountain ranges

Climate Extreme continental climate with sub-zero winters and very hot summers; average temperature (Irkutsk) January –20°C, July +20°C

Administrative divisions Republic of Buryatiya along the eastern and northern shores, Irkutsk oblast along the western and southern shores

Main cities Irkutsk, Ulan-Ude

Other major settlements Severobaikalsk, Nizhneangarsk, Ust-Barguzin, Angarsk, Slyudyanka, Kyakhta

People Russians, Buryats, Evenks, others (Ukrainians, Poles, Chinese, Byelorussians, citizens of all other former Soviet republics).

Life expectancy 73 years for females, 59 years for males

Languages Russian, Buryat, Evenk

Religions Orthodox Christianity, Buddhism, shamanism

Currency Russian rouble (RUB)

Exchange rate €1 = RUB43, £1 = RUB47, US$1 = RUB30 (Oct 2009)

International dialling code +7

Time GMT + 8 hours

Electricity AC 220V, 50Hz

Flags Russia: three equal horizontal bands of white (top), blue, and red. Buryatiya: three horizontal bands of blue (occupying the top half of the flag), white and yellow; in the upper left hand corner is a yellow soyombo, the traditional symbol of Buryatiya representing the moon, the sun and a hearth. Irkutsk oblast (region): three vertical stripes, two blue bordering a larger white middle stripe. In the centre of the white stripe is an unidentified animal called a 'babr' facing left and holding a red sable in its mouth. This is sometimes ringed with a wreath of cedar twigs.

Background Information

GEOGRAPHY

> How good it is to have Baikal! Mighty, rich, majestic and beautiful in so many ways, regal and untamed – how good that she is ours.
>
> Valentin Rasputin (see box on page 72)

THE REGION Very rarely will a local talk about 'the Baikal region', as strictly speaking no entity of this name exists. You may occasionally hear people speak of the 'Pribaikalye' (the area around Baikal) and 'Zabaikalye' (a large area east of Baikal), but in this guide, for simplicity's sake, we will use the term 'Baikal region', meaning the lake and the surrounding area.

The region occupies an area to the north of Mongolia approximately the size of Germany and located roughly 4,300km east of Moscow and 1,600km northwest of Beijing as the crow flies. The western side of the lake is dominated by the Irkutsk oblast (region), with Irkutsk as its capital; the eastern shore by the Republic of Buryatiya, centred around the city of Ulan-Ude (see *Administrative Divisions*, page 20). Most of the region, save for around the two main cities and along the Trans-Siberian Railway, is sparsely populated, and some areas in the north are completely uninhabited.

THE LAKE Take a look at a map of Siberia, and the banana-shaped slit of blue in its southern reaches immediately stands out as the most discernible natural feature. Some 636km long and 27–81km wide, Lake Baikal's shores create a gently curving arc of almost 90° (west to north), from Kultuk at the bottom to Yarki Island at the top, and at 31,500km^2 Baikal is the eighth-largest lake in the world by area.

The above figures would be remarkable on their own, but Lake Baikal is not an extraordinary place for its area or location alone. Further statistics relating to this 'glorious sea', as the Russians call Baikal, are simply mind-boggling: it's estimated that the lake first appeared 25–30 million years ago, making it by far the world's oldest and one of the most ancient geographical features on the planet. It's also the deepest lake on earth, with a maximum depth near Olkhon Island of 1,637m (over a mile!). With a total volume of over 23,000km^3 (more than all of the Great Lakes of North America put together), Baikal contains over a fifth of the earth's fresh water, enough to cover the entire surface of the planet in a 20cm-deep puddle. Another amazing statistic is that it would take a year for all the rivers in the world – the Nile, Amazon, Mississippi, Danube and Siberia's own great waterways included – to fill Baikal's empty basin. Scientists also think there may be several kilometres of sediment at the bottom, though accurate measurements have proved impossible to take. Baikal's incredible array of facts and figures make North America's Great Lakes look like shallow ponds, Lake Victoria a youthful puddle and Loch Ness a bathtub with a worm at the bottom.

Call Baikal a lake in the presence of anyone who lives on its shores and you will be corrected – 'Baikal is a sea' they say, and in many ways they're right. In millions of years' time the fault line which runs along the western shore, and tugs apart the two sides of this rift valley by four to six millimetres a year, will have rent asunder the continent of Asia, creating the world's fifth ocean. As the earth's crust performs its slow-motion split, the region experiences high levels of seismic activity, especially around the Selenga Delta in the north, though powerful earth tremors are rare.

Baikal's tributaries drain an area the size of Britain and France put together, reaching well over the border into Mongolia. The lake is fed by over 300 rivers and streams, but quite incredibly is drained by just one, the mighty Angara. This in turn is a tributary of the even mightier Yenisey, which eventually conveys Baikal's waters to the Arctic.

Natural features Baikal's crystal-clear waters are interrupted along both shores by a number of natural features which are both ancient shamanistic sites and popular tourist attractions. Two deltas seep into the lake – the Selenga Delta on the eastern shore, popular with birdwatchers, and the Verkhnyaya Angara Delta in the north. Thirty islands dot its shimmering waters, the largest of which is Olkhon on the west coast, the only inhabited island. The Svyatoy Nos Peninsula is a remarkable sight – a 1,877m-high mountain stranded offshore like a beached humpback whale. Only the sandbar linking it to the shore prevents it from joining the ranks of Baikal's islands. Some 174 capes, regiments of high cliffs and innumerable shallow bays give way to long beaches of both the pebbly and sandy type, ideal for summer wild-camping fun.

Sister lake Khövsgöl in northern Mongolia is often regarded as Baikal's sister lake. Similarly of the rift variety, Khövsgöl is also considered sacred by local shamans, though it's far less popular among tourists (mostly as it's hard to reach). The lake is also linked physically with Baikal as it's drained by the Egiin gol, a tributary of the Selenga which enters Baikal at the Selenga Delta.

THE LAND Lake Baikal's 2,000km of shoreline is ringed with a hinterland wall of mountain, carpeted in many places with impenetrably rich taiga (coniferous forest). To the south the landscape opens out into steppe as Russia fades and Mongolia takes over. This transition and the lake itself create an incredibly diverse range of landscapes, from alpine valleys and lakes to delta wetlands, and from the wilderness of the endless forest to the open spaces of the parched southern plains.

Mountains Baikal views are given the 'wow' factor by the countless peaks which rise from its shores and which become ever more dramatic the further north you progress. In the south the **Khamar Daban** range, visible from Listvyanka across the lake, reaches a height of over 2,100m and divides Baikal from the dry plains south of Ulan-Ude. The western shore is lined by the peaks of the Primorsky and the Baikalsky ranges, while northeastern vistas are generated by the Barguzinsky range, separating Baikal from the wide Barguzin Valley. However, the best known range in the region is the Eastern Sayan Mountains, which hem the Tunka Valley to the southwest. Their highest peak is Munku Sardyk (3,491m) near Mondy (see page 117).

Rivers Two of Siberia's great rivers have their source in the Baikal region. The Angara flows out of Lake Baikal between Listvyanka and Port Baikal, and begins its 1,779km journey across eastern Siberia via Irkutsk and Bratsk to join the Yenisey near the town of Lesosibirsk. But the real star of the show is the Lena, the world's tenth-longest river, which rises in the Baikalsky Mountains on Baikal's western shore. From there it flows an incredible 4,472 (mostly navigable) kilometres via Yakutsk to the Laptev Sea, where it creates a truly huge delta. In summer, it's possible to take a cruise ship from Ust-Kut on the BAM Railway (see page 150) all the way to Yakutsk, a journey of several thousand kilometres! Other rivers include the Barguzin, which rises to the west of Lake Baikal and flows 480km via the Barguzin Valley and the towns of Barguzin and Ust-Barguzin before emptying into the lake; the Verkhnyaya Angara, which creates a delta at the very northern tip of the lake; and the Selenga, which drains a huge area of Mongolia before meandering across the border to dump its cargo of water and sand into Baikal at the Selenga Delta.

CLIMATE

Eastern Siberia's extreme continental climate means fridge-freezer cold winters and oven-hot summers, with very short-lived autumns and springs squeezed in between. Winter is the longest season (as you might expect in Siberia), starting in late October/early November and not relinquishing its tight grip until well into April. Temperatures at the lakeside and in the surrounding region can differ enormously, with the large body of water taking the harsh edge off winters and summers alike. The average July figure in Irkutsk and Ulan-Ude is around 20°C;

in January this sinks to –20°C in Irkutsk and –25°C in Ulan-Ude. The summer value is slightly misleading, as the mercury often stays above 30°C for days on end in June and July. Winter lows reaching –45°C are common though never last for long. Whatever the temperature is in Irkutsk, for Lake Baikal take off five to ten degrees in summer, and add the same in winter. This difference is particularly pleasant in summer when the gentle breeze wafting across the water provides relief from the dust-plagued, superheated city streets.

The wettest months of the year are normally June, July and August, and most snow falls in November and December before the extreme temperature lows begin to bite. On average it rains around twice as much in Irkutsk as it does in Ulan-Ude, and southern Buryatiya is generally drier than further north and west.

For five months of the year (January through to May) Baikal is frozen over with an ice sheet 40–120cm thick forming on its surface. Baikal dons its icy winter coat sometimes months after most of its tributaries have solidified, and it's not fully understood why this happens. What is certain, however, is that the lake is possibly at its most attractive for the four months you can walk and drive across it.

HISTORY

Swotting up on the region's past before you leave home may be a good idea, otherwise eastern Siberia's historical procession of Decembrists, kurgans and Kurykan tribes will make little sense, even to those with a generally sound overview of history. Baikal's story is often specific to the region, at other times needs an understanding of Siberia-wide events, and occasionally requires a comprehension of pan-Russian and even world affairs. The following pages provide an outline of these overlapping narratives, and you can easily add more flesh to these bones during visits to the many regional museums across the Irkutsk oblast and Republic of Buryatiya.

The single greatest impediment to examining the history of any Russian region is the relative lack of trustworthy 20th-century accounts. Soviet historians had a political agenda – to make the Soviet experiment and Moscow's Marxist-Leninist policies seem like the natural culmination of millennia of man's existence on the planet. Even in scholarly accounts of individual historical periods, whole chapters are dedicated to insignificant peasant revolts, minor strikes elevated to major political upheavals and the slightest notion of class struggle magnified tenfold, all at the expense of a balanced description of events. Guides, pamphlets, brochures and museum exhibitions still very often have visitors view history through this distorted Soviet prism, though newer material may be slightly more balanced in its approach.

One historical fact you can be sure of is that more has happened around the lake in the past four centuries than in the previous 30 million years! The arrival of the Cossacks in the 17th century set the region alight, and was perhaps the most significant event in Baikal's history to date. It brought under Muscovy a land which had for centuries maintained close ties with Mongolia and had little or no contact with European civilisation. Though the Russians and native Buryats clashed at first, today there is no sign of any historical animosity, unlike in many other corners of the vast former Russian Empire.

Baikal's story emerges from geology and seismology around 100,000 years ago when milder conditions reigned here than in Europe and most of Asia. This brought waves of migration to the area, the first in a long series of human movements across the steppe which, it could be said, is still ongoing today. Since that time Baikal's history has been a tale of migration and conquest, of exile and refuge, and of a mixing and blending of peoples, cultures and religions from the two worlds which make up the Russian Federation – Europe and Asia.

EARLY CIVILISATIONS

Scythians Baikal's first nameable inhabitants belonged to the Scythian culture which from 1000BC until around AD500 extended across central Asia to Ukraine and as far south as Iran and northern India. Normally depicted as savage nomads charging bareback across the Eurasian steppe, firing off poison arrows as they gallop along, the Scythians were, it has been discovered, more civilised and their society more structured than this image would have us believe. Their loose empire, described in brief by Herodotus, left the landscape dotted with so-called *kurgans* (burial mounds) and richly decorated standing stones (mainly found in Buryatiya). These tombs have been excavated across southern Siberia, with some of the most famous digs taking place in the Altai and Tuva republics of the Russian Federation. Permafrost preserved the mummified bodies of nobles buried alongside their horses, and some graves contained kilograms of intricately cast gold armour, hinting at the wealth and sophistication of this little-known civilisation. No such treasures have emerged from Buryatiya's *kurgans* but many have yet to be excavated.

Huns The marauding Huns called time on the Scythian Empire in this corner of Eurasia in the 2nd century BC. They arrived in waves from what is now Inner Mongolia following their defeat by the Han Chinese, and dominated the Baikal region for around three centuries. It would be simplistic to claim that this was the beginning of their migration west, culminating in the rule of Attila the Hun and their invasion of Europe, but some link must exist. Some of the best archaeological evidence of the Huns' presence in the region originates from a place called Ilmovaya Pad, 23km north of Kyakhta, where excavations have revealed around 320 graves dating from the second and first centuries BC.

Kurykan The Hunnic Empire evaporated in the 1st century AD, allowing Turkic-speaking nomadic tribes gradually to move into the region. This included the Kurykan people, who buried their dead in similar ways to the Scythians. The strongest evidence of their existence can be found on Olkhon Island, around Ust-Orda, along the Angara River, on the Svyatoy Nos Peninsula and in the Barguzin Valley. Cliffs and rocks across eastern Siberia are still daubed with their match-stick petroglyphs, often depicting animals and hunting scenes, and they also had a sophisticated writing system using a runic script.

Most of the above concerns the steppe of the southern Baikal region. But from the Neolithic period until the decades of Stalinist collectivisation, the **Evenks** (a Tungus-Manchu people) hunted and lived in their timber *chums* (tepees) in the forests of the north, as ignorant of the outside world as the Indians of North America with whom they share much. Today they are regarded as the 'original' Baikal inhabitants, though few remain and their nomadic lifestyle has been stifled by European bricks and mortar.

EMERGENCE OF THE BURYATS Minus the barbed wire, rubber stamps and Kalashnikov-toting guards of today's border, it's somewhat misleading to describe the Buryat-Mongol people as 'entering' the Baikal region from Mongolia. Without even a natural border to divide the two areas, the process was probably more of a filtering in over several centuries, as Mongol tribes joined a people on the shores of Lake Baikal with whom they shared much. Archaeological evidence such as pottery design and burial sites suggests that the Kurykan people and Mongols probably existed side-by-side from around the 10th to the 12th centuries, before both assimilating into one ethnicity. It's thought some Kurykan headed north and assimilated with Tungus-Manchu tribes to form the Yakut people, while many stayed around Lake Baikal and merged with the Mongols. Evidence of this assimilation process comes from the fact that the Buryat language contains many Turkic elements which Mongolian does not. One thing is clear – by the end of the 12th century the Kurykan were no more, and a new ethnic group had come to dominate.

GENGHIS KHAN Decades before Batu Khan's dreaded Mongol hordes arrived at the gates of the cities of eastern Europe, it was the great Genghis (Chinggis) Khan who had managed to unite the Mongol peoples in the late 12th century. This naturally included the Buryats, who rode with him and his descendants against China, Moscow, Kiev and countless other states and cities until they hit the buffers in central Europe. Legend has it that Genghis' mother came from the wide Barguzin Valley on the lake's eastern shore, and that Genghis himself made several visits to Olkhon Island, the Svyatoy Nos Peninsula and the Tunka Valley, but there's no historical proof. The figure of Genghis Khan was a source of tension during the Soviet period (and for the imperial authorities before that) as the Buryats (and naturally the Mongols) see him as a hero who conquered half the earth in their name, while the Russians have, equally understandably, suppressed his legend, depicting him as a savage warlord from the untamed east. Mongolia has renamed its main international airport after its most (in)famous son, his emotionless face peers out from the 1,000 tögrög note and he has become a symbol of a resurgent Mongolian national identity (and dubious tool for the tourist industry), while Buryat parents now name their little boys in his honour and drunken Buryats slur his name in the direction of Western tourists – all to the Russians' mild dismay. In

MONGOL

Anyone with an interest in the Genghis Khan epoch should get hold of a copy of *Mongol*, a thrilling movie released in Russia in late 2007 and directed by Russian filmmaker Sergei Bodrov (www.mongolmovie.com). The film, apparently the first in a series, traces Genghis's early life and was shot in epic style on location in Mongolia. *Mongol* almost swept the board at the 2008 Russian equivalent of the Oscars, winning awards for Best Film, Best Director, Best Cinematography, Best Sound, Best Production Design and Best Costumes. Just like Genghis himself, Bodrov never does anything by halves.

fact it's a wonder the Russians so readily tolerate the naming of restaurants and cafés in Ulan-Ude after him and the general adoration for Eurasia's greatest warlord among the Buryat populace.

ARRIVAL OF THE COSSACKS Three centuries after the Mongols had murdered and pillaged their way across Eurasia, it was the Russians' turn to head east and invade the lands of the once feared hordes. The Cossacks' conquest of Siberia was incredibly swift, sweeping from the Ural Mountains in the west to the Pacific Ocean in the east in little more than half a century. The Russian imperialist conquest of Siberia was of colossal historic, political, cultural and geopolitical significance and is still acting as a significant influence on our own times (most of Moscow's oil and gas is drilled in Siberia). During their land grab to end all land grabs, the Cossacks added an incredible ten million square kilometres of territory to an already bloated empire.

The Cossack leaders who led a motley crew into the unknown were extraordinary men in terms of what they achieved, though the way they achieved it can leave little doubt that they were a ruthless and brutal bunch. Mostly illiterate, criminally minded but God-fearing, these *zemleprokhodtsy* (overland explorers) committed acts of genocide on the local indigenous populations, exploited their labour and resources, and engaged in environmental plunder on a scale not seen in the region before. They took sable and other pelts from the natives in tribute (called the *yasak*, from the Tatar language meaning 'tribute') and gave them disease and alcoholism in return. Most (though not all) of this went on with the blessing of the tsar in Moscow.

First European settlements The Cossacks based their new foothold colonies along the only passable routes across Siberia, namely the great rivers such as the Yenisey, Angara, Lena and Amur. They built *ostrogi* (forts), *ostrozhki* (small forts) and small winter outposts called *zimovya* at strategic locations, mostly on high ground next to these rivers. As the *ostrogi* grew, they became cramped, insanitary places, knocked together in a hurry, usually under native attack, and centred around a *gostinny dvor* (central marketplace). Natives were very often taken as slaves, kidnapped in an attempt to force a tribe to pay the sable tribute, and transferred to the *ostrog*. As a result of the desperate lack of womenfolk, native girls were often spirited into the *ostrog* to serve as prostitutes, a social phenomenon that hadn't existed among the Buryats until that time.

Lake Baikal 'discovered' A Cossack named Kurbat Ivanov stumbled upon Lake Baikal in 1643 and claimed it for the tsar. He crossed Lake Baikal in the north and imposed the *yasak* on the Buryats of the Barguzin Valley. This was the beginning of Russia's relationship with Baikal and the surrounding region which was absorbed into the empire. Four years later a second expedition reached the far northern end of the lake and built the Verkhneangarsky fortress near today's Nizhneangarsk. The *zimovye* at Irkutsk was founded in 1652 to collect the *yasak*, but in 1661 an *ostrog* was constructed to fend off the Buryats, and by 1686 the now rapidly growing settlement had been granted a town charter. By 1699 Irkutsk had 1,000 inhabitants and was already established as the biggest and most important city in Siberia, mostly thanks to its position on the mighty Angara River, which links Lake Baikal and its tributaries with the Yenisey and eventually the Arctic Sea, and the newly formed *trakt* along which migrants from European Russia travelled. The Verkhneudinsky *ostrog* (now Ulan-Ude) appeared in 1666 and had also been elevated to town status by 1689. In addition to Irkutsk, Verkhneangarsk and Verkhneudinsk, the only other *ostrog* established around Lake Baikal was at Barguzin (1648), on the Barguzin River.

From the 1650s onwards the government encouraged settlement in *ostrogi* across the Baikal region in order to establish permanent Russian colonies. In the Cossacks' wake came all kinds of imperial officials, priests, nuns, monks, peasants, merchants and craftsmen. Only a small percentage of these were women, which led to many Russian men taking native wives and fathering mixed-race children. These first Russo-Buryat offspring sometimes worked as interpreters, go-betweens and spies, often able to keep the Russians informed on what the natives were up to.

Buryat resistance Despite what locals in Buryatiya might claim today, Buryat resistance to colonisation was not as fierce as in other parts of Siberia such as Chukotka or Kamchatka. Nevertheless sporadic skirmishes went on for at least 50 years in the middle part of the 17th century, though the Cossack *ostrogi* at Irkutsk and Ulan-Ude (then Verkneudinsk) were never really under serious threat. Buryats occasionally fled into Mongolia to escape the Cossack terror, and even asked their Mongol brothers to help them drive the Russians back whence they came, but to no effect. With superior firearms and better military organisation, the Russian settlers were able to easily subdue the nomadic Buryats and Evenks, who lacked a central social structure, national leaders and effective weapons. The Buryats gradually threw in the towel tribe by tribe, swore an oath to the tsar and paid the annual *yasak*. In 1689 the Treaty of Nerchinsk (a town in the Zabaikalye region beyond Chita) finally set the border between Russia and China, cutting the Buryats' umbilical cord to Mongolia forever.

Effects of colonisation on the Buryats Though far from wiping out the Buryats of the Zabaikalye, the Cossack annexation of their lands inevitably had a huge impact on their lives. Away from the obvious effects of the low-level war they waged against the invaders, fear of the future and the humiliation inflicted upon them by a more powerful foe, the native Buryats suffered in a number of other ways. The Cossacks forced them to overhunt and overfish the taiga, rivers and Baikal itself to supply the *ostrogi*, and when natural stocks ran low the natives became dependent on the Russians' 'western foods'. The Russians brought disease with them across Eurasia, and two epidemics are known to have killed hundreds of Buryats in the mid 18th century. Alcoholism became rife as vodka was introduced to a people not accustomed to drink, a problem which persists to this day. The Cossacks generally didn't consider native Siberians as humans unless they converted to Christianity, and suppressed the local shamanist beliefs wherever they could. Ironically, many superstitiously minded Russians later turned to the shamans for advice and for their ability to foretell the future in the unpredictable and harsh environment of eastern Siberia.

ARRIVAL OF BUDDHISM Thanks to earlier links forged between Genghis Khan and Tibet, the Gelupka School of Tibetan Buddhism was first introduced into Mongolia during the reign of Kublai Khan. This new religion began spreading out from the court and was soon gently pushing aside or merging with the local shamanistic belief system. It was only a matter of time before Buddhism would reach the Mongols' cousins by Lake Baikal, and Tibetan and Mongolian missionaries began to penetrate communities on the eastern shore in the 17th century. The centre of Russian Buddhism was established at the Tamchinsky temple south of Ulan-Ude in 1741, and around 200 *datsans* (temples) were built as the religion slowly took over from traditional shamanistic beliefs here too. However, Buddhism never quite reached communities on the western shore or on Olkhon Island, where shamanism still prevails to this day.

IMMIGRATION AND EXILE While many Cossack pioneers, gold prospectors, tea merchants, government officials and fortune seekers came to eastern Siberia through choice, over the centuries many groups from European Russia were forced to make the long journey across the Eurasian steppe. Soon after the Cossacks had established their wooden stockades across the region, the Muscovite imperial authorities realised that Siberia would serve as a distant place of exile from which criminals and anyone out of favour with the tsar would never be able to return. Exile was also later seen as both an alternative to capital punishment and a quick way of populating Siberia, but the two aims were to prove wholly incompatible.

Despite the Russian government's penal policy, it's a myth that Siberia, at least from the 17th to the 19th centuries, was peopled by exiles; between 1662 and 1898 only around 5–10% of Siberia's population was formed of banishees from European Russia. Most settlers went east of their own accord, and the population rose rapidly through migration and reproduction. However, criminals, though a small minority, had a disproportionate impact on Siberian society as they made the region a dangerous place to live, a little like the American Wild West or Australia under the British.

From the outset, banishment beyond the Urals became the sentence passed for a whole range of minor crimes, though murder and treason were at first still punishable by death. The abolition of capital punishment in 1753 by Empress Elizabeth caused an influx of the most dangerous psychopaths into Siberia. The exile system was poorly administered, and most exiles (in fact some suggest up to 90%) absconded soon after their arrival in Siberia, taking to the taiga to eke out a living murdering travellers, robbing honest settlers and generally terrorising the population. These were no romantic Robin Hood figures, and stripped rich and poor of their possessions without discrimination. Exiles billeted to serve out their punishment in a Siberian village were very often seen as a burden on community life, a drain on resources and not to be trusted; they were thus ostracised by more established settlers. Invariably men, they also exacerbated the already woeful imbalance of the sexes (for centuries there were vastly more men in Siberia than women). Irkutsk had a larger population of exiles and therefore a greater number of escapees, which led in turn to greater lawlessness. The pages of the city's newspapers during the 18th and 19th centuries carried a gruesome daily diet of murders, rapes and hangings.

Following the abolition of serfdom in Russia in 1861, large numbers of land-hungry immigrants started to fan out in all directions from the cramped conditions

Throughout 2008, Russians had the chance to vote in a poll called 'Name of Russia' (*www.nameofrussia.ru*; Russian only), cárried out by the Rossiya TV channel. Its format was similar to the original '100' Greatest Britons' TV programme. The results, announced in late December 2008, caused some astonishment in the Western media when it was revealed that Stalin had finished in third place. Many Russia watchers were equally surprised that he didn't win.

The line-up was as follows:

1 **St Alexander Nevsky** Medieval Grand Prince of Novgorod and Vladimir, who defeated the Swedes on the ice of the River Neva in 1240

2 **Pyotr Arkadyevich Stolypin** Reformist Russian Prime Minister from 1906 to 1911

3 **Joseph Stalin** General Secretary of the Communist Party and Soviet dictator from 1922 until his death in 1953

4 **Alexander Pushkin** Russia's greatest poet, who lived in the early 19th century

5 **Peter the Great** Russian tsar who attempted to Westernise Russia and founded St Petersburg as the new imperial capital in 1703

6 **Lenin** Leader of the 1917 October Revolution and the first Communist head of state

7 **Fyodor Dostoyevsky** One of the most famous Russian novelists of the 19th century

8 **Alexander Suvorov** A great 18th-century general, who never lost a battle

9 **Dmitri Mendeleyev** 19th-century chemist and inventor of the Periodic Table

10 **Ivan the Terrible** First Tsar of all Russia, who lived in the 16th century

11 **Catherine the Great** 18th-century Empress of Russia

12 **Tsar Alexander II** 19th-century tsar who abolished serfdom

and inequalities of European Russia. Many went to Ukraine and central Asia, but the vast majority made the arduous journey along the *trakt* to Siberia. In the late 19th century around 61,000 immigrants were arriving in Siberia every year, though figures for the Baikal region are hard to pin down.

While chain-dragging exiles and ill-fated peasants fade into the pages of history, several more colourful and romantic groups banished to the Baikal region stand out for the contribution they made to the culture of eastern Siberia. The Old Believers (see box on page 128) arrived here in droves from the late 18th century, escaping religious persecution in Europe, while aristocratic Decembrists (see box on page 88) were transported here to a gentile banishment following their botched revolt in 1825. Irkutsk still has a sizeable Polish community today, ancestors of those exiled here following uprisings in Russian-occupied Poland during the 19th century. Even Lenin himself was exiled to Siberia for a few short years in the early 20th century, though the village of Shushenskoe in Khakassia (far from Baikal) hosted his rather stress-free and fervently productive banishment.

EARTHQUAKE AND TSUNAMI In 1861 Russian and Buryat alike were reminded, literally with a jolt, of what a volatile region they inhabited. A truly massive earthquake, with its epicentre a few kilometres to the east of the Selenga Delta, slopped a huge tsunami on to the eastern shore, drowning 1,300 people. The tremor, which measured a whopping 7.5 to 10 (depending on whom you believe) on the

Richter scale, created the shallow Proval Bay east of the delta, instantly plunging 200km² of land under water. Earthquakes are common around the lake, the last biggie coming in 1999. In the north small tremors are almost a daily occurrence.

TRADE Throughout the 18th and 19th centuries, trade had an immeasurable effect on the region's cities, in particular Irkutsk, Ulan-Ude and Kyakhta. In 1762 Catherine the Great abolished the Imperial monopoly on the fur trade and the privilege of sending caravans to Peking. Local merchants began importing tea from China and sending it to Europe along the so-called 'Tea Road'. A million chests of tea a year flooded over the border at Kyakhta, a city which at its zenith boasted more millionaires than the new capital, St Petersburg. Tea bricks – enough to build Moscow and St Petersburg in compacted leaves – found their way to the teahouses of England, while in the other direction went caravans of leather and fur. Kyakhta's fine mansions and churches were financed by these wealthy merchants, and their faded glory can still be made out today. Gold mining helped build and rebuild Irkutsk, while Ulan-Ude creamed off some of the profits of the tea trade.

Some of eastern Siberia's wealthy used their riches to become gentlemen explorers, striking out from Kyakhta and Irkutsk into Mongolia, China and Tibet and stocking the region's museums with exotic paraphernalia on their return. Lacking a nobility and far from the stiff aristocratic conventions of European Russia, the Orthodox Church and the imperial court, Siberia's merchant–adventurers became the swashbuckling celebrities of their day and are still remembered with fondness and admiration.

19TH-CENTURY IRKUTSK By the 19th century the Cossacks' timber stockade had grown into a large city of absurd contrasts and boundless opportunity to make a fast rouble. Both prosperous and squalid, mansions and hovels stood side by side, and a cosmopolitan mix of rich and poor shared the muddy streets. Decembrists arranged literary soirées and built a theatre, while the murder rate soared. In summer the streets ran rancid with sewage, while gentlemen explorers filled salons with delicate works of art brought from across Asia or imported from Europe. Fortunes could be made overnight from gold, and lost almost as quickly in an orgy of drink and gambling – money fuelled a culture of crime, prostitution, vice and murder. But profits were also set in stone in the shape of grand residences; for instance, the White House (see page 89) was originally the Baroque palace of a gold merchant named Sibiryakov, and later became the residence of the governor of East Siberia.

THE RUSSIAN COLUMBUS

In the grounds of Irkutsk's Znamensky Monastery stands a grand monument bedecked in capstans, sextants and other maritime regalia. This is the grave of Grigory Shelikhov (1749–95), often known as the 'Russian Columbus'. In 1783 he sailed a mini-fleet of three ships into the Bering Sea and founded a fur-trading post on Kodiak Island, just off the coast of Alaska. Shelikhov had big ambitions for Alaska but died suddenly in 1795 and was laid to rest here in Irkutsk. His son-in-law, Nikolay Rezanov, took over the running of the Russian-American Trading Company, founded after Shelikov's death, and set up permanent forts all along the American west coast. Alaska became part of the Russian Empire, but in the early 19th century these far-flung Russian outposts became a drain on the imperial purse and the tsar finally sold the land Shelikhov had claimed for Mother Russia to the US government – one of the biggest geopolitical misjudgements ever made by St Petersburg.

By 1836 Irkutsk boasted some 19,000 inhabitants and 1,958 houses, only 62 of which were made of stone. By 1877 the number of dwellings and offices etc had risen to 4,500, but still only a couple of hundred or so were made of anything else but local, sap-rich timber. The city was a 1970s sofa waiting for a stray cigarette end, and the inevitable disaster struck on 22 and 24 June 1879. A hayloft accidentally caught fire on a very hot and windy day and the ensuing infernos destroyed three-quarters of the city, including many of the stone-built structures. In the typical Irkutsk live-for-today style of the period, the situation was made even worse by the fire crews' inability to get water from the Angara to the burning buildings (and their reported drunkenness). In total the city lost 11 churches, the city library, the Geographical Society library and museum containing 22,330 irreplaceable exhibits, the governor's archives and thousands of homes.

This was a major catastrophe for Siberia's greatest city, but Irkutsk was not abandoned. Far from it, for the resulting rebuild in stone produced a splendid spectacle (though unpaved roads and open sewers still ran between its buildings). Chekhov passed through the city in the 1890s and called it '... a fine town. Quite cultured', and many would still agree with him. Many of the grand Neoclassical buildings you see today in the city centre date from that period, and here and there some of the pre-fire timber structures survive. By the 1890s, few signs of the fire remained and the city was home to 50,000 souls. Irkutsk's resurrection and remodelling in grand Neoclassical style led to it being dubbed, perhaps somewhat exaggeratedly, the 'Paris of Siberia'.

ARRIVAL OF THE TRANS-SIBERIAN RAILWAY For centuries the Great Siberian Post Road or *Veliky Trakt* had been the only way of travelling between Siberia and Russia, a journey that could take the best part of a year. Much of the route was passable only in the winter when the rivers froze, but temperatures sank to wheel-splitting lows. In summer, when the ice melted and water stagnated in pools, swarms of bloodthirsty mosquitoes would almost eat travellers alive. The hazards and discomforts of travelling the *trakt* and its inability to handle the amount of traffic travelling along it – and the fear that Russia could lose Siberia to a foreign power as a result of its isolation from the rest of Russia – in 1880 persuaded Tsar Alexander II that a railway stretching from St Petersburg to the Pacific was needed. In 1891 the edict giving authority to build the railway was issued on the shores of the Pacific by Grand Duke Nicholas – amazingly, the first-ever heir to the throne, never mind tsar, to visit Siberia! Work on the world's longest railway line began that year and progressed at amazing speed, with the talented and shrewd minister of finance and former railway manager, Sergei Witte, overseeing the mammoth project. Interestingly the 6,000 rails laid between Krasnoyarsk and Irkutsk were produced in England, and Italian masons worked on the few bridges built in stone. The tight-fisted tsar wanted the job done on the cheap, and building standards were generally lower than those in European Russia, with bridges fashioned from locally abundant wood, tunnelling kept to a minimum and the line single-track. Prison labour was used on most of the route. By 1898 the Moscow to Irkutsk section had been completed ahead of time, though there was still much work to be done on the tricky stretch around the southern shore of Lake Baikal, the so-called Circumbaikal Railway (see box on page 113) which wasn't finished until 1905. Possibly the greatest moment in the history of the Baikal region since the arrival of the Cossacks was the day the first steam engine arrived at Irkutsk station, thus forging an iron link between European Russia and eastern Siberia.

As a result of the new railway, immigration into Siberia went through the roof. The influx of settlers more than doubled from an average of 61,000 per year in 1895 to 134,000 per year in 1900. Although this initial boom did not last (numbers fell back to 45,000 per year in 1905), the early years were nothing compared with the post-1905 Revolution period, when the imperial authorities, in a bid to diffuse revolutionary fervour among the peasants, encouraged them to pack up and buy a ticket for any point east. By 1914 the number of land-hungry peasants arriving to start a new life beyond the Urals had reached 220,000 per year. Many who made the journey did so in conditions almost as bad as those encountered on the old *trakt*, with fifth-class box cars little more than cattle wagons. In fact, on the side of each wagon a sign read, 'For 12 horses or 43 men'.

REVOLUTION AND CIVIL WAR (1917) Although the now almost legendary October Revolution took place in 1917, Soviet power wasn't fully established across Siberia until 1922. Siberian peasants were slightly better off than their European counterparts, mainly because of their commune system, their money-spinning sideline in furs and even more lucrative contracts to supply the Russian army during World War I. As a result of their higher standard of living, Siberian peasants were more satisfied with their lot, considerably less unruly, and lacking in the revolutionary fervour that had gripped European Russia, where the 1917 revolution started. For this reason Siberia and the Baikal region greeted the Bolshevik revolution half-heartedly and sided almost from the outset with anti-revolutionary forces. Well-heeled Irkutsk put up serious resistance to the Bolsheviks as early as November 1917, but fell to superior forces, as did Ulan-Ude across the water.

That might have been that, were it not for two events which led to the start of civil war. The first was the landing of Japanese troops at Vladivostok, Emperor Yoshihito's government perceiving Bolshevik control of Siberia as a threat to his country's interests in Manchuria. The Japanese then made their way from Vladivostok along the Trans-Siberian Railway as far as Lake Baikal. The second event was the May 1918 revolt of a 50,000-strong Czechoslovak corps which was being evacuated on the request of the Allies on 259 trains through Vladivostok. It was this that really kicked off the Civil War, as with outside encouragement this well armed and well trained force managed to drive the Bolsheviks back and cut off Siberia from European Russia. The corps then took strategic control of the railway and all movements along it.

Following the rapid retreat of the Bolsheviks, Siberia splintered into 19 different governments, but was united in September 1918 in the Provisional All-Russia Government which pledged to free Russia of Soviet power. However, this was soon brought down in a coup led by the Siberian war minister, Admiral Kolchak, after political differences emerged. Kolchak established himself as White military dictator for 14 months, possibly with clandestine British assistance.

Over the course of 1919 the Reds advanced from the west, defeating Kolchak's Whites with greater troop numbers and better equipment, and gradually winning back large swathes of western Siberia. Kolchak's government was weak, ill-organised and incompetent, and troop supply lines from the east became blocked in the confusion. His capitalist allies did little to help, despite wide-ranging promises. Economic woes spread across Siberia as inflation skyrocketed and speculation increased. Dissatisfaction led many peasants to defect to the Reds, and uprisings across Siberia further sabotaged the Whites' efforts. In November 1919 the Red Army finally reached Irkutsk where Kolchak had retreated in his train carrying the imperial gold reserves (which he had captured in Kazan). The Czechs, still in control of the Trans-Siberian and eager to get home to their newly independent country, decided they had had their fill of Kolchak's war and handed him and his prime minister, Pepilyaev, over to the Reds, before negotiating their way out of the country with Kolchak's gold bars. Fearing the Whites were about to take Irkutsk back, the Reds shot Kolchak and Pepilyaev on 7 February 1920, but it was over 2½ years before the Bolsheviks took the final piece of Siberia's east.

During the Soviet decades, Admiral Kolchak was erased from the history books, but following the fall of the USSR, a statue to Siberia's White leader was raised outside Irkutsk's Znamensky Monastery (see pages 90–1) near the place he was executed. However, Kolchak remains a controversial figure and still triggers impassioned debate. Communist diehards and left-wingers see him as a military dictator who stood in the path of the juggernaut of Soviet power, causing the loss of thousands of lives in the process. Liberals and those leaning to the right hold him up as a hero who at least attempted to stop the Bolsheviks, however dictatorial his methods may have been. It's said the plinth his statue stands on was built high to keep the statue safe from vandalism.

STALINISM Quiz anyone in the West today on their idea of Siberia, and their description will undoubtedly be tinged by the Stalinist period of the 1920s and 1930s. Under Stalin, Siberia became a byword for terror as political prisoners, intellectuals and, as Stalin's paranoia grew, just about anyone who committed the smallest of misdemeanours, was banished to the Gulag as an 'enemy of the people'. A joke about the great leader or a complaint about the price of bread overheard by a neighbour or colleague could see you accused of treason, conspiracy or sabotage and shipped off to Siberia for 25 years' hard labour, from which you weren't likely to return. Siberia once again became a place of banishment, but this time in a vastly more horrific and large-scale capacity. Gulags sprouted across Siberia, although there were relatively few in the Baikal region itself. The greatest excesses of the Soviet period are responsible for the image of Siberia which still lingers today – a sinister place of cold exile and anonymous death.

Stalin regarded forced collectivisation as the best way to modernise Russia's agricultural and to feed the rapidly industrialising cities. This policy hit the region hard, thanks especially to the relative wealth of the peasants (called *kulaks*) in the region and their resistance to land seizures. 'Dekulakisation' (*raskulachivanye*) – the liquidation of wealthy peasants – saw thousands of Buryats flee to Mongolia as their herds were collectivised into *kolkhozy* (collective farms). The nomadic Evenks were driven into specially built communities in Kholodnaya and Baikalskoe in the north, losing forever their traditional reindeer-herding way of life.

The Soviets also saw no place in their brave new world for religion, whether it be the Orthodox Church, Buddhism or shamanism, though there was some tolerance at first of Buddhism, with many lamas claiming common ground between their belief system and Communism. But by the outbreak of World War II virtually all churches and, perhaps ironically, all Buddhist temples across Buryatiya had been closed down, with monks and priests sent into exile, transported to labour camps or shot. Even the centre of Russian Buddhism, the Tamchinsky Datsan near Goose Lake (Gusinoe Ozero), wasn't spared. One of the greatest losses to the Orthodox Church was the destruction of Irkutsk's Lady of Kazan Cathedral, which once rose proudly on the site of today's regional assembly building (on ploshchad Kirova). Once the dominant feature on the city's skyline, it was damaged during the Civil War and blown up on Stalin's orders in 1932. From old photographs it's evident what a huge and magnificent structure this was – it's said to have held 5,000 worshippers, and at 60m tall was one of the highest buildings in all Russia.

WORLD WAR II Eastern Siberia was a long way away from the World War II battlefields of western and eastern Europe, and wasn't directly affected by fighting. However, some key factories in European Russia were dismantled and hauled along the Trans-Siberian Railway beyond the Urals, to be reassembled out of range of Luftwaffe (and Japanese) bombers. These plants played a huge part in defeating Hitler, producing ammunition, aircraft and weapons for the war effort. The most easterly site of such installations was Ulan-Ude, as the Soviets regarded any point further along the railway as too close to China and Japan.

The human cost of the 'Great Patriotic War', as Russians and others insist on calling World War II (and, somewhat insultingly to countries involved from the beginning, often followed by 'of 1941–45'), was huge, with hundreds of thousands of local men sent to serve in the Red Army far from their Siberian homelands. Many never returned, killed in battles around Stalingrad and across eastern Europe. When the war was over, every city, town and village across the Baikal region erected its own war monument in their honour, a little like British communities did after World War I.

One little-known story of World War II is the fate of thousands of German and Japanese prisoners of war who were transported to Siberian camps and to labour on construction projects long after the war was over. You'll often hear that such-and-such a building was constructed by Japanese captives, and plaques to these forgotten prisoners adorn some 1940s and 1950s façades. There are also around 80 Japanese prisoner-of-war cemeteries in the Irkutsk oblast alone.

COLD-WAR YEARS Stalin died in March 1953 and was embalmed and laid to rest alongside Lenin in the specially designed tomb on Moscow's Red Square. Three years later, at the 20th Party Congress, he was denounced as a dictator and mass murderer by first secretary of the Communist Party, Nikita Khrushchev. His body was removed from the tomb (in 1961) and all traces of his rule (busts, statues, portraits) were dismantled, shelved or destroyed. Victims of Stalin's purges who survived the Gulag were rehabilitated and allowed to rejoin the Communist Party.

In the race to overtake the West, Siberia was seen throughout the Cold War as a place of boundless natural resources just waiting to be harvested in the name of the anti-capitalist struggle. The Soviets looked to harness Siberia's almost limitless energy resources in the form of hydro-electric power, with dams built along the region's great rivers. Lake Baikal's delicate ecosystem suffered a huge shock in the 1950s with the construction of the Angara hydro-electric power station. The building of a dam in Irkutsk to push river water through the turbines caused a large rise (one metre) in the lake's water level, which had what we can only assume were unforeseen consequences for both man and nature around the lake (the Soviet engineers seem to have done few impact studies). Rising water levels seriously affected *omul* breeding in Baikal's tributaries and silenced the singing sands (see page 157) on the eastern coast; the Trans-Siberian had to be rerouted between Irkutsk and Kultuk, water began lapping higher up flood defences in Slyudyanka and Listvyanka, and the Shaman Rock at the mouth of the Angara River almost disappeared under the strong currents. The town of Ust-Barguzin had to be relocated in its entirety from the low-lying north bank of the Barguzin River to the higher sandy southern bank. The hydro-electric plant produces a lot of energy and emits no harmful pollution, say its supporters.

The post-war years saw the cities of eastern Siberia expand with the construction of huge suburban high-rise housing projects to accommodate workers. Many migrant factory workers, labourers, engineers and other employees arrived from across the USSR to earn the 'long rouble', higher wages paid to those willing to toil in Siberia's extremes of climate. Some came to labour on temporary projects such as the BAM Railway or the Angara and Bratsk hydro-electric projects before returning home; others brought their families and stayed. Fed by cheap electricity and a ready supply of labour, Irkutsk and Ulan-Ude were industrialised with aluminium, chemical and cellulose plants. Ulan-Ude also gained the largest rolling stock and carriage repair works in all Siberia (LVRZ) as well as secret military factories producing aircraft.

In the 1970s, when Russia became nervous about the proximity of the highly strategic Trans-Siberian Railway line to then hostile China, the decision was taken by the then party leader, Leonid Brezhnev, to build another set of tracks further north. This line, which became known as the BAM (Baikalo-Amurskaya Magistrala, see box on page 150), skirts the northern shores of Lake Baikal and led to the founding of one of the biggest lakeside settlements, Severobaikalsk (see page 145).

In the sphere of state-controlled tourism, the 1980s saw Buryatiya opened up to some extent to foreign tourists despite its military plants, though always under the watchful eye of Inturist, the state tourism organisation.

BAIKAL AND SIBERIA SINCE 1985
Perestroika and glasnost
Following the death of Konstantin Chernenko in 1985, Mikhail Gorbachev became general secretary of the Communist Party and within a year had set about reforming the ailing Soviet system. In the years leading up to 1991 a raft of policies under the umbrella titles *perestroika* (restructuring or rebuilding) and *glasnost* (openness) were introduced to kick-start the stalled Soviet economy and introduce limited free speech. Some private ownership was permitted once again, and democratic elections to the new Congress of People's Deputies were held in 1989. However, the reform process began to split the country into Communist hardliners who hated to see how the old system was being dismantled, and liberals who thought the reforms too slow. The economic situation was also deteriorating, with food shortages, queues for life's basics and power blackouts a part of daily life. Old hostilities between ethnic minorities and between whole republics were also rearing their ugly heads, and the picture was confused even further by the fall of the Berlin Wall in November 1989. Eastern European Communist regimes from Prague to Bucharest tumbled like dominoes in the autumn and early winter of that year, with mass anti-regime movements able to take to the streets in the knowledge that Gorbachev had given assurances not to intervene in the affairs of eastern European states any longer. Now holding the new office of Soviet president, Gorbachev was awarded the Nobel Peace Prize in October 1990.

Collapse of the USSR
Faraway from Lake Baikal's shimmering waters, in August 1991 hardliners opposed to Gorbachev's new Treaty of the Union, which would loosen the glue binding the 15 republics of the USSR, staged a coup by taking the Soviet leader hostage at his Crimean *dacha*. These apparatchiks included generals and high-ranking politicians bent on stopping Gorbachev's reforms and reinstating Soviet power. Though the coup eventually failed, it led to all 14 of the other republics (all except Russia) declaring independence. The USSR was in effect no more, and in December of that year Boris Yeltsin took over as Russian president.

It usually comes as a surprise to Westerners that Gorbachev is widely reviled across Russia. While the former Soviet leader collects honorary degrees in the US and engages in international lecture tours, ordinary Russians hold him responsible for the fall of Russia from superpower status, the collapse of the economy and the dismantling of the old order.

Post-collapse
After the collapse of the Soviet Union and its command economy, Siberia went into freefall. State farms went belly-up, the wheels of industry ground to a halt, wages and pensions weren't paid for months and many turned to fishing in the lake for *omul* just to feed their families. Some politicians and intellectuals

seized upon the chaos to float the idea of Siberian independence, though this was never realistically going to happen. There's little doubt that if this huge chunk of the federation had attempted to break away the Russian army would have put a stop to matters very quickly. Ordinary Siberians were too busy trying to survive from day to day to devote their time to political pipe dreams – the idea never caught on.

Things improved slowly throughout the 1990s until the 1998 financial crisis pulled the rug from beneath the region's feet once again. Inflation soared, people saw their savings obliterated overnight and newly formed businesses went to the wall. Boozy President Yeltsin was widely blamed for bringing Russia to its knees once more.

The Putin era Former KGB officer and late 1990s Prime Minister Vladimir Putin took over as president on the last day of 1999, when Boris Yeltsin unexpectedly resigned. This marked a symbolic end to post-Soviet anarchy and ushered in a new era of order and resurgent patriotism. Putin won two more elections, serving two terms in the Kremlin before the constitution dictated he step down. Few expected the incredibly popular Putin to retire to his *dacha* to pen his memoirs, and they were right. Even before he had handed over the presidency to Dmitri Medvedev, he had already declared his intention to return to the role of prime minister, and it's widely expected he will retake the reins from Medvedev when he's served out his first term, or perhaps even earlier.

Slated in the West for curtailing press freedoms, reducing the Chechen capital Grozny to landfill, recentralising decision-making and using the gas and oil industries to hold former Soviet republics to ransom, Putin at home enjoys almost idol status, and you'd be hard-tasked to find a Russian who has a bad word to say about him. A strong leader (just what the doctor ordered for many a Slav nation), he has reasserted Russia's power on the international stage as well as serving the despised oligarchs their just desserts and generally raising living standards across the country. In early 2009 some commentators were predicting the world economic crisis could undermine his popularity, but Putin has too many tools at his disposal to allow this to happen. Most would gladly accept Vladimir Putin as president for life.

UNESCO and tourism The protection of Lake Baikal as a place of global importance received a boost in 1996 when it was listed by UNESCO as a World Heritage Site. The lake fulfilled all the criteria for inclusion and UNESCO status has lent the safeguarding of this unique natural phenomenon legal clout.

An inevitable upshot of the end of Soviet rule has been a noticeable influx of foreign visitors and domestic tourists during the long Russian summer holidays in July and August. Despite the need for a costly visa, as well as minor issues with independent travel which persist despite almost two decades of 'free movement' around the country (visa registration, border area restrictions), travellers from across the globe, but most numerously from Germany and France (though no official figures are available), have found their way to the lake's pebbly shoreline. From the point of view of sustainable tourism, a very positive development in recent years has been the Great Baikal Trail initiative (see box on page 105), which has received international plaudits for its work.

GOVERNMENT AND POLITICS

THE NATIONAL SCENE Much has been written in recent years about Russia's apparent rejection of classic Western democracy and the virtual personality cult around President, now Prime Minister, Putin. Whatever doubts the liberal West may harbour about Putin's methods, his *Yedinaya Rossiya* (United Russia) party enjoys immense popularity across Russia, and he and the party are generally credited with having lifted the country free of the humiliating financial and political quagmire of the 1990s. Russians (and indeed many other Slavs) believe a strong man is needed at the helm and are more than satisfied with the job Putin and those around him are doing. A slow drip of mild propaganda on TV and suppression of an opposition voice in the media are, in the Russian mind, a small price to pay for greater respect across the globe and relative stability at home. While criticised in the West, Putin's plan to legally become president for a third term after the incumbent Dmitri Medvedev steps down is widely supported. In the 2008 national presidential elections, Yedinaya Rossiya candidate Medvedev polled a massive 70% of votes, with the Communist Party's Gennady Zyuganov way behind with just 17%.

With the above in mind, those expecting to experience the kind of kitchen-table 'not in front of the kids' dissident conversations, typical of the 1970s and 1980s, will be disappointed. Russian nationalism is on the rise, and you may meet Siberians who will try to convince you that the West should even fear Russia, now a force to be reckoned with once again. The UK seems to be a target for particular criticism these days, with many Russians regarding Britain a spent power punching above its weight. The war in Chechnya, gas supplies to Ukraine, the independence of Kosovo and the 2008 war with Georgia are the most common subjects where Russian and Western views part company on less than friendly terms. Depending on your company, it's probably best to avoid opinionated discussions altogether (especially with inebriated males) and claim you have no interest in, or knowledge of, politics or world affairs.

ADMINISTRATIVE DIVISIONS The Baikal region is divided between the Irkutsk oblast (*Irkutskaya oblast*) and the Republic of Buryatiya (*Respublika Buryatiya*), both of them administrative divisions within the greater Russian Federation. The majority of Lake Baikal's shoreline (70%), from Vydrino in the south to Cape Elokhin in the north, belongs to Buryatiya. The capital of the Irkutsk oblast is (you guessed it) Irkutsk; the administrative centre of Buryatiya is Ulan-Ude. Each of these administrative regions is further divided into districts (*rayon*) centred around a town or very large village. As a republic, Buryatiya has a president while Irkutsk, as an oblast, has a governor. Buryatiya's parliament is called the *Narodniy Khural* (People's Khural; http://egov-buryatia.ru); in Irkutsk the equivalent body is known as the *Regionalniy Soviet* (*www.govirk.ru*).

Until 2006 the western Buryat town of Ust-Orda served as capital of the Ust-Ordinsky Autonomous Region, contained within the Irkutsk oblast. This administrative entity was flushed down the squat toilet of history in a local referendum that year, and merged with the surrounding oblast.

ECONOMY

NATIONAL PICTURE Most travellers to Russia will know about the jumbo economic meltdown this country suffered following the collapse of the Soviet-command economy. This complete system failure makes Russia's current recession look like a bounced cheque, as almost every part of economic machinery ground to a halt. It left people to fend for themselves and created a huge black hole which the Russian mafia soon filled. State farms crumbled, workers weren't paid for months, life's essentials weren't delivered to shops and prices skyrocketed. In the ensuing chaos, farm managers and factory bosses 'privatised' whatever they could lay their hands on. This was the situation across the former USSR (and Russia was far from the worst case) throughout the early part of the 1990s, but just as things looked like they were recovering, President Yeltsin was forced to devalue the rouble due to Russia's crippling foreign debt, and the whole thing came crashing down again.

Although the 1990s left deep scars, the economy has slowly recovered over the last five years, and across Russia as a whole stability has returned in some measure, partially funded by overheated oil and gas prices. However, not everybody has reaped the benefits, and the old, disabled, ill and homeless are still as bad off as they ever were. In late 2008, the Kremlin admitted that Russia was heading into recession due to the wider global economic downturn, and analysts predicted trouble on the horizon for the country's finances.

National facts and figures Nationwide, inflation is still relatively high at around 11%, but this is outweighed by increases in personal income, which has been growing at 12% per annum for the last six years. A quite remarkable figure is Russia's economic growth rate, which averaged 7% a year from 1998 until 2008. GDP per capita stands at almost US$15,000. Despite Russia's perceived economic strength, the country's reliance on oil, gas, timber and metals, which constitute 80% of exports, expose it to the swings and roundabouts of international commodity prices and the type of economic downturn the world saw in late 2008.

BAIKAL REGION The economic good times, rolling nationally since the beginning of this century until very recently, have also had a positive effect on eastern Siberia, though relative poverty and lack of infrastructure are still the norm. Timber export to China is a lucrative business, as is the extraction of precious metals such as gold and zinc which takes place at various locations around the region. Other industries you might see sending up plumes of smoke into pristine Siberian skies are the oil refineries at Angarsk, the cellulose plant at Baikalsk and aluminium plants just outside Irkutsk. Another major employer is the railways, often described as a 'state within a state'. Despite almost endless supplies, the fish industry hardly registers.

Tourism Tourism is a growing sector of the economy though very few people benefit directly. Despite the potential to attract many more visitors to Baikal's shores, there are virtually no government-funded initiatives to promote tourism in the Irkutsk oblast, and Buryatiya makes a mere token effort in the form of the special economic zone around Lake Kotokel. Work on the latter seems to be progressing at snail's pace, mercifully some might say.

While Baikal is a tourist Mecca for visitors from all across the Russian Federation, it remains very much a niche destination in the Anglo-Saxon world. This cannot be said of Europe, where in Germany the lake has become a see-before-you-die destination, and in France it's also on many travellers' wish lists. The fact that the book you are holding is the first dedicated solely to Lake Baikal, while there have been guides published in French and German for years, illustrates the difference in awareness.

Russia in general does little to promote tourism, one interesting theory being that it costs very little to export a barrel of oil, while a great deal of effort and cost goes into attracting a tourist to stay a night in a mid-priced hotel, both activities generating similar profit margins.

Poverty Despite what you may have heard about Russia's oil and gas wealth, as yet very few of the country's petrodollars have fluttered down into ordinary people's lives. Russia is still light-years behind the West when it comes to caring for the elderly, the sick and the disabled, and its healthcare facilities are of a shockingly low standard. Today the average monthly wage is around RUB18,000 (£360, US$600), though you'd hardly tell from the gas-guzzlers on the streets and the overpriced goods in the shops. While the cities have a semblance of economic normality, out in the sticks countless people have shunned money altogether, surviving by catching fish and harvesting their vegetable plots, a world away (literally) from Moscow's oli- and minigarchs and the oil-stained Kremlin.

PEOPLE

Three distinct ethnic groups inhabit the shore of Lake Baikal: the Evenks have been here for millennia, the Buryats for at least eight centuries and the Russians just 350 years. Despite their relatively recent arrival on the scene, the Russians are by far the biggest group. Everyone seems to get on OK in this corner of central Asia, though the relationship and history between Russians and Evenks is mildly reminiscent of white settlers and Native Americans in North America.

RUSSIANS Of the approximately four million people who call the Baikal region home, Russians make up the vast majority. A handful might be able to trace their DNA back to the original Cossacks who settled the region in the 17th century, but the bulk of Baikal's population are descendants of Russian peasants, political exiles, prisoners of war, Jews, BAM builders, workers who came to Soviet Siberia for higher wages and those who emigrated from former Soviet republics after the collapse of the USSR. Another group is the so-called Old Believers, who live mostly to the east and south of Ulan-Ude (see box on page 128). Although all of these people would describe themselves as Russians, they represent a hugely diverse gene pool from across the steppelands of Eurasia and beyond.

BURYATS Buryats are a Mongol people who first settled the Baikal region in the 10th and 11th centuries. It would be wrong to think that Buryats and Mongolians are the same, though it may seem that way to the outsider. The ancestors of the Buryats may have migrated from what is now Mongolia, but having arrived at the shores of Lake Baikal they assimilated and interbred with the Turkic Kurykan tribes who had inhabited the region for centuries. Their language also differs considerably from Mongolian, with some speakers of dialects in southern Buryatiya able to effortlessly read medieval Mongolian texts, which Mongolians themselves decipher with difficulty. The Buryat people are divided geographically and culturally into Western (Irkutsk, Olkhon, Ust-Orda) and Eastern (Buryatiya), and further into several ethnic groups, each of whom originally possessed its own dialect, customs, culture and religious practices. The ethnic lines have become slightly blurred, especially in Ulan-Ude, but any Buryat you ask will certainly know to which group he or she belongs.

In total there are some 520,000 Buryats around the world, 250,000 of whom live in Buryatiya. Surprisingly, they form less than a quarter of the population of their own republic, and a mere 3% of the inhabitants of the Irkutsk oblast call themselves Buryat. The population of the erstwhile Ust-Ordynsky Buryat Autonomous Region to the north of Irkutsk is only one-third Buryat.

DID YOU KNOW... ?

The world-famous ballet dancer Rudolf Nureyev was born March 17 1938 near Irkutsk aboard a train on the Trans-Siberian Railway. His mother was travelling to Vladivostok at the time to visit his father who was serving in the Soviet military.

EVENKS According to some theories, Lake Baikal is the original home of the Evenks who have inhabited its shores for 3,500 years. Today's Evenks, who can be found principally in the Barguzin Valley and around Severobaikalsk, are the remnants of the Tungus-Manchu people pushed north by the Buryats in the 10th and 11th centuries. They once lived as nomads in the endless taiga across Siberia, where they hunted, caught fish, and dwelt in skin-covered and wooden tepees. Their traditional way of life, in perfect harmony with nature and the seasons, came to an end in the 1930s when the Soviet authorities collectivised their reindeer herds and herded their families into brick-and-mortar villages. There are only around 30,000 Evenks left in the world and their numbers have halved over the last century.

The Evenk language is related to both Buryat and Yakut and has elements of Mongolian and Turkic tongues. Written Evenk only appeared in the 1920s and uses the Cyrillic script.

OTHERS As in most other regions of the former Soviet Union, the remaining population comprises a diverse ethnic mix of Estonians, Lithuanians, Latvians, Byelorussians, Ukrainians, Georgians, Armenians and a whole host of others from across Eurasia. This is particularly true in the north (Severobaikalsk, Nizhneangarsk), which is, for the most part, peopled by those who came to lay tracks and blast tunnels on the BAM railway in the 1970s and 1980s.

Poles form a small but interesting minority across Siberia. Many were exiled here after the 18th-century partitions of Poland, and more were banished across the Urals after uprisings and revolts throughout the 19th century. A 3,000-strong Polish community still exists in Irkutsk and even maintains its own Catholic church (see page 89).

LANGUAGE

The vast majority of people in the towns and villages around Lake Baikal speak Russian, as their mother tongue or as a second language to Buryat. Russian and Buryat are linguistically unrelated, though they are linked by the Cyrillic alphabet. This expresses Russian sounds well but does a pretty poor job as far as Buryat is concerned. While Russian is an eastern Slavic tongue like Ukrainian and Byelorussian, Buryat is closely related to Mongolian and is linked to the large Altaic group of languages which includes many tongues in central Asia and the Russian Federation. These languages are also very distant relatives of some European languages such as Finnish, Hungarian and Estonian. With some rare exceptions among the elderly in remote mountain villages in the south, Buryats speak good Russian (albeit with a heavy accent). Despite clear differences in language and culture between the two groups, there is little or no friction between Buryats and Russians, and no sign of a Ukraine-style language war. Buryats seem happy to be part of the Russian Federation and to speak its lingua franca when required.

With no Russian (and even less Buryat), making yourself understood and comprehending what's going on around you can be frustrating, to say the least. Most Siberians involved in the tourist industry speak some English, with the exception of waiters and some hotel reception staff. You may, however, come across the odd tour company where not a single person speaks a word of your language; and don't expect bus or taxi drivers to understand you. French and German are popular second languages, and some Buryats speak Chinese and/or Mongolian (as if that helps!). You won't see many signs, menus or even place names in Siberia written in the Latin script, and taking time to learn the Cyrillic alphabet before you leave home will pay huge dividends and be of immeasurable use in numerous situations from the ferry quay to the restaurant table. Learn a few words of Buryat

Whatever language you speak, a large share of communication uses no words at all. Russians, in particular, use slightly more gesticulation when speaking than the English or Americans and the following are some of the most common Russian gestures you may have difficulty deciphering:

- **Flicking the side of the neck just below the jaw** Indicates the drinking of alcohol or that someone you are talking about is an alcoholic or has been drinking.
- **Rubbing three fingers together** Indicates money changing hands.
- **Tapping the forehead with forefinger** Indicates someone is stupid or deranged.
- **Pushing thumb between index and middle finger in a fist** A 'screw you', 'not a chance' gesture.
- **Pretend spitting three times** Equivalent to knocking on wood for good luck.
- **Slapping right hand down onto top of left fist** 'You're going to get it' gesture.

Here are some gestures common in Anglo-Saxon societies, but considered rude in Russia:

- **Pointing** Never point at anyone unless you want to annoy them.
- **US 'everything's OK' sign** Just don't do it – it has a very rude meaning, though some Russians we spoke to didn't think there was anything wrong with it (but didn't know what it meant).
- **Winking at women** If you're a man in the habit of winking at women, don't – she'll think you think she's a prostitute.

and your hosts' eyes will pop out in amazement (especially if they're Russians). Who knows, you might be reading an untranslated copy of the *Geser Epic* (see box on page 107) by the time you board the plane or train home.

RELIGION

The three belief systems of Orthodox Christianity, Tibetan Buddhism and Siberian shamanism exist side by side around Lake Baikal, and in certain aspects replicate and merge seamlessly into one another. While Orthodox churches, with their onion domes and icon- and incense-filled interiors, are a common sight across the entire region, the biggest concentration of Buddhist temples (datsan, дацан) and stupas is in Buryatiya. Ancient shaman sites can be found everywhere, though they are less obvious around Irkutsk. Buddhism and shamanism are in many ways interwoven, and sometimes it's difficult for the untrained eye to lever the two apart. Even devout Orthodox Christians can sometimes be seen sprinkling coins and vodka at a roadside obo (holy place), a sight their European cousins would find very odd.

SHAMANISM Shamanism is an ancient belief system based on the power of nature and human ancestors, and if you had arrived on the shores of Lake Baikal a millennia or two ago, this is the 'religion' you would have encountered. Shamanism is still going strong in Buryatiya, despite three centuries of Buddhist encroachment and 70 years of Communist rule which banned shamanic practices.

Shamanism generally divides the world into three basic levels – the material world of people and animals, an upper level inhabited by gods, and the underworld populated by a host of spirits. The soul can inhabit any of these levels. Central to the belief system is the shaman, who the dictionary defines 'a person regarded as having access to, and influence in, the world of good and evil spirits'. These figures in their shaggy robes, thumping their tambours and speaking in tongues as they convulsed into a half-conscious state, acted as mediators between the world of the spirits and the world of people. In their trance-like state they could cure illness and foretell future events, but these were just some of their roles in society. In Buryatiya they were also guardians of the national cultural heritage, performing myriad rituals and magic, reciting poetry and keeping alive songs, myths and legends. Sadly, no shaman survived the seven decades of Soviet rule, and today's kitchen-table holy men and women are far tamer individuals. However, Buddhists and Christians alike often consult the local shaman (every village and high-rise estate has one) if they encounter a problem in life, are enduring bad health or want to know what the future holds.

Evenk and Buryat shamanism differ slightly, mainly due to Buddhist influences in the south. The world according to Buryat shamanism has a whopping nine levels, populated by a pantheon of spirits and gods, headed by Khukhe Munkhe Tengri (endless blue sky) in the upper world and the dark Erlin in the underworld. In Evenk culture the world's three levels are linked by a river.

During your time at Lake Baikal you may not witness a shaman in full flow (and if you do, he's likely to be an actor putting on a show for the tourists), but you can't fail to notice trees draped in rags and pieces of cloth along every road, the ground beneath them carpeted in coins. These sites – called *obos* – are places such as rocks, rivers, lakes, springs and hilltops where the spirits reside. It's customary for drivers to flick a coin out of the window of their car as they hurtle past, or even to stop and pour a little vodka on the ground (and some down their throat in the process) in order to attract good luck for the journey. Christian and Buddhist alike can be found at these places, which often have wooden benches and small pavilions where families come to picnic on sunny days.

ORTHODOX CHRISTIANITY The first Cossacks to claim eastern Siberia as Russian soil brought their Orthodox Christian faith with them, and the region's first church appeared in Barguzin (see page 140) not long afterwards. The first Orthodox mission to the Baikal region arrived in the late 17th century, and on the orders of Tsar Feodor III established the Posolsky Monastery (see page 120). It was from here that priests and monks set out to convert the heathen Buryats, with limited success. Many more churches were built in Buryatiya and Irkutsk by wealthy merchants,

BUDDHIST SYMBOLS

Above the entrance to most datsans you'll notice two deer sitting either side of an eight-spoked wheel. The deer represent the first sermon given by Buddha in the deer park at Benares; the wheel symbolises the noble eightfold path according to which Buddhists are meant to conduct their lives. The stupa, examples of which are sprouting on the hilltops of Buryatiya like gleaming white mushrooms after rain, is a symbolic grave monument where the remains of a holy monk are kept. It also symbolises the universe. The lotus flower is a symbol of purity and can be any colour except blue.

These are the most common symbols you might spot at temples across Buryatiya, but there are many more. A frequent spectacle you may see these days is the words 'Om mani padme hum' written in oversize Tibetan script using white painted rocks, on the sides of prominent hills above villages. This is the mantra of the *bodhisattva* (enlightened being) of compassion, and the words are often found inside prayer wheels. The meaning of the actual Sanskrit is very complicated.

and soon Siberia had its very own patron saint – St Inokent (see box on page 90). During the Soviet decades almost all the churches were closed and some destroyed, while Ulan-Ude's Odigitria Cathedral was to have become a museum of atheism displaying Orthodox icons and Buddhist art to a godless proletariat. It never happened, and while no churches destroyed by the Soviets have actually been rebuilt in the Baikal region, all those left standing have been returned to their former glory and are once again perfumed with billowing incense and bright with the gold of icons. The most impressive Orthodox churches in the region are at the Znamensky Monastery in Irkutsk, the Posolsky Monastery in the Selenga Delta and the Odigitria Cathedral in Ulan-Ude.

BUDDHISM Buddhism was the last religion to arrive in the region, brought to Buryatiya in the 17th century by Tibetan and Mongolian missionaries. It soon began to push out the local shamanistic and animalistic beliefs, sometimes with force but usually just through peaceful conversion. St Petersburg seems not to have fretted too much over the arrival of a foreign religion on its soil, in many ways encouraging the lamas in their work and even recognising Buddhism as an official state religion in 1741. Temples, monasteries and stupas were built throughout the 18th century, and the centre of Russian Buddhism was established at the Tamchinsky Datsan in the village of Gusinoe Ozero (see page 130). Books, medical texts, statues of the Buddha and countless works of Buddhist art were carted in from Tibet, India and Mongolia to fill the new places of worship and newly created monastery faculties. Though Buddhism took a firm hold on Baikal's eastern shore, it has never made great inroads on the western shore where shamanic beliefs are still strong. Many Buryats still practice Buddhism infused with shamanic rituals and beliefs, a mix which could be compared with Christianity in Europe which superimposed its major feasts, such as Easter and Christmas, on old pagan festivals. Buddhist temples very often appeared at sacred shaman sites, just as Christians built their churches in places of pagan ritual.

All of Buryatiya's Buddhist temples were destroyed, and the monks shot or sent to the Gulag, during Stalin's repressions of the 1920s and 1930s. It wasn't until 1945 that the then new Ivolginsky Datsan (see page 128) was allowed to open, one of only two in the entire USSR (the other was in the town of Aginskoe near Chita). This became the new centre of Russian Buddhism and remained so even after the collapse of the USSR, despite the reopening of the Tamchinsky Datsan. Tens of temples big and small have been built in the last two decades, some new, some copies of those that stood on sites at the beginning of the 20th century. Buddhism has witnessed a strong resurgence during that time, attracting Buryats and even some Russian converts to the temples.

Westerners with an interest in Buddhism as a philosophy or way of life may be a trifle nonplussed by Buddhism as a practiced religion. The custom of coming to the local temple to cleanse one's sins or ask for good luck even seems to contradict the Buddha's teachings and the noble eightfold path. But this is no stranger than Christians who 'covet their neighbour's ox' in some modern way or work a Sunday shift at the local supermarket.

Buddhist temples Most temples have essentially identical layouts, with a row of brightly coloured tables and benches covered in silks leading up to a large glass case covering an end wall packed with *thangkas*, pictures of the Dalai Lama, Buddha figures and various other regalia. On the tables and in front of the case you'll find offerings of butter lamps, rice, sugar, tea, vodka and money. At the bigger datsans there's a cash register chuntering in a back corner with mini-prayer wheels, butter lamps and Buddhist texts for sale.

All of the Baikal region's Buddhist temples are open to the public and don't charge admission to tourists. There are a few basic rules you should follow when visiting: always walk in a clockwise direction around the complex, enter temples by the left door (the central entrance is only for lamas) and feel free to leave a donation in the form of money or a butter lamp. Never turn your back on the *bodhisattvas* and Buddhas as you leave, and behave in a humble and reverent manner at all times. Lamas, especially at the smaller out-of-the-way temples, are usually more than willing to talk to foreigners, and visitors who show a real interest or knowledge of Buddhism may be asked to stay the night at the monks' dorm or eat at the refectory.

OTHERS Polish Catholics, Old Believers, Jews, Protestants, Baptists and the odd Tatar or Uzbek Muslim make up the 1% of others. For more information on the fascinating Old Believers, see box on page 128.

CULTURE

Across the former Soviet and Russian-speaking world, you'll soon discover that most people lead a Jekyll-and-Hyde kind of life. Long faces, grumpy demeanour and the occasional absence in public situations of what the British would describe as 'good manners' are swapped for generosity, humility and genuine hospitality in family or one-to-one situations. Deal solely with receptionists, bus drivers and security guards on a trip to Siberia, and you'll come away with a wholly negative view of the local psyche. Take up an invitation to a home and get to know Irkutskites or Ulan-Udeans around their kitchen tables over a shot or two of vodka, and your impressions will be entirely different.

It may be a wild generalisation, but most visitors find Buryats a jollier lot than Russians, the result perhaps of the former's Buddhist faith and tight-knit family networks. Rural Buryats in particular seem very content with their lot and have a constant smile across their Mongol features. You may even find you receive smilier service from those in officialdom and tourism in Buryatiya than across the water in the Irkutsk oblast.

LIFESTYLE

Town v country The vast majority of city dwellers live in dreary and often crumbling high-rise blocks on huge Soviet-era housing projects. While the communal spaces are dank and smelly, the actual flats in these seemingly soulless blocks can be cosy and very comfortable, if small. On any visit to a flat, you are sure to hear the word *remont* which can mean anything from a lick of paint to knocking out supporting walls. Siberians love to do up their abodes, no matter how humble, and will take pride in showing you their handiwork.

Employment for the average city-dwelling Siberian means long days in an office or factory, with pot-holed roads to be negotiated to get there by bus or in their own car, both probably secondhand and shipped from Japan or Korea. Lunch is a quick dash into a *stolovaya* (canteen) and the commute home a slow crawl in gridlocked traffic. Siberians are big readers, and the bus journey back to the *mikrorayon* (high-rise neighbourhood) provides opportunity to escape into the pages of a novel. TV is the most popular form of evening entertainment despite the schedule's poor procession of ersatz pop and insipid news broadcasts.

Families are close, but many in Siberia also have relatives living thousands of miles away in European Russia or further east along the Trans-Siberian. From the first signs of spring to the last falling leaves of autumn, weekends see these families head out to their *dachas*, country cottages usually surrounded by allotment-type

In this corner of Eurasia with its mix of shamanist and Orthodox Christian beliefs, it's often hard to see the dividing line between religion and superstition. Buryats have also adopted many of the countless Russian superstitions, of which there are almost enough to fill this entire book! Here is just a selection of the most frequently cited:

RUSSIAN

- Don't whistle indoors – you'll whistle your money away.
- Sit in silence for a moment before departing on a long journey as rushing out can bring bad luck on the road.
- Never shake hands across a threshold.
- Never give an even number of flowers.
- Always look in the mirror if you return home to collect something you forgot.
- Black cats bring bad luck and, much to the chagrin of British visitors, are shooed away unceremoniously.
- Never give a knife as a gift.

BURYAT

- Sprinkle milk, tea or vodka, or throw a coin, cigarette or sweet out of the car window when passing a special sacred place (*obo*) for good luck on your journey.
- The first drop of tea or the first piece of meat is given to the spirit-keeper of the house.
- Hold a person respectfully by the elbow when giving something.
- Never extinguish a fire with water or throw rubbish into the fire – it is believed the spirit-keeper of the home lives in the hearth.

RUSSIAN AND BURYAT

- Don't step on the threshold.

gardens where they grow vegetables, fruit and flowers, sometimes to survive, sometimes just for pleasure. Some of these *dachas* can be luxurious affairs such as those now sprouting up around Listvyanka for the *nouveau riche* of Irkutsk; others are simple timber dwellings left to city folk by elderly relatives, or rudimentary huts surrounded by vegetable patches.

Siberian country folk very often inhabit log-built houses, usually made of pine or larch, with beautifully carved sky-blue window frames. The plot of land around the house is usually cluttered with various outhouses for animals but mostly occupied by a garden for growing staples such as potatoes and cabbages. Many villagers are virtually self-sufficient in the basics, only venturing to the local shop to buy tea, pasta and vodka. *Omul* fishing also provides a source of food in shoreline communities, and tourism (homestays, sale of food) brings in a little extra money, but not much.

Following the collapse of Communism, collective farms and other rural employers were shut down and have never really been replaced. Unemployment is the norm in the sticks, and young people escape village life as soon as they can. This means rural communities are aging and emptying fast. Alcoholism and, to a lesser extent, drug addiction are major problems among those who stay.

Death of the nomadic life Many Buryats gave up their felt yurts and nomadic way of life in the 18th and 19th centuries and moved into octagonal timber yurts and static log cabins, though they continued to be expert hunters. After 70 years of Soviet rule, the Buryats are now almost completely urbanised or lead static lives in villages, and the nomadic and even semi-nomadic ways of life have all but vanished (unlike in Mongolia or Tuva). The Evenks' nomadic existence in the taiga north and east of Lake Baikal survived until collectivisation by the Soviets in the 1930s. Since the end of Soviet rule few have left the comfort of purpose-built villages set up for them in the Stalinist era to return to traditional ways in the forest.

RUSSIAN IDENTITY Russians are once again staunchly proud of their country and at no other time since the early 1980s has there been such an upsurge of patriotism. Recent successes in wars, ice hockey, football and even the Eurovision Song Contest have confirmed Russia as top of the pile in the local population's mind. Most Russians think the West should show greater respect for Russia and should even fear its might. This sits incongruously with the way Russians bemoan their standard of living, though this might be blamed on Gorbachev, Yeltsin or anonymous oligarchs (rarely Brezhnev, Stalin or corruption). Russians, and Siberians in particular, seem to pride themselves on succeeding in conditions that would have long defeated lesser peoples, sometimes even appearing to prefer the hard way of doing things.

COMMUNAL MINDSET Despite its size, Siberia still possesses a communal mentality, with everyone interested in everyone else's business and nobody afraid to speak up in front of strangers, ask for information or tell others off if they're doing something wrong. This may contribute to Russia being a very verbal place, with the spoken carrying greater weight than the written. For example, information, such as bus times or ticket prices, is very often dispensed by an official behind a glass screen rather than displayed publicly, and the practice of telephoning to find things out is still more common than looking them up online. This can be particularly taxing if you don't speak Russian, or are English and prefer not to communicate with your fellow human beings. On the other hand the Russian communal spirit can make getting to know the locals easier and will afford a more fulfilling travel experience.

QUESTIONS Get ready for some odd and sometimes uncomfortable questions on your trip around Baikal – don't be surprised if the elderly in particular quiz you on subjects such as 'Is there a war in your country?', 'Do people go hungry in England?', 'Why aren't you married?', or 'How much land do people in London receive from the state?'. Siberia is a long way from Tesco-isation and elderly Russians may look at you in disbelief as you explain that pensioners back home buy all their food from supermarkets, your family owns no land and Hitler never invaded Britain (nothing to do with Tesco, of course). After 70 years of being spoon-fed Soviet propaganda and a lifetime of growing vegetables just one summer away from hunger, 5,000km from the capital, it's easy to see how some Siberians (even the odd 30-year-old) could formulate some bizarre ideas of life outside Mother Russia.

NATURAL HISTORY

The Baikal region's diverse range of habitats creates a home for thousands of species of flora and fauna, many of which are endemic to the region. Millions of years of isolation from their original ancestors have produced some weird and wonderful variations such as the freshwater nerpa seal and the fat-rich *golomyanka* fish. If diving to skull-crushing depths or losing yourself in the never-ending taiga seem too much like hard work to spot a bit of wildlife, try the Baikal Museum in Listvyanka, which keeps many specimens both living and preserved. Also see below for an overview of the environmental threats faced by Lake Baikal and a detailed list of the protected areas which line its shores.

FLORA Everywhere you look around Lake Baikal you'll see trees, millions of them, which provide a home to hundreds of species of flora and fauna as well as berries, mushrooms, building materials and firewood for humans. Both the western and eastern shores are dominated by large areas of pine forest, interrupted by stretches of birch, cedar, spruce, larch and mixed woodland. Of all the trees found in Siberia, the larch is the most fascinating. Though it resembles an evergreen like the pine or spruce, its needles turn a fiery yellow in late autumn before falling to the ground.

The forest floor, riverbank and valley meadow are home to thousands of species of shrub, herb, flower and bush too numerous to even begin to list here. Endemic species include a type of pink orchid, the Baikal anemone, and an odd mushroom with a mesh skirt and an unbearable odour. The autumnal forest floor is rich in edible fruits such as blueberries, cranberries and wild strawberries (from which the Buryats make the most delicious jam) as well as hundreds of mushroom species.

FAUNA

On land Baikal's backdrop of cloud-grazing mountains are home to hardy species of goat, snow sheep, alpine vole, marmot and lemming. Descend from the snowy peaks to find the taiga, alpine valleys, lowlands and shoreline of Lake Baikal teeming with elk, deer, Siberian roe deer, brown bear, wolf, wild boar, fox, otter, sable, white hare, Siberian skunk, muskrat, squirrel and numerous types of rodent. Around 250 bird species inhabit the protected areas around the lake, some spending the summer here, others arriving in winter. Rare species of fauna include the black crane, black stork, falcon, Pallas' cat and white-tailed eagle which, although not nearing extinction, are on the endangered list. After centuries of hunting, Siberia's animals prefer to avoid humans at all cost, and wildlife-spotting trips (except bird-watching) can yield little fruit. Bears and sable are particularly camera-shy.

In the lake A book twice as thick as this guide could be written on the fauna of Lake Baikal. Its deep and nippy waters are home to over 1,500 species, of which over 80% are endemic. Baikal's most sighted species is the nerpa seal (see box opposite), the only seal in the world to live in freshwater conditions all year round. The second most visible species inhabiting the lake is the *omul* fish, but you're far

SABLE – GOLD OF THE TAIGA

A sable is a small forest mammal native to Siberia, Mongolia, China and Japan whose single greatest misfortune is to possess a fine coat of fur. In the 18th and 19th centuries beautiful and durable sable was the pelt of choice for the production of hats and coats, and so prized was the animal's fur that the tax levied on locals by the Cossacks was calculated in sable skins. But by the early 20th century the animal had almost been hunted to oblivion, and numbers ran dangerously low. The Barguzin Nature Reserve and several other protected areas were set up to save the sable from extinction, and now populations are back to normal. Some 400,000 animals a year are trapped in a sustainable manner by licensed hunters, with each pelt they take worth up to US$3,000. Coats made from sable fur retail in Moscow for between US$15,000 and US$30,000, and sable hair is also used to make high-quality brushes for artists.

NERPA SEALS

Like shiny rotund torpedoes zipping through the water, the nerpa seal is Baikal's most recognisable inhabitant and one of only two species of freshwater seals in the world (the other lives only some of the year in freshwater). They are most easily observed basking on the Ushkanie Islands off the Svyatoy Nos Peninsula, but most have their first encounter with these cute creatures, with their big sad eyes and bristly whiskers, in aquaria in Irkutsk and Listvyanka's Baikal Museum. The nerpa thrives on a monotonous diet of *golomyanka* fish whose high fat content helps the seals survive the winter and give birth to their young (fluffy white balls with big black eyes) on the ice in March and April. When the lake freezes they keep holes open to breathe through, and when Baikal reverts to liquid form they swim or bask on rocks around the shore, usually well away from human populations.

Around 100,000 seals inhabit Baikal, mostly in the north where there are fewer people and less pollution. Studies have shown they are related to Arctic seals, but it's a mystery how they came to populate Lake Baikal. Scientists think that millions of years ago there may have been a water route linking the lake with the Arctic, along which seals made their way. The Evenks hunted the nerpa sustainably for millennia, using their fur for clothing and eating the meat. But with the arrival of the Buryats and then the Russians, people began killing seals for furs which they could sell. Hunting quotas have been introduced but are regarded as too high by conservation groups and could push the seals into the endangered species category. Over the huge expanse of lake ice, it's almost impossible to police hunting (seals are caught by netting their ice holes) and more needs to be done to protect this unique species.

more likely to encounter this on a restaurant plate than in the lake itself. There are several different types of *omul*, all of different sizes and named after the rivers where they spawn. Tens of other fish species live at varying depths, including roach, whitefish, bream, rotan, carp, sturgeon, orfe, catfish and eelpout.

One of the most interesting and by far the most numerous fish species is the *golomyanka*, which forms the staple diet of the nerpa seal. This scaleless fish is endemic to Lake Baikal, and as it's only found between 200m and 500m, your chances of spotting one are slim. Transparent and viviparous (females give birth to live young rather than laying eggs), their bodies are almost half fat, which helps them thrive at such varying depths. In the past, when *golomyanka* were flipped on to Baikal's beaches during storms, locals would collect their greasy carcasses and use the oil for lamps and even traditional remedies.

ENVIRONMENTAL ISSUES AND CONSERVATION

In addition to low-level sources of pollution such as agricultural run-off, emissions from lakeside settlements, water-borne craft and litter, over the last few decades Baikal has faced a number of more serious threats to its drinkably pure water, the majority of which have been successfully dealt with by the government or by prevailing economic conditions. Until recently the proposed Transneft oil pipeline posed the greatest environmental danger, the original barmy route passing just 800m from the lake's north shore in an area of frequent seismic activity. Putin stepped in to save the day and 'persuaded' the company to divert the pipeline. In late 2008 the Baikalsk cellulose plant, for decades Baikal's biggest polluter, was on the brink of bankruptcy, but this may in future years be replaced by an even greater threat – a proposed international uranium enrichment plant in Angarsk.

In July 2008 a team of Russian submarine explorers (the same group which in 2007 rather comically planted a Russian flag on the bottom of the Arctic Ocean) probed the bottom of Lake Baikal using a special type of submarine. Many suspect the team was secretly testing for oil reserves, prompting fears that the 'sacred sea' could one day be blighted by oil platforms and burn-off flares.

BAIKAL'S NATIONAL PARKS AND PROTECTED AREAS The five national parks (народный парк, narodny park) and large reserves (заповедник, zapovyednik) in the immediate vicinity of Lake Baikal protect fragile habitats, home to thousands of species of indigenous animal and plant life. Though all have zones set aside for visitors, getting into these sometimes seemingly trackless and impenetrable areas can usually be done only in the company of an official guide. Contact the various park headquarters (details given below) to arrange visits and tours. The five protected areas are:

Baikal–Lena Reserve (*Headquarters: ul Dekabrskikh sobyty 47, Irkutsk;* ↘ *3952 350 615;* e *zapoved@irk.ru*) Established in 1986, this reserve, the 14th-largest in Russia, is a huge chunk of taiga on the western shore with virtually no human population. The area of almost 660,000ha contains the upper reaches of the River Lena, Russia's longest and the tenth-longest in the world. It's also home to thousands of plant species and a large bear population, as well as 50 other mammals and 240 types of bird including the black stork, scoter and white-tailed eagle.

Baikal Biosphere Reserve (*Headquarters: ul Krasnogvardyeyskaya 34, Tankhoy;* ↘ *30138 93 720;* e *bainr@burnet.ru; http://zapovednik.e-baikal.ru/english/about.html*) This reserve, inland from the Baikal village of Tankhoy in the Khamar Daban mountain range, was set up in 1969. Its 34,000ha were declared a UNESCO Biosphere Reserve in 1986. It's quite easy to arrange a guided walk with rangers organised through the reserve headquarters.

Barguzin Biosphere Reserve (*Headquarters: ul Kozlova 61, Nizhneangarsk;* ↘ *30130 47 992;* e *bargnr@burnet.ru*) This was the first protected area created in Russia, initially set up in 1916 by Zenon Svatoš (see box on page 144). The almost 375,000ha of mountainous terrain (highest point 2,472m) and taiga (from 600m to 1,250m) is situated on the northeast coast and includes a huge mountain range between Lake Baikal and the Barguzin Valley. Large bear populations as well as sable and squirrel roam these impenetrable forests and 243 types of bird (and even two types of amphibian!) also call it home. The reserve is incredibly difficult to access as you must first reach Davsha (see page 143) by supply ship or private boat.

Pribaikalsky National Park (*Headquarters: Mikrorayon Yubileyny, House 83A, Apt 185, Irkutsk;* ↘ *3952 467 442;* e *pribpark@angara.ru; http://pribpark.narod.ru*) Established in 1986 and by far the most visited protected area around Lake Baikal, this park consists of a thin strip of coastline 1–8km deep stretching from Kultuk in the south to Cape Kocherikovsky north of Olkhon, and including the island itself. An area of 418,000ha makes it one of the biggest national parks in Russia and includes 22,000ha of cedar forest.

Zabaikalsky National Park (*Headquarters: pereulok Bolnichny 3, Ust-Barguzin;* ↘ *30131 92 575;* e *zabaikal@burnet.ru*) Also set up in 1986, the 267,000ha which make up this small national park include Chivyrkuysky Bay, the Svyatoy Nos Peninsula (see page 139), the Ushkanie Islands (see page 140) and a large area of mountain and taiga north of Ust-Barguzin. It's fairly accessible to visitors

PUTIN PLUNGES TO NEW DEPTHS

In summer 2009, Russian Prime Minister, Vladimir Putin, embarked on a journey few have made – to the murky bottom of Lake Baikal. The special Mir submarine is being used to investigate the lake's silted depths and Mr Putin displayed his legendary machismo by informing reporters of his 1.4km vertical-trip into what he described as 'plankton soup'. Over two years, two Mir subs were to make 160 dives at various locations to gather information on tectonics and Baikal's ecosystem and to inspect shipwrecks and other things that have plunged to lake's floor (possibly treasure). Despite reassurances from Russian environmentalists, many suspect the subs may have actually been looking for oil and gas reserves at the lake's bottom.

accompanied by guides from the park headquarters, and is home to many species of fauna and several very rare bird types.

In addition to these national parks and reserves, there are several smaller protected nature reserves (заказник, zakaznik), such as around Lake Frolikha (see page 157) and in the Selenga Delta (see page 136).

2

Practical Information

WHEN TO VISIT

SPRING Early spring sees the ice roads add an extra and very welcome layer of infrastructure which the region lacks when Baikal reverts to liquid form. However, spring is a short season in Siberia and the chill of winter can hang on in these parts well into May. Late spring is one of the best times to come as you'll avoid the crowds, though public transport, especially to places such as Olkhon Island, is scarce. As shoulder seasons go, autumn is better.

SUMMER July and August are possibly the worst months to be in Siberia. In addition to bloodthirsty mosquitoes which descend on animals and humans alike like a cloud of post-sundown mini-Draculas, this is when most Russians take their summer holidays. Flights, trains and hotels are overbooked and overpriced, every bus and *marshrutka* is crammed to bursting point, the sultry weather brings out the worst in the Russian character, tempers fray, litter plagues the most popular spots and travel becomes a trial. The heat also plays its part away from the lake's shores, though by the water itself things are cooler and a dip in its still-chilly waters will make you appreciate the high temperatures.

AUTUMN Early autumn is by far the best time to explore Baikal's shores – the worst of the heat has abated, the vast majority of Russian tourists are safely back in their schools and offices, the days are still warm and sunny (though the nights can be pretty chilly) and the landscape plays out an autumnal drama where fiery cedar trees with their yellow needles and black trunks, forest floors carpeted with berries and mushrooms and the snow-topped mountains are the principal characters. Even the mosquitoes have given up the fight by mid-September. Despite the lack of tourists, public transport works almost at its summer peak until late September, meaning even out-of-the-way places can still be reached but without the crush and ticket shortages of the summer.

WINTER If cold is not your thing, a Siberian winter is probably best avoided for pretty obvious reasons. That said, the landscape is perhaps at its most attractive during this season, and there's nothing better than curling up snug and cosy in a Russian Railways bunk and watching the snow-bound taiga crawl by outside the carriage window. Russia is at its most Russian when the air is crisp and clear, your breath immediately turns to tiny ice crystals and a fur hat no longer seems like a luxury.

A 150cm-thick crust of ice forms on Lake Baikal between January and May, lending the landscape a completely different character and facilitating a number of thrilling, if slightly foolhardy, outdoor activities. New Year is one of the most enjoyable times of the year to be anywhere in Russia, and Irkutsk or Ulan-Ude are no exceptions. An invitation to a Russian New Year party should definitely not be turned down – just

35

don't eat for a few days beforehand! Naturally there are fewer tourists around in winter, though cold-weather activities are becoming increasingly popular.

HIGHLIGHTS

BARGUZIN VALLEY Undervisited and with an atmosphere of timeless tranquillity, this wide valley of salt lakes, rock formations, water meadows and grazing wild horses is stunningly beautiful and as remote as it gets. See page 141.

OLKHON ISLAND Join the backpacker crowds on Baikal's biggest island and spiritual retreat. The views across the lake and the mountain-backed Maloe More will smack any gob. See page 105.

IRKUTSK The capital of eastern Siberia is the cultural hub of a huge region and a superb base for Baikal adventures. It's a major stop on the Trans-Siberian Railway, where overlanders leave their compartments to savour the grand 19th-century architecture, rows of timber dwellings and party atmosphere in a city boasting a large student population. See page 79.

SVYATOY NOS The relatively easy climb up the Svyatoy Nos Peninsula which rises from Baikal's eastern shoreline is rewarded with some of the most spectacular wide-screen views of the lake. See page 139.

ULAN-UDE The Buryat capital's Asian faces come as a surprise, as does the biggest Lenin head in the world which gazes across the city's main piazza. With some excellent tour agencies and a couple of fascinating museums, this is the best place to base yourself for some exploration of Buryatiya's remote wilderness areas, Buddhist heritage and long, sandy Baikal shoreline. See page 121.

ARSHAN High up in the Tunka Valley, this pretty alpine spa town is out on a limb, but those who make it here are rewarded with hikes into the Eastern Sayan Mountains, lonely peak-backed Buddhist temples and a warm Buryat welcome. See page 115.

BAIKALSKOE This fishing village on the northwestern shore of the lake is like many others in the region, but its setting between the snow-dusted peaks of the lonely Baikalsky mountain range and the deep blue waters of Baikal itself is simply breathtaking. Hike from Baikalskoe back to Severobaikalsk for an outdoor experience you'll never forget. See page 153.

LISTVYANKA Touristy and much hyped, but still a pretty setting and one of the best places to pick up souvenirs, taste Baikal's *omul* fish and learn a little about the lake's flora and fauna at the local museum. See page 97.

CIRCUMBAIKAL RAILWAY Board a train from Slyudyanka to Port Baikal on the original route of the Trans-Siberian along the southern shores of Lake Baikal. Hiking the route is also a rewarding experience, wild camping and bathing in the lake as you go. See page 113.

IVOLGA As the epicentre of Russian Buddhism, the temple complex is a must-visit for anyone in the region. Show the monks you are genuinely interested in their religion, and they may even let you stay the night at the temple guesthouse and attend morning prayers. See page 128.

1 Take a hike across mythical Olkhon Island.
2 Walk the Great Baikal Trail along the shores of Lake Baikal.
3 Meet the monks on a visit to a Buryat Buddhist temple.
4 Catch a ride on the Circumbaikal Railway from Port Baikal to Slyudyanka.
5 Don't miss a photo opportunity with the world's biggest Lenin head in Ulan-Ude.
6 Call in to see the Old Believers in one of their distinctive villages near Ulan-Ude.
7 Tuck into a plate of steaming hot pozy (Buryat dumplings).
8 Brave the ice roads on a journey across frozen Lake Baikal.
9 Sleep it off during an overnight train ride on the Trans-Siberian or the BAM Railway.
10 Wonder at a Siberian winter sunset over the world's deepest lake.

SUGGESTED ITINERARIES

IN TRANSIT The majority of visitors to the Baikal region do so as part of a stopover while travelling along the Trans-Siberian Railway from Europe to China or Mongolia, or vice-versa. Irkutsk is the most popular halfway stop on the Trans-Siberian, primarily thanks to its transport links and services just a short bus ride away from Lake Baikal. From the city, travellers might make a one-day trip to dip their toes in the chilly waters of the lake at Listvyanka before heading back to Irkutsk to board a train to Moscow, Ulaanbaatar or Beijing.

TRANSIT FOR THE MORE ADVENTUROUS With more time to spare, a few days touring Olkhon Island combined with the more touristy pleasures of Listvyanka is feasible. Another halt, at the less popular though possibly more interesting Trans-Siberian stopover of Ulan-Ude, adds a bit of Asian spice to your journey. Another possible and slightly more adventurous transit route travelling west-to-east is to take a through service from Moscow (or change at Tayshet from the Trans-Siberian on to the BAM) as far as Severobaikalsk. After several days exploring the north of the lake, take a flight down to Ulan-Ude where you can rejoin the Trans-Siberian. If the BAM has tickled your fancy, there are also flights to Ulan-Ude from Taksimo (not covered in this guide), east of Severobaikalsk.

TWO WEEKS In addition to Irkutsk, Listvyanka (and Port Baikal) and Olkhon Island, two weeks is sufficient time to explore Ulan-Ude, the Buddhist temples of Buryatiya, the Barguzin Valley and the less frequented north.

ONE MONTH Four weeks or so are probably sufficient to pay a visit to almost every place in this book. In winter, thanks to the extra transport option provided by the ice roads across Lake Baikal, getting to places such as Ust-Barguzin and other towns and villages on the remote east coast becomes much easier and gives you a lot longer to explore the more mainstream destinations.

TOURIST INFORMATION

ABROAD The official Russian National Tourist Offices are, to be frank, pretty hopeless and seem to be little more than a front for an expensive visa and tour agency. They give out little practical information and maintain badly written, uninformative websites. Tourism is a pretty low priority for the Russian authorities so most travellers fall back on guides, Russian tour company websites (often inaccurate puff) and excellent internet projects maintained by enthusiasts on subjects such as the Trans-Siberian Railway or conservation. Proper tourist information about Buryatiya is virtually non-existent, even in Russia.

Official Russian Tourist Offices

London 70 Piccadilly, London WIJ 8HP; ℡ 020 7495 7570; www.visitrussia.org.uk
Edinburgh 16 Forth St, Edinburgh EH1 3LH; ℡ 0131 550 3709; www.visitrussia.org.uk

New York 224 West 30th St, suite 701, New York, NY 10001; ℡ 877 221 7120; www.russia-travel.com

IN SIBERIA One of the greatest problems encountered by the independent traveller around Lake Baikal (and indeed in the whole of the Russian Federation) is the complete absence of official, impartial, state-funded, accountable tourist offices. Most visitors rely on their hotel or tour company for information, the quality of which can vary wildly. Entities advertising themselves as information offices are simply tour companies trying to reel in customers. Private entities providing a reasonable service can be found in Listvyanka and Severobaikalsk, but Ulan-Ude has nothing and Irkutsk is 'served' by BaikaliInfo, who'll kindly tell you where to buy a map!

MAPS Extremely rarely will you be given a free map in Siberia, and it's a good idea to print town plans off the internet, if possible, before you leave. Good quality maps are hard to source, even in Russia. In most small places (and a good few big ones) around Baikal, locals may have never set eyes on a map of their town/village, so expect a degree of surprise and curiosity if you arrive with one in hand.

If you haven't sourced what you need before you arrive, Irkutsk's **Knigomir Bookshop** (*ul Karla Marksa 28*) always has piles of dusty Irkutsk street plans and an unpredictable assortment of regional maps on sale. This normally includes the best wall map of the lake, produced by the Irkutskaya Kartograficheskaya Fabrika and simply called *Lake Baikal* (1:500,000). Maps of both Buryatiya and the Irkutsk oblast (1:1,000,000) exist but are hard to track down, and street maps of Ulan-Ude, Severobaikalsk and possibly a couple of other larger towns and cities (Angarsk, Slyudyanka) are sporadically available *en lieu*. One surprisingly comprehensive source of cartography is the website of the **Children's Regional Centre for Tourism and Culture** (Областной центр детско-юношеского туризма и краеведения – *www.sutur.irk.ru*) based in Irkutsk, but you'll probably need a good command of Russian to browse and order by email. You'll not find a more exhaustive list of detailed area maps for sale than on this site, and prices are very low, so it could be worth seeking out their headquarters at ul Krasnokazachya 9.

Pre-departure, the ever reliable Stanfords in London (*www.stanfords.co.uk*) stock the excellent *Lake Baikal* (1:550,000), produced by the German publishers Reise Know-How, as well as atlases and maps of the entire Russian Federation, road atlases of Buryatiya and the Irkutsk oblast, and even a street map of Irkutsk, most printed by Roskartografia. Stanfords offer a mail-order service, and it's well worth investing before you set off. Another rather more specialised source is the limited mail-order service provided by Baikalplan in Dresden. You can browse their catalogue of obscure Russian maps at http://shop.baikalplan.de.

TOUR OPERATORS

All of the following tour operators can arrange Trans-Siberian itineraries with stopovers anywhere around Lake Baikal. Be aware that railway tickets purchased from these companies will be much more expensive than those purchased in Russia itself.

UK

Audley Travel New Mill, New Mill Lane, Witney, Oxon OX29 9SX; ✆ 01993 838000; www.audleytravel.com. Trans-Siberian Railway tours & Russian river cruises.

Great Railway Journeys Saviour Hse, 9 St Saviourgate, York YO1 8NL; ✆ 01904 521936; e grj@greatrail.com; www.greatrail.com. Luxury trips from London to Vladivostok via Lake Baikal.

Imaginative Travellers 1 Betts Av, Martlesham Heath, Suffolk IP5 3RH; ✆ 0845 077 8802; e online@imtrav.net; www.imaginative-traveller.com. Trans-Siberian Railway adventures via Lake Baikal.

Intourist 7 Princedale Rd, Holland Park, London W11 4NW; ✆ 020 7727 4100; e info@intourist.co.uk; www.intourist.co.uk. The former state tourist agency is now in the business of helping travellers tour Russia, not preventing them from doing so. Potentially the people most experienced in organising travel to Russia, they can arrange any type of tour you may think of, or just flights & visas.

Just Go Russia ✆ 020 3355 7717; e info@justgorussia.co.uk; www.justgorussia.co.uk. Russia specialists with tours across the country, including a cycling break on Olkhon Island & a multi-sport 11-day activity holiday taking in Baikal & the Tunka Valley.

Muir's Tours Nepal Hse, 97a Swansea Rd, Reading RG1 8HA; ✆ 0118 950 2281; e info@nkf-mt.org.uk; www.nkf-mt.org.uk. Trekking & horseriding trips in the Eastern Sayan Mountains & rafting on the Oka River.

On the Go 68 North End Rd, West Kensington, London W14 9EP; ✆ 020 7371 1113; www.onthegotours.com. Tailor-made Trans-Siberian tours.

Regent Holidays Mezzanine Suite, Froomsgate Hse, Rupert St, Bristol BS1 2QJ; ✆ 0845 277 3317; e regent@regent-holidays.co.uk; www.regent-holidays.co.uk. Four-day Baikal cruises out of Irkutsk, all inclusive (without flights) from £450.

Russian Gateway 83 Willes Rd, Leamington Spa, Warwks CV31 1BS; ✆ 01926 426460; e travel@russiangateway.co.uk; www.russiangateway.co.uk. Don't currently include Lake Baikal in their brochure but may in future.

Scotts Tours 141 Whitfield St, London W1T 5EW; ✆ 020 7383 5353; e independenttravel@scottstours.co.uk; www.scottstours.co.uk. Russia specialists offering independent itineraries & a visa service.

The Russia Experience Research Hse, Fraser Rd, Perivale, Middx UB6 7AQ; ✆ 020 8566 8846; e info@trans-siberian.co.uk; www.trans-siberian.co.uk. Possibly the best agency to contact about travel to Lake Baikal on the Trans-Siberian Railway.

NORTH AMERICA

Go to Russia 309A Peters St, Atlanta, GA 30313, USA; ✆ 404 827 0099; www.gotorussia.net

The Society of International Railway Travelers 1810 Sils Av, Louisville, KY 40205, USA; ✆ 502 454 0277; www.irtsociety.com

Sokol Tours ✆ 724 935 5373; www.sokoltours.com. An excellent agency that can set up visits to Irkutsk, Ulan-Ude & Olkhon Island, rides on the BAM & Circumbaikal Railways & hikes around Lake Baikal.

Intours Corp 2150 Bloor St West, Suite 308, Toronto, Ontario M6S 1M8, Canada; ✆ 416 766 4720; www.torussia.com

Trek Escapes 223 Carlton St, Toronto M5A 2L2, Canada; ✆ 416 922 7584; www.trekescapes.com

LOCAL TOUR COMPANIES AND HELPERS

Alyona Maryasova ✆ +7 9148 759818; e kolonok2004@yandex.ru. Based in Severobaikalsk, Alyona can help with accommodation & other services in the north, runs her own hostel (Baikal Trail Hostel) & information centre in Severobaikalsk, & is heavily involved with the Great Baikal Trail project & the local School for Tourism & Ecological Education. She speaks good English & is very helpful.

Baikal Adventures e info@baikaladventures.com; www.baikaladventures.com. Small baseless tour company offering a range of ecotours, horseriding trips, safaris & various Baikal excursions. May be slow to answer emails & there's no phone number.

Baikal Discovery ✆ +7 3952 200 550; e travel@baikal-discovery.ru; www.baikal-discovery.ru. Irkutsk-based tour agency which facilitates entry into the Baikal ice marathon. Takes its green credentials seriously.

Baikal Ecotour 196-12 Gagarin Mikrorayon, Baikalsk; ✆ +7 902 576 7319; www.baikaltur.com. An English-speaking tour company based in Baikalsk & running a limited number of multi-day tours, mostly around the south of the lake.

Baikaler ✆ +7 3952 336240, +7 9085 439 686; e baikaler@mail.ru; www.baikaler.com. Jack Sheremetoff is well versed in travellers' needs & is the person to contact in Irkutsk if you are looking for budget accommodation (hostel or homestay) or trips to Listvyanka, Krestovka, Olkhon Island & many other places on request. A friendly English-language welcome to the region is his most appreciated service.

Buryat Intour Kirova ul 28a, Ulan-Ude; ✆ +7 3012 216954; www.buryatintour.ru. Tours of Ulan-Ude & the surrounding area, excursions to the major sights in Buryatiya, botanical & birdwatching tours.

Baikal Naran Tour Hotel Buryatiya, Office 105, Kommunisticheskaya ul 47a, Ulan-Ude; ✆ +7 3012 215097; e baikalnarantour@mail.ru; www.baikalnarantour.com. Svetlana (Sesegma) & her well-regimented staff can organise any type of trip, from a city tour of Ulan-Ude to birdwatching in the Selenga Delta, from an evening in an Old Believers' village to hunting trips into the taiga. Ask about their incredibly off-the-beaten track horseriding trips from the village of Verkhnyy Torey across the Khamar Daban mountains to Vydrino on Lake Baikal, an unforgettable experience. This superb agency regularly wins the award for best tour operator in Buryatiya, & they are the best people to turn to in the Buryat capital.

Baikal Trekking ✆ +7 9086 662744; www.baikaltrekking.com. Small Irkutsk-based agency organising all kinds of treks & expeditions, including ice trekking & ice cycling.

Firn Travel Ul Babushkina 13a, Ulan-Ude; ✆ +7 3012 555055; www.firntravel.ru. Another trustworthy agency that specialises in ecotourism & adventure tours.

GoBaikal Ul Oktyabrya, Block 16, Apt 2, Severobaikalsk; ✆ +7 30139 21 560; e rashit.yahin@usa.net; www.gobaikal.com. Former BAM worker & tour guide Rashit Yahin has been welcoming independent travellers to the north of Lake Baikal for donkey's years. Rashit suffered a stroke a few years back, but can still arrange tours, & is forever coming up with exciting new ideas (such as tours for the disabled). He is usually quick to answer emails.

In the World of Fantasy Office 2, 11 pereulok 8 Marta, Irkutsk; ✆ +7 3952 204 250; www.baikal.iwf.ru. A large agency with offices in Moscow, St Petersburg & Irkutsk, dealing mainly with Russian clientele.

Irkavia Ul Shiryamova 9; ✆ 3952 287730; www.irkavia.ru. This tiny air company offers helicopter tours from Irkutsk to various points around the south of the lake. Flight times range from 90mins to 5hrs.

Khatan Dangina Ul Pushkina 4, Ulan-Ude; ✆ +7 3012 260 592; www.baikalkhan.ru. A small local outfit which also owns the Baatare Urgöö yurt restaurant on the outskirts of Ulan-Ude. Mainly focuses on Buryat culture tours.

Meridian 109 Ul Rabochaya 143 (airport), Nizhneangarsk; ✆ +7 30130 47 700; www.109meridian.ru. An experienced & well-organised tour company based at the airport in Nizhneangarsk. Staff organise inexpensive excursions to places such as Dzelinda, Goudzhekit & Baikalskoe as well as permits to land on the northeastern shore. Unfortunately none of the staff speak much English.

Valery Semeykin Ul Akademicheskaya 2, Apt 8, Listvyanka; e baikal-inform@irk.ru; www.etur.ru/experts/31. English-speaking tour guide & Baikal expert who runs a small homestay in Listvyanka & personally leads fascinating hikes, horse rides & canoe trips around Listvyanka & further afield.

RED TAPE

VISAS The biggest headache prior to any trip to Russia is obtaining a visa. There are basically three types of visa: private, tourist and business. To obtain a private visa you must have an official invitation from a person ordinarily resident in Russia. These are the most complicated to obtain and a real hassle for the Russian citizen involved. Tourist visas are valid for 30 days, just about long enough to visit the entire Baikal region. The best visa to have is a business visa, which can be multi-entry and valid for up to one year. These are tough to organise on your own and it's best to go through a visa agency. They cost more, but the extra validity can be useful for longer exploration. All travellers to Russia should be aware that overstaying a visa results in a fine, automatic deportation and a ban from returning to the country for five years. There's no right of appeal and only a huge bribe, or the intervention of a person in very high political office, will get you off the hook.

Visa agencies The simplest way to obtain a Russian visa is to let someone else do it. There are numerous agencies that can apply for the visa on your behalf and generally make the process a whole lot simpler and less stressful. You'll pay a charge for the service, but as anyone who has tried to get a visa unassisted will tell you, it's money well spent. Agencies can also arrange many other aspects of travel to Russia and neighbouring countries, such as (expensive) visa registration, flights, hotels and railway tickets.

Real Russia 3 The Ivories, Northampton St, Islington, London N1 2HY; ☎ 020 7100 7370; f 020 7900 3633; www.realrussia.co.uk
Alpha–Omega Travel 16 Eldon Pl, Bradford, West Yorkshire BD1 3AZ; ☎ 01274 760 600; f 01274 760 633; www.alpha-omega.ru

Zierer Visa Service 60 East 42nd St, suite 1250, New York, NY 10165; ☎ 866 788 1100; www.zvs.com. Other offices in Houston, San Francisco, Washington, Europe & Australia.

On arrival Before landing in Moscow or as you approach the Russian border by land, you'll be required to fill in an immigration card, similar to that completed by non-EU visitors to the UK. You must complete both halves (in Latin letters or Cyrillic) as the card (or piece of paper) is ripped in half by the border official who keeps one section and inserts the other into your passport (bring a paperclip). You must keep this safe as you'll need it to get out of the country. Your passport is stamped (either on the visa itself or on the facing page) and you're in.

Visa registration Visa registration is a thorn in the side of every traveller to Russia. This farcical process affords travellers a small taste of the tiresome bureaucratic absurdity Russians have to endure on a daily basis to get anything done. Officially, the law requires all foreigners to register in any large town or city where they spend three or more working days. Therefore, if you arrive in Irkutsk and plan to stay a week, it's a good idea to register. Staying at large expensive hotels means you won't have to worry as the process is done for you by reception staff. Problems arise when staying in homestays and hostels which don't offer the service. In this case, forget trying to register with the police directly; usually a few hundred roubles slipped discreetly to a hotel receptionist or travel agency staff will suffice to obtain the necessary paperwork. In theory it should be possible for your host (if you have one) to register you through the post office but this is rarely done in practice.

According to the law, it would be possible to get off the Trans-Siberian at numerous places, spend less than three days in each and never register. But not having even one registration stamp after a month in Russia exposes you to the risk of being fined or even deported at the border, even if you have an explanation. So what's the best strategy to beat the system? Well, in the Baikal region it is only realistically possible to register visas in Irkutsk, Ulan-Ude and, at a push, Severobaikalsk. The most hassle-free course of action is to register in Irkutsk or Ulan-Ude if you plan to use either as a base. This will give you at least one stamp to satisfy the police and immigration. If you are then heading to Mongolia or China, there's no need to register again; if travelling west to Moscow, register again in the capital. It must be said that in Siberia, unlike Moscow and St Petersburg, you'll hardly ever see a policeman in the streets, and the chances of your documents being scrutinised by the *militsiya* are low. In recent years the police seem to have been warned off hassling foreigners about visas and registration anyway.

CUSTOMS If you're flying into Irkutsk or Ulan-Ude via Moscow, you'll have already gone through customs in the capital and will not have to repeat the process on landing in Siberia. Officers are pretty uninterested in foreign tourists these days, and if you pass through the Green Channel you'd be unlucky to be pulled over for a search.

The rules on import and export limits are complicated and arcane, but there are a couple which occasionally trip up the unsuspecting traveller. You are only allowed to bring in US$10,000 in cash or travellers' cheques, but can take out US$3,000 – credit cards, debit cards etc don't count. If you buy an item made more than 100 years ago you must clear export with the Ministry of Culture in Moscow. This could also apply to antiques and culturally valuable items irrespective of when they were originally produced. Otherwise you may, without paying duty, import/export two litres of spirits (from 21 years of age), 250g of sturgeon roe in factory cans, 50 cigars, 100 cigarillos, 200 cigarettes and 250g of tobacco.

If you're considering taking anything valuable into Russia that you may have to declare (professional camera equipment, vehicles, large amounts of cash, rifles etc), it's worth checking out the official website of the Russian Federal Customs Service at www.customs.ru/en/ (in English), before you leave. Duty levied on such items is high, and you may even need a licence or carnet.

E EMBASSIES

RUSSIAN DIPLOMATIC MISSIONS ABROAD

Australia (Embassy) 78 Canberra Av, Griffith, ACT 2603; ✆ 6295 9474; www.australia.mid.ru. (Consulate-General) 7–9 Fullerton St, Woollahra, Sydney, NSW 2025; ✆ 9326 1188

Canada 52 Range Rd, Ottawa, Ontario KIN 8J5; ✆ 613 236 7220

China 100600 Beijing, Dongzhimennei Beizhong St 4, Sanlitum; ✆ 10 6532 1267

France 40–50, Bd Lannes, F-75116 Paris; ✆ 01 45 040 550

Germany Unter den Linden 63–65, 10117 Berlin; ✆ 030 229 1110

Ireland 186 Orwell Rd, Rathgar, Dublin; ✆ 01 492 3525

Israel 120 Rehov Hayarkon, 63573 Tel Aviv; ✆ 03 522 6744

Japan 1-1 Azabudai 2-chome, Tokyo 106-0041; ✆ 03 3583 4445

Mongolia A 6 Enkhtayvany gudamzh (Friendship St), Ulaanbaatar; ✆ 1 327 071

New Zealand 57 Messines Rd, Wellington; ✆ 04 476 6113

South Africa 316 Brooks St, Menlo Park, Pretoria 0001, PO Box 6743; ✆ 2712 362 1337/8

UK 5 Kensington Palace Gardens, London W8 4QS; ✆ 020 7229 8027; www.great-britain.mid.ru

Ukraine Vul. Kutuzova, Kiev; ✆ 044 294 7936

USA 2650 Wisconsin Ave NW, Washington, DC; ✆ 202 298 5700; www.russianembassy.org

FOREIGN DIPLOMATIC MISSIONS IN MOSCOW The telephone code for Moscow is +7 495 from abroad.

Australia Podkolokolny pereulok 10A; ✆ 956 6070; www.aus.ru

Canada Starokonyushenny pereulok 23; ✆ 105 6000; www.dfait-maeci.gc.ca

China ul Druzhby 6; ✆ 938 2006; http://ru.china-embassy.org

France Bolshaya Iakimanka 45; ✆ 937 1500; www.ambafrance.ru

Germany Leninski prospekt 95; ✆ 933 43 11; www.moskau.diplo.de

Ireland Grokholsky pereulok 5; ✆ 937 5911; e moscowembassy@dfa.ie

Israel Bolshaya Ordynka ul 56; ✆ 230 6700; http://moscow.mfa.gov.il

Japan Kalashny pereulok 12; ✆ 291 8500; www.ru.emb-japan.go.jp

Mongolia Borisoglebsky pereulok 11; ✆ 290 6792; e mongolia@glasnet.ru

New Zealand Povarskaya ul 44; ✆ 956 3579; www.nzembassy.msk.ru

South Africa Granatny pereulok 1; ✆ 540 1177; www.saembassy.ru

UK Smolenskaya Naberezhnaya 10; ✆ 956 7200; www.britaininrussia.ru

Ukraine Leontievsky pereulok 18; ✆ 229 1079; www.ukremb.ru

USA Bolshoy Devyatinsky pereulok 8; ✆ 728 5000; http://moscow.usembassy.gov

FOREIGN CONSULATES IN THE BAIKAL REGION
Mongolia ul Lapina 11, Irkutsk; ℡ 342145, ul Erbanova 12, Ulan-Ude; ℡ 220419

GETTING THERE AND AWAY

In a time when Siberia teems with audacious individuals circumnavigating the globe by bike, on foot, by motorbike (*Long Way Round*-style), on horseback or in a number of other curious ways (jogging, unicycling, in a gypsy caravan, by 2CV, walking backwards), most travellers (though sometimes one wonders) take the train – the famous Trans-Siberian – from Moscow, Beijing or Ulaanbaatar. Others prefer to fly, though an air ticket to Irkutsk or Ulan-Ude from Europe or America comes with a hefty price tag.

BY RAIL The most common way travellers reach Lake Baikal is on the Trans-Siberian Railway from Moscow, Beijing or Ulaanbaatar. Romantic rail journey to some, claustrophobic nightmare to others; if your idea of travel hell is being

---

PACKING FOR THE TRANS-SIBERIAN

Embarking on a three-day train trip without some vital pieces of kit can turn the journey into an uncomfortable ordeal. Here are some tips on what to take (and not take) to survive the Trans-Siberian with ease.

THINGS TO TAKE
- Loose-fitting clothes such as a tracksuit – so you can join your fellow travellers' pyjama party
- Slippers or flip-flops – so you don't have to keep lacing up your walking boots 20 times a day
- Copy of Tolstoy's *War and Peace* which should just about last you the three or four days it takes to get from Moscow to Irkutsk or Ulan-Ude. As you read it, tear out the pages to use as loo roll (NB: a potential cultural faux pas in the company of educated Russians)
- Tea, coffee, sugar, instant noodles, cup, fork, spoon, food to share with others in your compartment
- Russian dictionary and/or phrasebook
- Cards, travel chess – so Russian passengers can thrash you at both (NO playing for money with strangers)
- iPod for when language barrier or boredom kick in
- Soap – to avoid using the slimy grey communal bar in the toilets
- Glasses case – so you don't wake up after the first night served on a bed of crushed specs
- Toilet paper – essential should you not have a half-read copy of *War and Peace*
- Standard British gas meter box key – opens windows, toilet doors etc

THINGS TO LEAVE AT HOME
- Cavernous wheeled suitcase
- Personal DVD player; look out of the window or talk to fellow passengers instead (plus it won't be stolen)
- Shower gel (showers are very rare)
- Sleeping bag (bedding is included in the ticket price)
- Any notion of personal space or privacy

imprisoned for days in a swaying cupboard with three strangers who drink vodka for breakfast, never shower and don't speak your language, forget it – fly. If you are the type who likes to go native, meet the locals, down '100-gram' shots of vodka at seven in the morning and doesn't mind body odour, snoring, constipation-inducing food and a complete lack of privacy, then you'll survive the Trans-Siberian with many a riveting travel tale to tell.

Train and carriage types There are basically four types of carriage on intercity express trains used for the vast majority of journeys – SV (СВ) with two berths (most expensive); *kupe* (купе) with four berths; *platskart* (плацкарт), an open dorm carriage with around 50 bunks; and the rare *obshchy* (общий) class (seats). Most foreigners plump for *kupe* as it affords some degree of privacy but is considerably cheaper than *SV* (which is, more often than not, hopelessly sold out anyway). All Trans-Siberian services are allotted numbers, and basically the rule is that the lower the number, the faster (and possibly better) the train. The flagship service is the *Rossiya* (No 1 westbound, No 2 eastbound) which travels the entire Moscow to Vladivostok route, but there are dozens of other trains plying sections of the line from, say, Irkutsk to Ulan-Ude or Moscow to Khabarovsk. *Elektrichki* are slow trains which trundle at a leisurely pace between small towns and big cities, stopping at every village and hamlet along the way. These have just one type of carriage, with rows of six seats, but there are up to

PLATSKART VERSUS KUPE

Platskart for some, *kupe* for others, the debate rages on between Trans-Siberian aficionados. Here are some of the pros and cons:

PLATSKART: PROS
- It's cheaper.
- You meet more people.
- Your gear is safer as there are more people around to watch it.
- You're likely to get more free food from your fellow passengers (there are more of them).

PLATSKART: CONS
- You have a lot less privacy than in *kupe*.
- Your gear is less safe as there are more people around to see it.
- The air is stuffier, smellier and hotter.
- There are the same number of toilets as in *kupe* but more passengers.

KUPE: PROS
- You get more privacy with only four bunks per compartment.
- Your stuff is safer as you can lock the door.
- The toilets are not overflowing with people, loo roll and...
- It's quieter minus the kids, drunks, small farm animals and incessant comings and goings of *platskart*.

KUPE: CONS
- It's more expensive.
- You can get stuck with three people you'd rather not share a confined space with.
- You meet fewer fellow travellers.

three different classes to choose from. Second class is comfortable enough; third class should probably be avoided.

Buying tickets Russian railway tickets can be bought in your home country prior to departure (most expensive; see *Tour operators* on page 38), at service centres, local travel agents and private ticket kiosks in Russia, and from ordinary ticket windows at the railway station (cheapest). Tickets go on sale 45 days in advance and can be bought up to departure time. Purchasing tickets for your entire journey before you leave home gives peace of mind but ties you down to sometimes unrealistic schedules. Doing things as you go along is usually cheaper and gives you time to spend an extra day in a place you like, or take up an unexpected invitation to someone's home. Even in July and August tickets rarely sell out completely, though you may not get the specific train or carriage type you want.

If you're buying tickets from stations as you go but speak no Russian, do a little research before you set off (you'll find a comprehensive online timetable at *www.rzd.ru*) and write down on a piece of paper exactly what you want (you could even get a local to scribble it down in Cyrillic). You should include the destination, date, train number, carriage type and how many tickets you need. Big-city railway ticket sellers are quite used to foreigners, but never seem to understand or speak a word of English.

Getting to Moscow If you're doing the trip to Lake Baikal on the Trans-Siberian Railway from Europe, you'll first have to get to Moscow. The easiest way is to fly and most European national carriers operate flights to the Russian capital with prices starting at £200 return from London. BMI, Transaero, Aeroflot and British Airways all have scheduled flights between Moscow and London's airports. An expensive if more romantic mode of transport is to take the train. The internet rail-travel bible Seat 61 (*www.seat61.com*) explains how to do this with the best-price tickets coming in at £150 one way. A tried-and-tested ultra-cheap route is to take a Ryanair flight (*www.ryanair.com*) from Stansted to Riga, then an Ecolines bus (*www.ecolines.net*) from there to Moscow. Booking the flight well in advance, it has been known for some travellers to get all the way from London to Moscow for as little as £35.

Useful rail services

Moscow–Irkutsk Train No 2 *Rossiya* (*departs: every odd date; journey time: 75hrs*) is the quickest and most comfortable, though tickets (around RUB10,000 for *kupe*, no *platskart* carriages) can be hard to come by in summer. Train No 10 *Baikal* (*departs: on even dates; journey time: 75hrs*) is only marginally slower and has *platskart* carriages (RUB3,400) and *kupe* berths (RUB8,000–10,000). Many other cheaper but slower services make the approximately three-day run.

Moscow–Ulan-Ude Train No 2 *Rossiya* (*departs: every odd date; journey time: 83hrs*) continues to Ulan-Ude on its way to Vladivostok. Other useful services include trains No 222 (*departs: on even dates; journey time: 89hrs*), No 44 (*departs: on odd dates; journey time: 93hrs*) and No 350 (*departs: on odd dates, journey time: 96hrs*), but some slower trains can take over five days. Ulaanbaatar- and Beijing-bound expresses also call at the Buryat capital but tickets are normally scarce if booked at short notice.

Moscow–Severobaikalsk The only two direct services are trains No 76 (*departs: on odd dates; journey time: 90hrs*) and 92 (*departs: on odd dates; journey time: 90hrs*), with *platskart* (RUB3,500) and *kupe* (RUB6,500) carriages. Otherwise a change in Krasnoyarsk is necessary.

Severobaikalsk–Irkutsk Train No 71 (*departs: on odd dates; journey time: 32hrs*) loops round via Tayshet. Tickets cost RUB1,300 for a bunk in *platskart*, RUB2,600 in *kupe*. In the opposite direction (*departs: on odd dates*) the number of this service stays the same.

Other routes Although taking the train from Moscow is the most convenient route, you can (and may need to) join the Trans-Siberian somewhere else. There are now direct trains from Berlin via Warsaw to Irkutsk (contact German Railways; *www.db.de*); and coming from the east there are, of course, direct trains from Vladivostok, Beijing and the Mongolian capital, Ulaanbaatar. In December 2008, the no-frills airline Wizzair (*www.wizzair.com*) launched eagerly anticipated flights from the UK to Kiev (Ukraine), from where it's just a short express train hop to Kharkov and direct services (train No 53) to Irkutsk and Ulan-Ude. Be warned, however: this train passes through a tiny corner of Kazakhstan and you might need an extra visa plus a multi-entry visa for Russia.

✈ **BY AIR** For those on a tight schedule or with an aversion to almost four days on the Russian rails, the plane is the only alternative. Flights to Irkutsk and Ulan-Ude from western and eastern Europe always require a change of planes (and usually airport) in Moscow as there are no direct connections. Fares from the UK start at around £500 return with Aeroflot, and there are virtually no bargains or last-minute deals to be had. Sometimes a combination of flight to Krasnoyarsk or Omsk and train can save you money.

The following airlines operate scheduled flights to the region:

Aeroflot (*www.aeroflot.co.uk*, *www.aeroflot.ru*) Russia's national airline has almost shaken off its Soviet image (though its logo still bears the hammer and sickle) and vastly improved its safety record. Now a member of the somewhat second-division group of airlines called SkyTeam (alongside such illustrious names of the airline world as Alitalia and KLM), on-board service is nonetheless excellent and aircraft are of a high standard on international flights. Planes used on domestic runs can be slightly below the standard you may be used to in Europe or the US. Aeroflot operate services from most European capitals to Moscow, with planes landing at Sheremetyevo 2, and onward services to Irkutsk (5½ hours) taking off from Sheremetyevo 1 (a free shuttle bus runs between the two Sheremetyevo airports). This is by far the best routing as Aeroflot are a big scheduled operation and unlikely to cancel flights due to an oligarch owner's refusal to write a cheque for aviation fuel (it does happen).

S7 (*www.s7.ru*) Known in the early noughties as Sibir Airlines, S7 is now Russia's largest domestic carrier, operating over 120 flights a day. It is the most user-friendly of Russia's airlines and has a budget airline-style website, e-tickets and a relatively high standard of customer service. S7 flights link Moscow with Irkutsk, Ulan-Ude and Bratsk, and Irkutsk with St Petersburg, Bratsk, Beijing and Shenyang. However, S7 has an unfortunate safety record, though it must be added this has not always been the airline's own fault. In July 2006, one of its planes skidded off the runway at Irkutsk Airport and slammed into a building, killing around 120 of the 192 passengers and crew on board. In 2004 one of the two airlines brought down by Chechen terrorists near Moscow was a Sibir flight, and it was one of this airline's planes that was accidentally shot down by a Ukrainian surface-to-air missile over the Black Sea in October 2001. So make sure you fasten your safety belt.

KrasAir (*www.krasair.ru*) The unfortunately named KrasAir operates flights from Moscow to Ulan-Ude and Irkutsk via Krasnoyarsk. You could combine a flight from Moscow to Krasnoyarsk with a short onward Trans-Siberian trip to Lake Baikal to at least get a flavour of life on the rails. In mid 2009 this airline looked to be on the verge of going out of business.

VIM Airlines (*www.vim-avia.com*) Virtually unknown in the West, VIM is one of the biggest Russian domestic carriers, with flights from Moscow to Ulan-Ude and Bratsk (on the BAM Railway).

BY CAR During your time around Lake Baikal you are sure to notice the odd car with a non-Russian number plate (usually a VW Campervan or Citroen 2CV) which has made it all the way from Europe to this far-flung region. As the crow flies it's 6,650km from London to Irkutsk, or around 8,000–9,000km by road. Several vehicles make it every year, and a good book to read if you are thinking about embarking on an overland trip is *Linger Longer – Driving the Trans-Siberian* by Chris and Simon Raven, who did the trip from the UK to Vladivostok in an old Ford Sierra. Other good overland driving stories are told at www.4wd4life.com.au/johnandcarys and at www.dreamers1.com/russia/practicalities/.

BORDERS The only border anywhere near Lake Baikal is with Mongolia to the south. The two crossings open to foreigners are at Kyakhta (road from Atanbulag) and Naushki (Trans-Mongolian rail line from Sukhbaatar and Ulaanbaatar). The bad news for travellers who want to see Khövsgöl, Baikal's Mongolian sister lake, then continue on to Siberia, is that the border at Mondy is closed to foreigners, meaning a convoluted trip via Darkhan in Mongolia. There is no border between the Irkutsk Region and the Republic of Buryatiya.

Note that if you are heading from Ulan-Ude to Ulaanbaatar or vice-versa, it's much better to go by bus, as this service negotiates the border in less than an hour, while trains can loiter for several hours.

✚ HEALTH with Dr Felicity Nicholson

RISKS Minor irritations such as sunburn or a bout of travellers' diarrhoea aside, the vast majority of visits to Lake Baikal pass without the need for helicopter evacuation. However, serious threats to your health come in the form of sunstroke, hyperthermia and tick-borne encephalitis (see box on page 50), all of which are potentially fatal. Diseases which can be avoided easily are HIV/AIDS and others of the sexually transmitted type, rife across the former Soviet Union, especially among sex workers.

IMMUNISATIONS Becoming seriously ill in eastern Siberia is a travel experience you'll probably want to avoid, so getting a few pre-departure jabs is advisable. It would be wise to be up to date with **tetanus, diphtheria and polio**, which come as an all-in-one jab (Revaxis) which lasts for ten years. **Hepatitis A** vaccine may also be recommended. One dose covers for a year but can be boosted at least six months after the first dose to give at least 20 years of cover.

Other vaccinations that may be relevant include hepatitis B, rabies and tick-borne encephalitis. **Hepatitis B** is recommended for those who are working with children or in a medical setting, and **rabies** for people working with animals or for more extensive trips. Travellers wishing to visit more rural parts of Siberia from late spring to autumn should take precautions against **tick-borne encephalitis** (see box on page 50). If you're travelling during the Russian 'flu season' (winter and early spring) a **flu** jab is a very good idea. Only if you intend to stay for a protracted period of time should you consider inoculation against **Japanese encephalitis** and **typhoid**.

Dr Felicity Nicholson

Any prolonged immobility, including travel by land or air, can result in deep-vein thrombosis (DVT) with the risk of embolus to the lungs. Certain factors can increase the risk and these include:

- Having a previous clot or a close relative with a history
- People over 40, with increased risk in over 80s
- Recent major operation or varicose-veins surgery
- Cancer
- Stroke
- Heart disease
- Obesity
- Pregnancy
- Hormone therapy
- Heavy smokers
- Severe varicose veins
- People who are tall (over 6ft/1.8m) or short (under 5ft/1.5m)

A deep-vein thrombosis causes painful swelling and redness of the calf or sometimes the thigh. It is only dangerous if a clot travels to the lungs (pulmonary embolus). Symptoms of a pulmonary embolus (PE) – which commonly start three to ten days after a long flight – include chest pain, shortness of breath, and sometimes coughing up small amounts of blood. Anyone who thinks that they might have a DVT needs to see a doctor immediately.

PREVENTION OF DVT
- Keep mobile before and during the flight; move around every couple of hours
- Drink plenty of fluids during the flight
- Avoid taking sleeping pills and excessive tea, coffee and alcohol
- Consider wearing flight socks or support stockings (see www.legshealth.com)

If you think you are at increased risk of a clot, ask your doctor if it is safe to travel.

TRAVEL CLINICS AND HEALTH INFORMATION A full list of current travel clinic websites worldwide is available on www.istm.org/. For other journey preparation information, consult www.nathnac.org/ds/map_world.aspx. Information about various medications may be found on www.netdoctor.co.uk/travel.

UK

Berkeley Travel Clinic 32 Berkeley St, London W1J 8EL (near Green Park tube station); ☎ 020 7629 6233; ⏰ 10.00–18.00 Mon–Fri; 10.00–15.00 Sat
Cambridge Travel Clinic 41 Hills Rd, Cambridge CB2 1NT; ☎ 01223 367362; f 01223 368021; e enquiries@travelcliniccambridge.co.uk; www.travelcliniccambridge.co.uk; ⏰ 10.00–16.00 Mon, Tue & Sat, 12.00–19.00 Wed & Thu, 11.00–18.00 Fri
Edinburgh Travel Health Clinic 14 East Preston St, Newington, Edinburgh EH8 9QA; ☎ 0131 667 1030; www.edinburghtravelhealthclinic.co.uk;

⏰ 09.00–19.00 Mon–Wed, 9.00–18.00 Thu & Fri. Travel vaccinations & advice on all aspects of malaria prevention. All current UK prescribed anti-malaria tablets in stock.
Fleet Street Travel Clinic 29 Fleet St, London EC4Y 1AA; ☎ 020 7353 5678; www.fleetstreetclinic.com; ⏰ 08.45–17.30 Mon–Fri. Injections, travel products & latest advice.
Hospital for Tropical Diseases Travel Clinic Mortimer Market Centre, 2nd floor, Capper St (off Tottenham Court Rd), London WC1E 6AU; ☎ 020 7388 9600; www.thehtd.org; ⏰ 09.00–16.00. Offers consultations

& advice, & can provide all necessary drugs & vaccines for travellers. Runs a healthline (020 7950 7799) for country-specific information & health hazards. Also stocks nets, water purification equipment & personal protection measures. Travellers who have returned from the tropics & are unwell, with fever or bloody diarrhoea, can attend the walk-in emergency clinic at the hospital without an appointment.

MASTA (Medical Advisory Service for Travellers Abroad), at the London School of Hygiene & Tropical Medicine, Keppel St, London WC1 7HT; 09068 224100; e enquiries@masta.org; www.masta-travel-health.com. Calls to the premium-line telephone number are charged at 60p per minute. For a fee, they will provide an individually tailored health brief, with up-to-date information on how to stay healthy, inoculations & what to take.

MASTA pre-travel clinics 01276 685040. Call or check http://www.masta-travel-health.com/travel-clinic.aspx for the nearest clinic; there are currently 30 in Britain. They also sell malaria prophylaxis, memory cards, treatment kits, bednets, net treatment kits etc.

NHS travel website www.fitfortravel.nhs.uk. Provides country-by-country advice on immunisation & malaria

prevention, plus details of recent developments & a list of relevant health organisations.

Nomad Travel Stores 3–4 Wellington Terrace, Turnpike Lane, London N8 0PX; 020 8889 7014; f 020 8889 9528; e turnpike@nomadtravel.co.uk; www.nomadtravel.co.uk; walk-in or appointments 09.15–17.00 daily, late nights Thu. Six stores countrywide: 3 in London, plus Bristol, Southampton, Manchester. As well as dispensing health advice, Nomad stocks mosquito nets & other anti-bug devices, & an excellent range of adventure travel gear.

InterHealth Travel Clinic 111 Westminster Bridge Rd, London SE1 7HR; 020 7902 9000; e info@interhealth.org.uk; www.interhealth.org.uk; 08.30–17.30 Mon–Fri. Competitively priced, one-stop travel health service by appointment only.

Trailfinders Immunisation Centre 194 Kensington High St, London W8 7RG; 020 7938 3999; www.trailfinders.com/travelessentials/travelclinic.htm; 09.00–17.00 Mon, Tue, Wed & Fri, 09.00–18.00 Thu, 10.00–17.15 Sat. No appointment necessary.

Travelpharm www.travelpharm.com. The Travelpharm website offers up-to-date guidance on travel-related health & has a range of medications available through their online mini-pharmacy.

Irish Republic

Tropical Medical Bureau Grafton St Medical Centre, Grafton Buildings, 34 Grafton St, Dublin 2; 1 671 9200. Has a useful website specific to tropical destinations: www.tmb.ie.

USA

Centers for Disease Control 1600 Clifton Rd, Atlanta, GA 30333; freephone 1 800 232 4636 or 1 800 232 6348; e cdcinfo@cdc.gov; www.cdc.gov/travel. The central source of travel information in the USA. Each summer they publish the invaluable *Health Information for International Travel*.

IAMAT (International Association for Medical Assistance to Travelers) 1623 Military Rd, #279, Niagara Falls, NY 14304-1745; 716 754 4883; e info@iamat.org; www.iamat.org. A non-profit organisation with free membership that provides lists of English-speaking doctors abroad.

Canada

IAMAT (International Association for Medical Assistance to Travellers) Suite 1, 1287 St Clair Av W, Toronto, Ontario M6E 1B8; 416 652 0137; www.iamat.org

TMVC Suite 314, 1030 W Georgia St, Vancouver, BC V6E 2Y3; 905 648 1112; info@tmvc.com; www.tmvc.com. One-stop medical clinic for all international travel medicine & vaccination needs.

Australia, New Zealand, Thailand

TMVC (Travel Doctors Group) 1300 65 88 44; www.tmvc.com.au. 22 clinics in Australia, New Zealand & Thailand, inc Canterbury Arcade, 170 Queen St, Auckland; 09 373 3531; 75a Astor Terrace, Spring Hill, Brisbane, QLD 4000; 07 3815 6900; brisbane@traveldoctor.com.au; Dr Sonny Lau, 393 Little Bourke St, 2nd floor, Melbourne, VIC 3000; 03 9935 8100; melbourne@traveldoctor.com.au; Dr Mandy Hu, Dymocks Bldg, 7th floor, 428 George St, Sydney, NSW 2000; 02 9221 7133; f 02 9221 8401

IAMAT PO Box 5049, Christchurch 5, New Zealand; www.iamat.org

South Africa

SAA-Netcare Travel Clinics e travelinfo@netcare.co.za; www.travelclinic.co.za. 12 clinics throughout South Africa.

TMVC NHC Health Centre, Cnr Beyers Naude & Waugh, Northcliff; ℡ 0 11 214 9030; traveldoctor@wtmconline.com; www.traveldoctor.co.za. Consult the website for details of clinics.

Switzerland

IAMAT 57 Chemin des Voirets, 1212 Grand-Lancy, Geneva; e info@iamat.org; www.iamat.org

HEALTHCARE FACILITIES Siberia's healthcare facilities are in a dire state and decades behind the West in every respect. You should do whatever you can to avoid admission to state hospitals in particular, though outside of Moscow there are few alternatives, with privately run Western-standard clinics thin on the ground. City hospitals in Irkutsk and Ulan-Ude have limited equipment; out in the sticks expect chilly threadbare wards but little else except the whiff of chlorine. Although healthcare is meant to be free across Russia, you will very often have to express 'gratitude' to doctors and nurses (in banknotes) to gain every stage of your care,

---

TICKS

Tick-borne encephalitis (TBE), as the name suggests, is spread by the bites of ticks, which live in long grass and the branches of overhanging trees. The disease, which affects the brain, starts with a flu-like illness followed a few days later with headache, neck stiffness, confusion and occasionally coma. Brain damage and death have been known. Infected ticks are common, so if you intend to visit the country in spring or summer, ensure you have the right clothing. Wearing long trousers (tucked into boots) and hats, and applying tick repellent, can all help. Likewise, checking for ticks after forays into grassy areas is sensible. Any ticks should be carefully removed as soon as possible (see below). Medical help should always be sought as soon as possible, even if the tick has been safely removed.

Pre-exposure vaccine against tick-borne encephalitis is not licensed in the UK, but it can be obtained by some GPs or travel clinics on a named-patient basis. (It is unavailable in the USA.) If you can locate the vaccine, a course of three doses over 21 days should suffice. However, taking the preventative measures described above is also very important. Go as soon as possible to a doctor if you have been bitten by a tick (whether or not you have been vaccinated), as tick immunoglobulin may be needed for treatment.

TICK REMOVAL Ticks should ideally be removed as soon as possible, as leaving ticks on the body increases the chance of infection. They should be removed with special tick tweezers that can be bought in good travel shops. Failing that, you can use your fingernails, grasping the tick as close to your body as possible and pulling steadily and firmly away at right angles to your skin. The tick will then come away complete, as long as you do not jerk or twist. If possible douse the wound with alcohol (any spirit will do) or iodine solution. Irritants (eg: Olbas oil) or lit cigarettes are to be discouraged since they can cause the ticks to regurgitate and therefore increase the risk of disease.

It is best to get a travelling companion to check you for ticks. If you are travelling with small children, remember to check their heads and particularly behind the ears. An area of spreading redness around the bite site, or a rash or fever coming on a few days or more after the bite, should stimulate a trip to the doctor.

including diagnosis. Bedside manner is distinctly lacking, patient facilities rudimentary and lone travellers are in real trouble as hospital food is no better than starvation rations, and most small pieces of equipment such as sheets, syringes etc must be supplied by patients' friends and families. Hygiene is OK and staff relatively well trained, though overuse of unnecessary drugs, especially antibiotics, is endemic.

Should you need to see a doctor, your best option may be to enquire at hostels and tour companies who deal with Westerners and where staff will certainly know of a trustworthy practitioner who may even speak English. Chemists (аптека) are a common sight in the larger towns around Lake Baikal and stock many foreign drugs and remedies. Western prescription medicines including asthma inhalers and antibiotics can often be bought over the counter. If you need to source prescription drugs, having the generic Latin name of the drug or its ingredient at hand (usually found on the packaging) can make things easier.

SAFETY

CRIME Theft is a danger you should take seriously anywhere in Siberia, and it's truly shocking just how many travellers have something stolen while passing through Russia. There are countless methods thieves use to put distance between you and your belongings, from skilfully executed scams involving almost Dickensian guile to pulling a clumsy blade up a backstreet.

Bag snatching, camera swiping, pick-pocketing and (extremely rarely) mugging are all travel experiences you'll obviously want to avoid. Never leave valuable items such as your passport, air tickets and money in a hotel room or hostel dorm; always stash them in the hotel safe if there is one. Never stuff your wallet in your back pocket. Never leave cameras or video equipment lying on restaurant or café tables. Always keep an eye on your bags; on busy trams and city buses never keep a daypack on your back but hold it in front of you. Don't flash large sums of money or expensive equipment in public places. In general, use common sense and take the same precautions as you would back home.

Theft on the train deserves a chapter unto itself and the Trans-Siberian compartments and bunks are where most travellers lose their gear (see box on *Kupe versus platskart* page 44). On the railways, always keep your passport with you and store your cash in a money belt. Cameras and other valuables left on bunks are just asking to be pilfered, so keep them out of sight under beds or at least beneath a pillow. If everyone is getting off to stretch their legs at a station, ask the *provodnitsa* (carriage attendant) to lock the compartment door.

Also, don't always assume that thieves, criminals and other assorted troublemakers will be Russian. During research for this guide we witnessed an incident where a French national made off with a British girl's daypack from a hostel. This kind of 'traveller-on-traveller' crime is more common than you might imagine and usually befalls people when their guard is dropped (in hostels, on trains). It's also not a good idea to take packages back to the UK for people you meet, even if they allow you to look inside (unless it's absolutely obvious there's nothing suspicious afoot). Free travel to Siberia means it's no longer the preserve of Oxford dons researching the *kurgans* or anthropologists on their way to interview far-flung tribes, and all kinds of people now pitch up there. Many inexperienced travellers (especially British) who simply cannot get over the affordability of alcohol or availability of prostitutes, very occasionally get involved in nasty incidents with the police and locals. Steer well clear. Be aware that the Russian police take a very dim view of public drug-taking, and engaging in such activity will land you in a Russian jail – not an experience you'll savour.

TAXI SCAM

Watch out for the following scam, particularly at airports and train stations. Waiting for your luggage or a friend to emerge from the toilets, you are approached by a taxi driver who enquires where you are heading. He kindly informs you that public transport is out of action that day and offers, in sympathy, a very low fare which, of course, you jump at immediately. On arrival, after much friendly banter and now on first-name terms, he announces that actually that was the rate per kilometre.

SCAMS While Moscow and St Petersburg teem with crooks inventing schemes to part foreigners from their cash, Siberians seem to have better or more important things to think about. Even taxi drivers appear slightly more honest than their European counterparts, though many try to wangle more roubles out of you than you agreed at the beginning of the ride. If you do encounter a scam, it's most likely to happen at a railway station or anywhere else foreigners pass through in any numbers, but even in Irkutsk or Ulan-Ude this is unlikely.

That said, there are a couple of tricks you should be aware of. Never pick up a wad of cash someone drops in front of you. You'll be accused of pilfering notes from it. A new friend at a railway station may offer to buy you a drink and, to while the time away, gets out the cards for a quick game. Another 'stranger' happens to notice and joins you ... see where this is going? You may meet 'officials' on trains heading into Mongolia who demand that you buy health insurance – it's fake.

To avoid being scammed, follow three basic rules – never get your wallet out under any circumstances; never hand over your passport (or other documents or tickets) to anyone; never let anyone persuade you to deviate from what you had planned ('Take a taxi, the buses aren't running', 'Don't sit here, come for drink with me').

THE POLICE The Russian police are called the *militsiya* (**милиция**) and, unless you are the victim of a crime, you'll probably want to avoid these guys, particularly if you haven't registered your visa. Officers sport a variety of ill-fitting uniforms depending on the season, but can usually be spotted amid all the other myriad uniformed personnel by their cap with a red band beneath the brim. They patrol in twos around railway and bus stations, and always seem to show up just after a drunk has been buttonholing people for money or there's been a tussle between a couple of inebriated market traders or bus drivers. Avoid eye contact with them if you're not registered, as a fineable foreigner is easy pickings.

Should you be unlucky enough to be stopped by the police, never hand over your passport or wallet. If they begin to hassle you for any reason, a good tactic is to make out you don't understand a syllable of any known Indo-European tongue, and generally pretend you have just arrived from Mars. After a few minutes of trying to get blood out of a stone they'll probably get bored and wander off to look for someone else to bother. Never, *ever* offer a bribe to a police officer under any circumstances, despite what you may have read in other guidebooks.

DANGERS
Alcohol
Drunks should always be avoided, but especially Buryats and Evenks who can turn unpredictably violent after just a few shots. You should also prevent yourself becoming inebriated (tricky in these parts) as dimmed senses make you more prone to accidents or becoming the victim of a crime. Avoid drinking sessions with new 'friends', especially at stations and to a lesser extent on trains – drink spiking is common. Always consume alcohol in moderation as the last thing you

want in Russia is to end up having your stomach pumped in hospital or spending the night sobering up at the *militsiya's* pleasure. Despite what anyone may tell you, strong spirits do not warm you up when the temperature sinks below zero; in fact, alcohol can have the opposite affect and bring on hypothermia even quicker. In a similar vein, vodka is a very bad cure for a prickly throat or Delhi belly.

Animals Animals present a small but potentially serious threat to your health and well-being. This can be anything from a bite from a tick infected with encephalitis or a mosquito sting which can cause swelling, to rabies caught from dog and fox bites. Wild and stray dogs in the cities are not the epidemic they once were and usually ignore people anyway. You'd be mighty unlucky to be mauled by a bear, though you should still heed locals' warnings, especially in remote places in late spring when they (bears, not locals) awake ravenous from their winter slumber.

Outdoor pursuits In August 2008 a female British tourist was killed after falling from a hiking trail on Baikal's shores. Despite the best efforts of Great Baikal Trail volunteers, hiking paths can still be quite dangerous and care should be taken on tricky cliff-top sections. Russian guides will occasionally go bounding off down a steep hill to show you some petroglyphs on a rock face, 40m above the seething waters of the lake – they're used to the terrain, you're not, so take care how you step. Ice fun on skidoos, skis, dogsleds etc brings its own dangers, but if you're mad enough to slither out on the frozen lake in the first place... When engaging in any outdoor pursuits, make sure the safety equipment you are using looks and feels safe. As with all physical activities, don't overestimate yourself ('sure, I can ride a horse') and err on the side of caution.

Roads and vehicles Of all the perceived dangers Siberia presents, possibly the last hazard most people would think of would be roads. You are considerably more likely to be injured or killed on city and rural roads than to be eaten by a bear, die in an earthquake, be battered by a drunk or drown in the lake. The standard of driving in Siberia leaves much to be desired, and you should watch out for speeding, dangerous overtaking, erratic behaviour and general disregard for other road users. The standard of roads, especially unpaved routes in Buryatiya and the north, only adds to the melée. Always wear your seatbelt even if those around you don't seem to know what they're for. Ice roads come with their own set of risks, and you should never try to drive across any part of Lake Baikal without a local who can spot dangers, such as places where the ice has parted. Several vehicles go to the bottom of Lake Baikal every year.

Weather In a part of the globe where winter temperatures regularly fall below –40°C, there is a high risk of hypothermia and frostbite. Always make sure you are dressed appropriately for any activity. It may sound odd in the context of Siberia, but heat stroke is a real danger in summer.

WOMEN TRAVELLERS Female visitors to the Baikal region should take the same common-sense precautions as they would back home. At night avoid parks, deserted streets and alleyways away from city centres, and use public transport rather than taxis. Russian men can be extremely courteous to women one moment (opening doors, helping with bags, etc), and be elbowing them (and children, for that matter) to the back of a bus queue the next; it just depends on the situation.

Lone female travellers may be taken under the wing of other females on trains etc, as travelling alone is still seen as risky (even for men). Rail carriage attendants are invariably women and therefore usually sympathetic to female requests to be moved from a compartment occupied by three men. However, Russian males observe unwritten rules of etiquette on the trains, usually vacating compartments if women need to change their clothes. No words are spoken.

Frequenting the showier nightspots of Irkutsk and Ulan-Ude alone puts you at a small risk of being mistaken for a prostitute. By all accounts, dating a Russian man is a real voyage of discovery, very often leading back to somewhere *circa* 1950.

TRAVELLERS WITH DISABILITIES It must be stated from the outset that Siberia is not a very advanced destination when it comes to disabled access and facilities. Wide boulevards roaring with traffic, steep steps down into underpasses, uneven walkways, cobbles, cars parked on pavements, no access to public transport and an absolute absence of ramps and lifts makes getting around with mobility problems almost impossible. No hotels in the Baikal region, with the possible exception of the Mayak in Listvyanka and Yevropa in Irkutsk, have special rooms for the disabled, and many do not even have lifts. Things may be slightly better (and safer) in the countryside, though you can hardly expect a humble homestay to have facilities for the handicapped. On your travels around Siberia, the only disabled people you may see will, in all likelihood, be begging for change outside churches, a fair indication of how the country treats its own disabled citizens.

The following companies and organisations can give advice on travel for those with disabilities, though their knowledge of facilities around Lake Baikal will be very limited.

Access Travel 6 The Hillock, Astley, Lancs M29 7GW; ☎ 01942 888844; www.access-travel.co.uk
SATH (Society for the Advancement of Travelers with Handicaps) 347 5th Av, New York, NY 10016; ☎ 212 447 7284; www.sath.org

Holiday Care Services The Hawkins Suite, Enham Place, Andover SP11 6JS; ☎ 0845 124 9971; www.holidaycare.org.uk
Tourism for All Shap Rd Industrial Estate, Shap Rd, Kendal, Cumbria, LA9 6NZ; ☎ 0845 124 9971; www.tourismforall.org.uk

WHAT TO TAKE

CLOTHING

Winter In winter, a professional expedition-standard down-filled jacket is essential kit. Quilted trousers, thick woollen socks, at least four layers of clothing (thermal underwear, shirt, fleece, outer shell), ski gloves, a warm hat with ear flaps, and sturdy walking boots are also must-packs. If you are just visiting cities, staying indoors and travelling by train, you'll be fine in normal winter clothes, but if you're going across the ice on foot, by dogsled or any other way, you should really invest in some proper professional arctic gear.

Rest of the year What to stuff into your rucksack depends very (very) much on when you are heading out to Siberia and what you intend to do there. The extreme continental climate Lake Baikal 'enjoys' means sweltering summers and chillier springs/autumns than most places on earth. In summer, essentials include shorts, T-shirts, sandals and a hat. Insect repellent is vital in summer and early autumn due to the large number of mosquitoes, midges and other assorted biting insects, not to mention ticks. A common item found in the backpacks of those heading to Baikal's beaches is swimwear – you can probably leave this at home as even at their warmest the lake's waters are only bearable for a few seconds.

TRAVEL KIT Carrying a few basic pieces of equipment when travelling can solve an infinite number of problems on the road. Recommended gear:

- Torch and spare batteries (for illuminating dark stairwells, village streets, long-drop loos)
- Insect repellent (indispensable in the summer months)
- Penknife
- Basic first aid kit (at least painkillers, plasters and diarrhoea tablets)
- Water bottle
- Sewing kit (strange how your clothes mutiny when you are travelling)
- Duct tape (for repairing damaged backpacks)
- Sunglasses (important even in winter)
- Pocket Russian dictionary (for decoding menus and timetables)
- British gas meter box key (for opening train carriage windows)
- Universal sink plug (though Russians perform their ablutions in slimy railway carriage bathrooms and low-cost hotel rooms under running water for good reason)

LUGGAGE The best type of luggage to take to the Baikal region is a medium to large rucksack (50–70 litres) or a travel bag (a rucksack with a smaller day-sack zipped to the back). This sort of baggage can be stuffed under seats in trains and tied onto roofs of buses most easily. It's also simple to carry if you have to walk somewhere, is easy to repair and will be less conspicuous. A suitcase is definitely not recommended as it can be clumsy and Siberia's cracked pavements and uneven cobbles will gnaw away the wheels, though it may actually attract less attention than a backpack as you haul it through crowded streets and along dirt tracks. A daypack (around 20–30 litres) is also a good idea for walks and city tours.

ELECTRICITY Russia works on 220V AC, 50Hz. To use electrical appliances from home you will need a simple adapter to fit standard continental two-pin sockets. These are available from travel shops, electrical goods retailers and these days even your local supermarket. The electricity supply can be patchy and power failures common. AA and AAA batteries are widely available and relatively cheap.

$ MONEY

THE ROUBLE The Russian currency is the *rouble* (sometimes spelt *ruble*), often abbreviated to RUB, RUR, ру or just p. The word is thought to be derived from рубец (*rubyets*) meaning 'seam', referring to the ridge left on the outer rim of silver coins by pouring the metal into the mould in two stages.

Banknotes come in denominations of 5,000, 1,000, 500, 100, 50 and 10 roubles, after which come 5, 2 and 1 rouble coins. One rouble is further divided into 100 kopeks, which come in denominations of 50, 20,10, 5, and 1 kopek coins, the last four of which have been rendered virtually worthless by today's prices. The one-kopek piece will possibly have disappeared from general circulation by the time you read this, as the metal used to produce one is worth more than the coin itself.

As cash is king in Siberia, you'll be seeing a lot of these notes, which are thankfully pretty easy to distinguish from one another. Most transactions are made with notes which, despite their frequent use, tend to be in better condition than some of their Western equivalents.

DOLLARS AND EUROS Although prices in hotels (and occasionally elsewhere) are sometimes quoted in dollars or euros, the bill you receive will normally be in roubles. Any unofficial transactions – such as paying taxi drivers, tour guides or even small guesthouses and hostels – which take place in a foreign currency are likely to be in the new king of currencies in Russia, the euro. But on the whole Russians tend not to be fussy about 'hard' currency anymore, and will accept roubles just as happily as foreign notes. Shops, hotels and restaurants will only take foreign currency if you offer, and probably at a poor rate. Don't even think about trying to pay for anything in British Sterling, as these days Russians rate the feeble pound about as highly as the Zimbabwean dollar or the North Korean won.

CHANGING MONEY Foreign currency can be changed at the vast majority of banks, though most now handle euros and US dollars only. If you are coming from Britain it's a good idea to exchange your pounds for roubles before you leave home, as you may end up going from bank to bank in an attempt to find one that will change Sterling. The same applies if you are arriving from China, and if you pitch up in Russia with a wodge of Mongolian tögrög, forget it. Some banks are exceedingly picky about the standard of notes they'll accept, and even if you ask for absolutely pristine dollars or euros in the UK or the US, keen-eyed cashiers and their bizarre arsenal of scanning machines can spot even the tiniest speck of ink, water or worse, and the note will be refused. Sberbank seems to be the least fussy and will exchange even the most moth-eaten greenback; VTB are the best bank for exchanging currencies other than the dollar and euro, including British pounds.

It's also possible to draw money directly from your home bank account using a debit card (or credit card), and ATMs (**банкомат**, bankomat) are very common, especially in large towns and cities. Instructions can usually be viewed in English, and terminals sometimes give the option of making the withdrawal in US dollars. Make sure you know your PIN and tell your bank or credit card company you intend making transactions in Russia, especially if you plan to be there for a long period of time. Travellers' cheques are no longer worth the hassle for the security they provide, and they're a pain to convert into cash, even in Irkutsk and Ulan-Ude.

CASH VERSUS CARDS Russia is still very much a cash-based society and throughout your trip you may only use your debit card to withdraw funds from an ATM. Plastic is accepted in an ever-increasing number of shops, restaurants and hotels, but you will be charged by your debit or credit card company for every transaction, and some establishments may only take one type of card. Transactions are sometimes slow to come through, and occasionally you may still encounter the old manual machines which make an imprint of your card on a document which you sign. Be particularly careful with this type of transaction, as the funds take up to a month to be debited from your account. Hostels rarely accept plastic, shops outside Irkutsk and Ulan-Ude definitely will not accept payment by card, and bus tickets cannot be purchased in this way. Rail tickets can in theory be bought with plastic, but it's definitely more convenient and quicker to just hand over the cash, especially if there's an impatient queue behind or around you. If you do intend to use your debit or credit card abroad you must inform your bank or credit card company before you leave home, as cards can be quickly blocked if you make cash withdrawals or use the card to book accommodation on the internet. Also, make sure you know the numbers to call should your cards be stolen, and set up a Skype account so it won't cost you a fortune to do so.

BUDGETING

As you may be aware, Russia is by no means the cheap destination it once was. Although Siberia is marginally less expensive than Moscow, St Petersburg and other large cities, few would regard the Baikal region as value for money. Accommodation in even the most basic of hotels is overpriced, and eating out in decent restaurants can seriously dent your budget. However, getting around is still relatively inexpensive, as are admission fees to museums, galleries etc, even when you factor in the practice of double pricing (see below).

Sleeping in hostels and homestays, dining in no-frills canteens and cafés, limiting yourself to a couple of sights a day and using public transport, you could get by on a self-imposed allowance of around RUB1,100 a day. Staying in mid-range hotels, eating in anything better than a *stolovaya*, seeing as many sights as you please and occasionally taking a taxi will see you parting with at least RUB3,000 per day. The sky's the limit at the upper end, with guides, taxi drivers and the odd upmarket hotel waiting to lighten your wallet.

DOUBLE PRICING Sadly the Soviet practice of charging foreigners more for admission to museums, galleries and other tourist attractions has survived the decade and a half since the end of Communism, and continues to be one of the most irritating aspects of travel in Russia. Sometimes the 'foreigner price' can be five times what a local pays, and ticket sellers and takers will gladly explain the twisted logic behind this system ('people in the West earn more than Russians'). This would mean billionaire Roman Abramovich would only hand over 20 roubles to get into the museum, while a cash-strapped student from the West would be hit with the full-whack of 100 roubles.

Don't think for one moment you will ever get away with paying the 'Russian price'. Even if your Russian is perfect and you dress like a Russian, the sour-faced guardian (almost always old and female) on the other side of the ticket office window can smell a foreigner from 100 paces. You will be spotted trying to merge inconspicuously into a large group of Russians, and even if you get a local to buy the tickets for you while you hide round a corner, somehow the ticket lady will just know she is being duped (how do they do it?). Pleading poverty or disability, slapping your OAP bus pass on the ticket window or even

WHAT'S FREE

Here are some ideas for things to do around Lake Baikal that won't cost you a single kopeck:

- Baikal views are free, numerous and ever-changing.
- Don an anorak and indulge in a spot of train-spotting at the grand stations that punctuate the Trans-Siberian line – just don't get arrested for taking snapshots of the locos!
- Spend half an hour perusing Ulan-Ude's free Geological Museum.
- Siberia has yet to come up with a way of charging to drink from the innumerable mineral-rich springs which dot the landscape.
- Hike a section of the Great Baikal Trail or the Circumbaikal Railway.
- Admire the region's timber architecture for nothing.
- Buddhist temples and orthodox churches never charge admission fees.
- Use the world economic downturn as an excuse to wild camp on the lake's shores.
- The Listvyanka Picture Gallery is free – as long as you don't buy any of the works displayed, that is.
- The Port Baikal railway station museum charges no admission.
- Stroke Lenin's giant goatee in Ulan-Ude at no cost.

attempting small-scale bribery will have little effect, and could result in your being thrown out.

TIPPING Those involved in providing services directly to tourists, such as waiters, drivers and tourist guides, are only too willing to accept a tip. In cheap and middle-of-the-road eateries, round the bill up to the nearest RUB50 or RUB100. In more upmarket restaurants you may want to give a bigger gratuity if you were really satisfied with the service. Don't tip if you are not happy with the way you have been treated – it's the only way waiters etc will learn how to give the service you expect. Tour guides, especially poverty-stricken students working to get themselves through university, should always be tipped. Taxi drivers from official companies appreciate a bit extra on top of the bill; some unofficial drivers may try to get more roubles out of you at the end of the journey than you agreed at the outset. Tips can be given in roubles, dollars or euros; British pounds are not so welcome.

OPENING TIMES

All businesses are required by law to display their opening times in a visible place on the door or window of their premises, and the overwhelming majority do so. Generally speaking, things tend to open in Russia when they're required by the populace, and it can be hard to generalise about opening times as the day is less structured than in the UK and most of Europe. Excuses to slam shut the doors, such as lunch breaks, 'technical pauses', 'sanitary days' and professional holidays, are all-too-common throwbacks to the Soviet era; 24-hour opening to a techno beat and flashing neon is the new order. Some businesses, especially small shops and cafés, give the impression of being permanently abandoned – tug open the heavy plate-steel door to discover otherwise.

BANKS These are generally open from 09.00 to 18.00 Monday to Friday, with the odd rare example opening its doors for limited hours on Saturdays. Be aware that foreign exchange counters occasionally keep different hours to the rest of the bank. Lunch breaks are rare, 'technical breaks' are decreasing.

SHOPS Russians generally begin work later than in the West and shops rarely open before 10.00. Typical hours are from 10.00 to 18.00 Monday to Friday, 10.00 to 19.00 Saturday and Sunday, but this should only be used as a general guide. Every town has at least one food shop open round the clock (*kruglosutochno*). Lunch breaks are common though less so than in the past. In another part of Russia, we came across a shop which had 'open 24 hours a day' emblazoned in throbbing fairy lights across its frontage, but a hand-written sheet of A4 taped to the door detailing the daily two-hour lunch break.

RESTAURANTS, CAFÉS, KIOSKS Sit-down restaurants tend to be open from 11.00 to midnight or later, though they may close earlier if there are no customers around. Cafés, bars and kiosks keep all kinds of odd hours, the rule of thumb being that the closer an establishment is to a railway station, the more hours of the day it will be open. Eateries very often open for shorter hours on Sundays.

TOURIST ATTRACTIONS Museums, galleries and other attractions do not have uniform opening times but are generally closed on Mondays. They also observe at least one regular 'sanitary day' in the month, whatever that may be. Lunch breaks are the norm, as is unscheduled closing due to staff shortages, technical problems and a multitude of other excuses.

BY BUS Buses are used for short to medium-length journeys around Lake Baikal, and the vast majority of places can be reached using this mode of transport. The standard of vehicles is acceptable, with many operators having exchanged their fume-belching Soviet buses with bed-spring suspension for secondhand Korean models still parading illegible Korean destinations and fading back-of-seat advertising. All reek of diesel fumes and breakdowns are a common occurrence. Tickets from cities such as Irkutsk and Ulan-Ude should usually be bought in advance, especially on popular routes such as Irkutsk–Arshan and Irkutsk–Kuzhir. Thanks to horrifically bad road surfaces, police road blocks, frequent stops, breakdowns and cigarette/coffee/*pozy* breaks, journeys are long.

BY *MARSHRUTKA* A *marshrutka* (plural *marshrutki*) is basically a minibus which acts as a taxi but with a fixed route. This popular mode of transport appeared on streets across the former USSR in the 1990s, mainly as a quick-fix substitute for failing public transport systems. Two types of *marshrutka* work Russia's highways and byways: first there are those that scurry around towns and cities, charging a flat fare and making almost unlimited stops. These tend to be slightly more expensive but faster than ordinary public buses. Then there are those that speed between towns, cities and villages and have a 'fare structure' and fewer stops. These make up for the relatively low number of intercity buses and the slowness and hassled ceremony of the train.

In towns, wait until passengers have got out, find a free seat and pass your fare via passengers in front of you to the driver (no tickets are issued). When you want to get out, tell the driver to stop and fight your way to the sliding door. These urban *marshrutki* are usually quicker than ordinary public transport, but it can be hard to obtain route information. For long-distance journeys *marshrutka* is the least comfortable mode of transport and for overnight trips (from Irkutsk to Ulan-Ude for instance) the train may be more expensive but the level of comfort incomparable.

Foreigners with no Russian language or guide sometimes find using *marshrutki* slightly daunting as it does require limited interaction with the driver. Communication between the man behind the wheel and passengers often involves a series of hardly audible grunts from both parties, from which (without eye contact or explanation) the driver somehow knows exactly where everyone wishes to alight. Failure to grunt at the required moment may bring the wrath of the otherwise phlegmatic chauffeur onto your foreign head.

Another big issue for travellers using *marshrutki* for long-distance trips is luggage. There is a very small space behind the back seats in most vehicles for rucksacks, and occasionally drivers may agree to tie your belongings to the roof rack, if there is one, which obviously brings its own risks.

BY ICE ROAD If the idea of steering two tons of Soviet-era van across a metre-thick crust of ice floating upon a 1½km-deep water-filled chasm doesn't freak you out, then Baikal's ice roads are for you. Several specially marked and maintained routes create some very convenient short cuts, and link villages on both sides of the lake which for the rest of the year may as well exist on different planets.

Several vehicles a year find themselves sucked to the bottom of the lake. These usually belong to locals who should know better but risk a crossing after the ice has started to thin. Cracks and gaps are caused when the wind shifts the ice sheet, and these pose the greatest danger to vehicles. Very rarely a strong gust will separate ice from shore, stranding everyone who finds themselves out on the lake at the time.

On old Soviet maps you may notice little airport symbols next to some unlikely places such as Ust-Orda, Khuzhir and Ust-Barguzin. These are rudimentary airfields which once handled domestic flights to and from regional capitals. Until the collapse of the Soviet Union, taking to the air to reach small towns and villages was common, but these services evaporated in the economic turmoil of the early 1990s. With most domestic airlines struggling to provide an economically viable service even on major routes, these short hops are unlikely to be revived any time soon.

BY TRAIN Three main rail routes cross the region – the Trans-Siberian, the BAM and the Trans-Mongolian. The Tran-Sib route from Irkutsk via Slyudyanka to Ulan-Ude is the main transport artery in the region and the best way to travel between the region's two major cities. Around 11 trains a day make the trip in both directions, with a journey time of approximately eight hours. Travel during the day to catch some great Baikal views. The Trans-Mongolian begins in Ulan-Ude and meanders down to the Mongolian border at Naushki via Gusinoe Ozero (for the Tamchinsky datsan). The BAM (see box on page 150) flirts with the northern tip of Lake Baikal on its 4,324km-long journey from Tayshet in the west to Sovietskaya Gavan on Russia's far eastern coast.

BY AIR The only domestic flights of interest to the Baikal explorer are between Irkutsk, Ulan-Ude and Nizhneangarsk. These are operated by Buryat Airlines, a tiny two-plane company based at Ulan-Ude airport. Tickets can be bought through travel companies in the above cities and fares are reasonable. A flight from Ulan-Ude to the north of the lake can save you two or three days on the train and is well worth the extra cost. All luggage must be loaded on the Antonov An-24 aircraft by passengers themselves, the interior is reminiscent of a 1970s air disaster movie, and the in-flight service is a stale sweet and a plastic cup of fizzy water (more than you get on Ryanair). Despite this, the hour-long flights across Lake Baikal are incredibly scenic, and take-off and landing surprisingly smooth. However, be warned – bad weather can cause serious delays, and it has been known for pilots to take off from Ulan-Ude, reach Nizhneangarsk successfully, circle the town several times, decide the landing is too tricky and fly all the way back again.

BY BOAT In the summer months hydrofoils zizz their way up and down Lake Baikal and the Angara River. All services operate from mid-June until late August with the exception of the Irkutsk–Listvyanka–Bolshie Koty service, which runs from late May until late September. The following is a rundown of the timetables, but check for changes before travelling:

Irkutsk–Nizhneangarsk (via Port Baikal, Olkhon Island & Severobaikalsk) Runs Tue & Fri; dep 08.50, arr 20.40; tickets RUB2,000

Nizhneangarsk–Irkutsk (via Severobaikalsk, Olkhon Island & Port Baikal) Runs Wed & Sat; dep 07.40, arr 20.00; tickets RUB2,000

Irkutsk–Listvyanka (via Port Baikal) Runs Wed & Sat; dep 10.30, arr 11.50; tickets RUB180

Listvyanka–Irkutsk (via Port Baikal) Runs Tue & Fri; dep 17.30, arr 18.50; tickets RUB180

Irkutsk–Bolshie Koty (via Listvyanka) Runs daily; dep 09.00, 12.30 & 14.30, arr 10.30, 14.00 & 16.00; tickets RUB240

Bolshie Koty–Irkutsk (via Listvyanka) Runs daily; dep 12.30, 17.00 & 18.00, arr 14.00, 18.30 & 19.30; tickets RUB240

HITCHHIKING Hitchhiking – as in getting a free ride from a friendly stranger who engages in light conversation, buys you a coffee and a sandwich at a service station and goes out of his or her way to drop you off at a convenient place of your choosing – doesn't really exist in Russia. Stand by a road in Siberia, arm extended, and the vehicle that stops for you will be nothing more than an unofficial taxi. Every car in Russia is a cab for the right price, and the driver will expect money for his services – give away the fact that you are a foreigner and he (drivers in Siberia are almost always men) will in all likelihood want even more of your roubles. Very often hitching works out just as expensive as the train or bus fare, meaning there's little to be gained from thumbing a ride. There's no such thing as a free ride in this country, and hitching should also be avoided, if at all possible, for obvious reasons of personal safety.

ACCOMMODATION

Gone are the days when Inturist, the erstwhile state tourism organisation, prescribed which hotels were for foreign eyes and which were definitely not. You're free to stay virtually anywhere you like these days, and the market has certainly diversified since those regimented Soviet days. Irkutsk boasts the full caboodle of accommodation choices, from backpacker hostels to luxury hotels, while out in the sticks homestays fill a gap in the market. Wild camping, station resting rooms and yurt camps are just some of the less conventional options.

HOTELS The cities and towns of the Baikal region have a wide variety of hotels, from Soviet dinosaurs to glitzy new Western-style establishments, and from uber-basic vodka-streaked crash pads to almost boutique lakeside guesthouses. Many of the old Soviet slab hotels have undergone at least partial refits, and Western-standard establishments such as the Yevropa in Irkutsk, the Mayak in Listvyanka and the Sibir and Ayan in Ulan-Ude offer high standards.

Prices When it comes to room rates, bargains are thin on the ground with the average price per night across the region around RUB2,000 for a double room. Very often the standard of facilities in mid-range and 'budget' places is low, with dodgy plumbing, less than friendly staff and sometimes unruly fellow guests up to no good until the early hours. The one advantage to staying in a hotel is that your visa will be registered with the police automatically by reception staff, but hostels and homestays are much better value for money unless you can dig deep for a top-notch place. Some hotels charge half price for stays of less than 12 hours, and some have an hourly rate (and not just for the reason that springs instantly to mind). Very often at reception you will be faced with a price list on which every single room is charged at a different rate. The price normally reflects the room's state of repair, range of facilities and size, though quite often a RUB50 or RUB100 difference is triggered by a 1980s hairdryer (which last dried any hair in that decade) or a small and noisy fridge. Double pricing (as far as we could see) is now a thing of the past, as is settling the bill in foreign currency.

Booking If booking by telephone from your home country, make sure you ask for some kind of written confirmation (email or fax). Some hotels charge a booking fee, normally 25% of the first night's accommodation. Booking through local tour companies takes a lot of the hassle out of the process and often doesn't cost much more (in fact it can cost less, depending on the relationship between the company and the hotel in question). Online bookings are yet to appear on the Siberian accommodation scene, with the exception of the region's hostels.

Checking in and out On arrival the receptionist will take your passport so that your visa can be registered. Some hotels have begun, somewhat cheekily, to charge for this 'service' with RUB200 the going rate. Don't forget to collect your documents again next day. It's essential that you ask to see the room before committing, as receptionists get very stroppy if you wander back down after five minutes to declare your bed is too hard. As a foreigner, you might be allocated the best room (as you're from the West) or the worst room (as you're from the West!). Most hotels take payment up front and you should never rely on being able to pay with plastic. Some older hotels still employ a *dezhurnaya* (floor lady, always women) on every floor who is responsible for handing out and collecting keys and generally keeping order. Nowadays these range from the polite and unintrusive to the old-style Soviet monsters who have been known to barge into rooms to tick off naughty guests, as well as taking a cut from prostitutes for guiding them to suitably single Western men's doors.

Make sure you ask when check-out time is, as some hotels charge per 24-hour period, while others want you packed and off by 10.00 next day. As bills are often paid in advance, check-out usually just involves leaving your key with the *dezhurnaya* or receptionist.

HOSTELS In Krasnoyarsk and Chita, tour companies scratch their heads and wonder: 'Why don't more people get off the Trans-Siberian in our city?' The answer could be, at least in part, the absence of cheap hostels which the Baikal region now has aplenty. Irkutsk can now pride itself on four backpacker digs, all of a high standard and run by owners who are in tune with the needs of independent travellers. A similar hostel recently opened in Severobaikalsk, Slyudyanka now boasts a hostel of sorts, and Ulan-Ude recently joined the party. These are by far the best places to stay, and are by no means the preserve of the young, with all manner of overlanders from across the globe sharing stories, food and advice over the hostel kitchen table. In fact, sometimes these places feel like a stationary extension of the Trans-Siberian compartments. Expect to pay around RUB700 for a dorm bed without breakfast; facilities usually include a kitchen, washing machine, luggage store and a PC connected to the internet. The Baikaler Hostel in Irkutsk offers free Wi-Fi.

HOMESTAYS To state the blindingly obvious, a homestay involves staying in someone's home. Many locals, especially in rural areas, have a spare room which they rent out to guests to earn a bit of extra cash. Despite its virtual demise in other parts of Russia, the homestay is still very much alive around Lake Baikal. Digs range from prearranged, internet-booked, full-board affairs to basic turn-up-and-ask beds in timber cottages (see box on opposite page). To book a bed in someone's home pre-trip, try the Host Families Association (*www.hofa.ru*). Expect to pay anything from RUB200 per bed per night in a very simple house in the countryside to over RUB1,000 for a pre-arranged stay with meals included. A house offering homestays might not be marked in any way or may have the words Сдаются комнаты (rooms for rent) or Сдаётся комната (room for rent) posted somewhere on the façade.

CAMPING There are no official campsites around Lake Baikal nor, indeed, in the whole of the Russian Federation. In a place as vast as Siberia, wild camping is the norm and you can in theory erect your tent wherever you like. There can be nothing better than pitching up on a deserted beach to watch the sunset in perfect isolation while cooking dinner over an open fire. However, when choosing a spot,

---

CHOOSING A HOMESTAY

Unless you meticulously plan your entire stay around Lake Baikal in advance or use a tour company to organise the trip for you, an unscheduled stop in the sticks, where there is little or no accommodation, is inevitable. Enter the homestay, the perfect way to meet local people and see how they live – a much more engaging experience than the four walls of a hotel and a supermarket dinner. Indeed, the homestay is in the best tradition of Russian hospitality, and long may it prosper.

Being unofficial accommodation, there is no set of standards for homestays and levels of cleanliness, friendliness and comfort vary wildly. The traveller takes the luck of the draw and puts himself or herself at the mercy of strangers. No contract is signed, no receipt is issued (no tax is paid) and there is no check-out time or receptionist. With this sometimes uncertain relationship with your hosts in mind, consider the following advice:

- Make sure on first contact with the owner that the homestay is not miles away from where you want or need to be.
- Look at the state of the house from the outside – this provides a good idea of what you're likely to find on the inside.
- Shop around, don't be afraid to look at several rooms and compare 'facilities' before making your decision.
- Choose younger owners – old people occasionally become paranoid and afraid of their guests, turfing them out in the middle of the night. Younger families tend to be more hygienic, too.
- Alcohol on the owner's breath or any other signs of vodka consumption should have you out of the garden gate at once.
- Don't bargain down the price too hard. Villagers taking in guests are usually quite poor and need every rouble they can get.
- Most houses have outside pit toilets. If you can't handle this, retreat to a hotel.
- Be careful what you eat and what you eat from. Dirty hands, lack of sewers, absence of running water and generally low hygiene levels make stomach and bowel problems a real risk. Diarrhoea at three in the morning on a pit toilet with no loo roll is a travel experience you will not savour.
- Always try to get a room with a lockable door, and never leave valuables lying around.
- Never hand over your passport to anyone.
- Mark the house on a map or at least try to remember where it is before setting out to explore. Many houses and indeed whole streets of timber cottages look very much the same, and street names are often difficult to read or missing altogether.

it's advisable to do so out of sight of a village unless you want drunks invading your nylon haven at three in the morning or kids hurling stones. Camping out in the wilds brings a number of dangers, especially in the form of hungry bears, ticks and mosquitoes. The latter pairing can be dealt with using sprays, the first on the list cannot, but you'd be mighty unlucky to attract a ravenous bear anywhere near human habitation. Only light a fire if absolutely necessary as forest blazes destroy millions of hectares around Lake Baikal every year (though these are rarely started by campers). It's OK to use water directly from the lake, and from streams if there's no settlement upstream.

OTHERS *Komnaty otdykha* (resting rooms) are basically crash pads at railway stations where you can sleep while waiting for a train or sleep off an early arrival. They are very cheap (as little as RUB50 an hour) but some have minimum-stay conditions. Most have showers and other (paid) facilities. A *turbaza* (holiday camp) is a collection of huts in a pretty spot such as by a lake or river, usually with dorms but sometimes with private rooms where Russians go in the summer months for a bit of R&R. There's often a canteen, a shower block, a place to grill meat, and outdoor tables and chairs, as well as perhaps a games room and play areas. This is often the cheapest type of accommodation but not one habitually frequented by foreigners. On Olkhon Island and possibly in other locations around Lake Baikal you may find *turbazy* consisting entirely of felt yurts. The form of accommodation you are least likely to encounter is a *sanatory* (sanatorium), a kind of workers' health spa, usually set by a lake or built on top of hot springs. These were once ultra-cheap but have shot up in price in recent years, and you usually need a doctor's prescription to get a room

✖ EATING AND DRINKING

RUSSIAN FOOD Although not one of the world's most celebrated cuisines, Russian food does throw up some tasty and filling dishes (but hopefully you won't!). Like all traditional national cuisines, Russian and Siberian dishes reflect the type of ingredients which are naturally available in the region. Pizzas, hamburgers, chips and instant noodles may now be convenient and widely available, but Siberians will always prefer a plate or bowl of their very own traditional hearty fare.

Siberia's signature dish is *pelmeny* (пельмени), a kind of ravioli traditionally stuffed with three types of minced meat and flavoured with onion, salt and pepper (though there are many vegetarian recipes around too). The word *pelmeny* originates from the Komi language and means 'ear bread', an accurate description. *Pelmeny* are usually eaten with a knob of butter, a dollop of sour cream, a dash of vinegar or these days a coating of ketchup.

For many Siberians breakfast is the previous night's leftovers, but sometimes consists of *tvarog* (sweet cottage cheese) or some kind of *kasha* (porridge) which can be made from buckwheat, oats, corn flour, rice, semolina or millet. The day starts late for most, meaning lunch isn't eaten until between 13.00 and 15.00, and dinner after 19.00. At both of these mealtimes you may encounter *ukha* (fish soup), *shchi* (cabbage soup), *lapsha* (noodle soup), *pirozhki* (pasties), *bliny* (pancakes with various sweet or savoury toppings), *ikra* (caviar), *kholodets* (aspic) served with horseradish or mustard, and *kotlety* (meatballs). For dessert you may be offered *syrniki* (fried sweet cottage cheese fritters), *morozhenoe* (ice cream) or *frukhty* (fruit).

Food across Russia is as diverse as the population, and just as the British have taken many dishes into their own national cuisine from former colonies, so have the Russians made foods such as *chebureki* (meat turnover from the Caucasus), *shashliki* (barbecued meat from the Caucusus), *plov* (pilau rice with meat from central Asia) and *borscht* (cabbage and beetroot soup from Ukraine) their own.

BURYAT FOOD Milk and meat from cows, sheep, horses and goats are still the major components of the Buryat diet, reflecting their herding tradition. Similar in some ways to the infamous Mongolian cuisine, going Buryat can range from the tempting (fresh clotted cream, spicy meatballs) to the downright unpalatable (raw liver, fermented milk), though most of what you will be served in Buryatiya is delicious and filling fare.

Pozy (позы), meatballs approximately the size of a golf ball wrapped in pasta-like dough and steamed until cooked (*buuzy* in Mongolian, *manty* in Russian), are both Buryat national cuisine and national obsession with almost every town possessing at least one *poznaya* (a café selling just *pozy*). During the steaming process the meatball separates from the dough, and the cavity fills with juices from the pork or lamb (or combination of both). They are eaten by hand with ketchup, soy sauce, mustard and bread, and are the region's favourite fast food, eaten in cafés, at roadside kiosks and in cheaper restaurants. Bite straight into a *poza* and a gush of scalding meat juice will flash-fry your chin. Instead, make a small hole in the dough case and slurp it out before devouring the meat and casing together. They are delicious, filling and especially good on bitingly cold days accompanied by a mug of steaming Russian tea.

Bukhuler (бухулер) is a very popular dish of meat broth made with mutton or lamb. The meat is boiled in large chunks, with only a pinch of salt added, until it's cooked through. It's then drained and served separately to the bouillon – a real carnivore's feast and tastier than it sounds. *Khushuur* (хушуур) are a delicious fried version of Russian *pelmeny*, only with a mutton or lamb filling. As a dessert or for breakfast you might be served *salamat* (саламат), a sour porridge made with flour and cream. Other dishes you could encounter are *erye'elzhe* (эрээлже, sausage filled with liver, blood, onion, mutton fat, garlic and milk), *ezgey* (эзгей, a kind of Buryat cheese), *khime* (химэ, beef sausage) and *sharbin* (шарбин, fried dumplings filled with minced mutton). Buryats traditionally love gathering food from the taiga whose floor is rich in wild berries (wild strawberries, cranberries, blueberries) and hundreds of different kinds of mushroom. Fresh clotted cream and homemade wild strawberry jam on freshly baked bread is a tastebud extravaganza you won't forget.

Omul Although considered a delicacy in European Russia, *omul* is fished out of Lake Baikal in industrial quantities, and is a staple source of protein for many lakeside communities. While tasty at first, you may have had quite enough of its salmon-like flesh after a few days, especially in places like Olkhon where locals seem to eat precious little else. *Omul* is prepared in a number of ways but is best grilled over an open fire in the traditional way.

DRINKING Think of Russia, think of drinks, and vodka, lots of vodka, immediately springs to mind. For the uninitiated, there is a ritual to vodka consumption which must be followed (see box below). Boozy sessions are lent a little extra Oriental touch by the Buryats who, before drinking, dip their third finger into the glass and flick drops into the air or pour a little onto the table (not the floor) as an offering to the spirits. Russians sitting at the same table can often be seen following suit. In addition to tens of straight vodkas on sale, you'll also find Russia's favourite firewater flavoured with lemon, peach, vanilla, cherry or mandarin and other uniquely Russian concoctions such as birch, pine and cedar nut. By far the purest and least hangover-inducing vodka in the region is distilled by Ulan-Ude's Baikalpharm (*www.baikalpharm.ru*). Among Russia's *nouveau riche*, cognac has replaced vodka as the *de rigueur* tipple, most of it distilled in Armenia.

VODKA

The Russian's love of alcohol is well known and you don't have to be in Siberia long to witness it with your own eyes. In fact, it is said that Russians are only Christians thanks to their love of a tipple – Prince Vladimir of the Kievan Rus, when deciding which religion to adopt to replace Slav pagan beliefs, plumped for Christianity as all the others banned or impeded the consumption of alcohol.

Russian men need little excuse to thump a bottle on the table and order a daughter/wife/grandma to fetch glasses – birthdays, national holidays, days dedicated to a certain profession, births, marriages, arrivals, departures, new flats, new cars… almost every day provides an excuse to get sloshed, and meeting a foreigner is as good a reason as any.

But Russian vodka drinking is no wild free-for-all – there is ritual and order to inebriating oneself which must be strictly obeyed. First, a designated man is responsible for pouring the drinks. After your glass is filled, you must wait until the first toast. Then down the contents in one, 'do dna', as the Russians say, no sipping or saving half for later. Follow this with a *zakuska*, a little piece of something – gherkin, bread, bit of cheese. Glasses loaded again, second toast, down the hatch, *zakuska* … and again, and again … until the toasts become slurred and dedicated to absurdities, empty bottles roll under the table and foreigners can discreetly pour their vodka on the floor/into plant pots/in their shoe without anyone noticing.

Not everyone you meet around Lake Baikal drinks this way, however. Slavs can take their liquor but the Buryats and Evenks, some lacking the enzyme in the body needed to break down alcohol, can react badly to even a small amount. Some young people are turning away from vodka orgies and towards less inebriating beer, though not to such a great extent as in Ukraine and Poland, for instance.

Sold out of wheeled tanks on street corners throughout the summer months, *kvas* (**квас**) is made from fermented rye bread, tastes a bit like weak beer, but contains virtually no alcohol. On hot days there's nothing more refreshing than a plastic tumbler of this traditional brown concoction which costs around RUB15 per half a litre. You can bring your own bottle and have it filled by the vendor, but the communal cup on a chain has long since disappeared. Long queues form at the tap around going-home time on sweltering Siberian evenings, though most of the tanks vanish if the weather turns nasty. In recent years mass-produced *kvas* has appeared in plastic bottles on supermarket shelves, but lacks the yeasty tang of the street version.

Russia brews some very quaffable ales, the most popular being the Baltika series. Each of the ten types of Baltika has a number and everyone has their favourite. Baltika No 0 is non-alcoholic, Baltika No 3 is the classic lager, No 8 is a delicious wheat beer and No 9 Extra is a strong 8% volume ale. Czech, German, British and Scandinavian beers are also widely available across the Baikal region. Unless it's imported from a well-known wine-producing country, or Georgia or Moldova, give wine a wide berth.

The Buryats have their very own spirits but you're unlikely to come across them very often. *Tarasun* is sour milk distilled into a vodka-like drink; *khurunga* is similar to Mongolian kumis only made from cow's milk rather than mare's milk.

Russians like their tea black, strong and with lots of lemon and sugar. Buryats, on the other hand, prefer green tea with milk. Even in good restaurants coffee is invariably instant, and by the time you get home you may be craving an authentic double espresso. Even Siberian city dwellers have little idea what good coffee should taste like, and Buryat villagers and farmers out in the sticks may never have tasted the stuff.

As far as soft drinks are concerned, all the usual culprits of the fizzy drink world are widely available, but the traditional Russian soft drinks are *kompot*, a sugary squash made with berries and other fruit, and *kvas*, a thirst-quenching concoction produced from fermented bread (see box above). Tap water (where there are taps!) is safe to drink across the region, just don't expect it to taste very pleasant. Boiling can help to rid tap water of its chlorine bouquet and kill off bacteria, but this is not essential. Bottled water is available everywhere but some of the Russian mineral waters have a very strong 'geological' aftertaste. Water can be drunk straight from Lake Baikal, although we wouldn't recommend you do this in or near lakeside towns and villages.

PUBLIC HOLIDAYS

The Russian Federation marks just seven national holidays, one less than even the overworked UK. However, the calendar blushes with many other red-letter days, especially in Buryatiya where there are several unofficial religious holidays. If a public holiday falls on a Thursday, people may work on a Saturday leading up to that day instead, creating a 'bridge' from the Thursday to the weekend.

1 January	New Year's Day
7 January	Eastern Orthodox Christmas
8 March	International Women's Day
1–2 May	International Labour Day/May Day
9 May	Victory Day
12 June	Russia Day
4 November	Day of National Unity

RELIGIOUS

Sagaalgan (Buddhist New Year, from the Buryat meaning 'White Moon') Celebrated in Buryat homes and at Buddhist temples on the first day after the first new moon in February. This means Buryats get to celebrate New Year three times (both Russian calendars and Buddhist).

Maidari Celebrated in July and is a Buddhist festival involving a colourful procession, the star of which is a large cloth horse.

SPORT

Baikal Marathon Held in Listvyanka on the first Sunday in June.

Baikal Ice Marathon A 26-mile run held in early March across the frozen lake, from Listvyanka on the western shore to Tankhoy on the eastern shore. For anyone who enjoys marathon running, this is one of the most extreme events on the planet and a challenge few know of. Those interested in taking part should contact Andreas Kiefer at BaikalExpress in Germany (*www.baikal-marathon.de*).

Surkharban Known as Naadam in Mongolia, this is the biggest traditional summer sporting event of the year among the Mongol nations. Held on the first Sunday in June at Ulan-Ude's hippodrome, it involves archery, feats of horsemanship and a lot of dressing up.

ARTS

Altargana Buryat cultural and folk song festival held in a different region with a Buryat population every year.

Crystal Seal Festival of Ice Sculpture This fascinating festival takes place in the first half of February in the port area of Listvyanka, and attracts sculptors from around the world with its generous cash prizes. In addition to the exhibition of amazing works chiselled and smoothed from Baikal's crystal clear ice, there's also an ice village with various attractions including an ice restaurant.

Jazz by the Angara Held in late May and early June at various venues around Irkutsk, eastern Siberia's only jazz festival once used to take place in Angarsk. The website www.jazz.ru is the best source of information on future dates etc.

OTHERS

Irkutsk City Day Usually held in early June, the city's official birthday is an opportunity for people to let their hair down a bit with music, street performers, food and balloons for the kids. Most of the action takes place along the riverfront.

Ulan-Ude City Day Same kind of thing in the Buryat capital, held on 12 June.

International Women's Day This essentially Communist-era relic is still one of the biggest excuses in the calendar to get smashed. Things usually start in a civil manner with much hand-kissing, flower giving and toasts celebrating 'our women', before descending into vodka-fuelled debauchery.

New Year's Eve For Buryat and Russian, this is the biggest party of the year and it's well worth making a special trip to Russia to experience the celebrations.

Russians take New Year's Eve seriously, with much vodka drinking, special dishes, music and a massive firework display bursting over every town.

Professional holidays In Russia someone has their day every day – firemen, miners, medics and even those who work in the tourist industry. These holidays are taken very seriously, with 24 hours of vodka consumption and mountains of food. Russians are convinced some of these professional holidays are international affairs – trying to explain otherwise will be met with some disbelief.

SHOPPING

The idea of going to Russia to shop a decade or two ago would have been completely absurd. The narrow selection of pickles, vodka and alcohol in dour state-run shops is not exactly what you would have called an exciting retail experience. Times have certainly changed, with everything you could possibly need, want and desire available even in Siberia's far-flung cities. Prices have replaced availability as the main obstacle to happy shopping, and wandering in supermarkets and large stores anywhere across Russia you will be astounded at the criminal mark-ups most retailers put on their goods.

SOUVENIRS Birch bark and cedar feature heavily in the range of typically Siberian souvenirs visitors take home. Versatile, supple but very strong, birch bark is fashioned into a whole host of items such as boxes, shoes, table mats, artwork, jewellery, baskets and even canoes. Robust cedar wood is carved into spoons, plates, jugs, cups and chopping boards with simple rural designs and patterns carved into the wood. Locals will definitely recommend you buy a bottle of cedar oil, which has many uses including ridding the skin of scars. Popular souvenirs from Buryatiya include Buddhas (though these are often made in China), mini-prayer wheels, Buryat dolls in national costume, colourful traditional Buryat clothes, mock shaman pendants and other shamanic decoration such as head-dresses and drums. Other souvenir ideas include colourfully decorated chocolate boxes, semi-precious stones and minerals from the Baikal region, vodka (especially the Baikalpharm brand from Ulan-Ude), pirate CDs and DVDs, coffee-table books, jars of exquisite honey and tins of red caviar (not as cheap as it once was). Russian nesting dolls, enamelled boxes and Khokhloma ware (red, gold and black wooden spoons etc) hail from European Russia, but can still be bought in department stores in Irkutsk and Ulan-Ude. Unlike in Moscow and St Petersburg, there's not much Soviet and Red Army junk (pin badges, fur hats, watches) around for sale, possibly as there aren't the numbers of foreigners around to buy the stuff in large enough quantities.

ACTIVITIES

The forests, mountains, slopes and trails of the Baikal region are an outdoor enthusiast's paradise, especially for those who like to escape the clutches of civilisation and feel truly out in the wild. The most popular land-based activities are hiking and horseriding; out on the lake itself, watersports are an obvious option, and all kinds of weird and wonderful opportunities present themselves when the lake turns into Siberia's biggest ice rink.

HIKING With the development and expansion of the **Great Baikal Trail** (see box on page 105) hiking on many stretches of the shore has become a lot more predictable, with markers pointing the way, footbridges crossing streams and the odd picnic table and info board. However, if this seems too civilised, most of the uninhabited shoreline remains as wild as it was millions of years ago, and with the water as your main navigational aid, you'll not get lost. Possible trekking routes are listed throughout the guide.

SKIING AND SNOWBOARDING Not many foreigners come to ski or snowboard by Lake Baikal and, to be frank, the increased risk of suffering a bad accident which your health insurance may not cover is probably not worth it. If you really must snap on your Rossignols to enjoy Siberia's guaranteed snow, there are small ski resorts at **Baikalsk** (*www.baikalski.com*) and **Listvyanka** (*www.eastland.ru*), and new centres are planned or already under construction just outside **Nizhneangarsk** and in the special economic zone on the eastern shore. Ski hire/lift pass costs RUB700/850 a day at Listvyanka, RUB400–1300/750–1300 at Baikalsk.

DOGSLEDDING Listvyanka's **Baikalsky Tsentr Yezdnovo Sporta** (✆ 3952 496 829; *www.baikalsled.ru, in Russian only*) is the place to head for a spot of exhilarating dogsledding in any season. Alternatively contact Jack Sheremetoff in Irkutsk (see *Local tour companies and helpers*, on page 39) who can organise a day's excursion from Irkutsk.

HORSERIDING Horseriding has taken off in a big way across the Baikal region, with almost every tour company offering trips on horseback. The terrain lends itself to adventures in the saddle, and it's a tranquil, sustainable and very fitting way of seeing the sights, given the Buryats' long association with the horse. It's also a good way of accessing places vehicles can't and which are too far to reach on foot. Local guides normally use small, stocky Mongolian horses which can carry heavy loads over long distances and are used to the terrain. Popular horseriding areas are the Tunka Valley, the Khamar Daban mountains and the Barguzin Valley, though the choice of potential routes across the region is immense. Be aware that Russian and Buryat men sometimes presume that every Westerner can ride. If you can't, make it clear from the outset.

ICE FUN Ask any of the tour companies listed under *Local tour companies and helpers* (see page 39) to find out if they can help you arrange any of the following winter activities. The ice is thick enough to walk and cycle on from early December through to mid/late March. Slippery black ice, deep snow, cracks and buckling ice crags blocking the way mean every trip turns into an adventure sooner or later.

Ice trekking Every year hundreds of walkers traverse Lake Baikal on foot. Trips almost always include a night camping in the middle of the ice sheet, an unforgettable experience by all accounts. Some tour companies prefer you to have at least some sub-zero camping experience before you sign up. Popular routes lead from the northernmost point of Olkhon Island to the southernmost point of the Svyatoy Nos Peninsula; from the eastern shore of Olkhon Island to Ust-Barguzin via the Ushkanie Islands, or just straight across from Listvyanka to Tankhoy. A day-trek across the Maloe More is for those who prefer not to sleep on the ice. Longer trips and expeditions are major undertakings, so make sure you are fit, healthy and suitably equipped before setting out.

Ice mountain biking Pedalling your way across the world's deepest lake is a relative newcomer to the Baikal activities scene, but an exciting addition. Tracks usually stick to the ice roads and snow, as black ice can be impossible to cross by bike. The advantage (or disadvantage perhaps to some) of cycling over trekking is that you probably won't have to camp out on the ice. Baikaler in Irkutsk can organise day rides from Listvyanka (see *Local tour companies and helpers*, on page 39).

Others **Skijoring** is Nordic skiing where the skier is pulled along by a dog or dogs. Listvyanka is the place to head if you fancy a go. **Snowmobiles** can be seen buzzing across the ice around lakeside villages all winter and can be readily hired. The gruelling **Baikal Ice Marathon** takes place in March (see *Festivals and special events* on page 68).

ARTS AND ENTERTAINMENT

MUSEUMS AND GALLERIES Museums and galleries across Siberia are generally poorly funded and have seen little investment or additions to their collections since the late 1980s. Often dry, uninspiring and certainly not interactive or multimedia, Russian museums are regarded more as solemn institutes of scientific research than as fun tourist attractions. Despite these shortcomings, anyone with a diehard interest in Russian history will find some of Baikal's better museums fascinating depositories of the region's history.

There are several different types of museum in the Baikal region. Irkutsk and Ulan-Ude boast typical regional and city museums. Smaller towns maintain museums dedicated to local history, but some are housed in schools and have no fixed opening hours or staff. The Baikal region's two open-air museums at Taltsy and just outside Ulan-Ude, which have preserved the region's traditional architecture for posterity, are two of the best and an unmissable part of any visit. Other museums include those dedicated to a single topic, such as the Decembrist museums in Irkutsk and Novoselenginsk, the Baikal Museum in Listvyanka and the BAM Museum in Severobaikalsk.

The region's indoor museums are interesting for their very quirkiness and antiquated appearance, sometimes worth paying the 'foreigner price' to see in itself. Often as the only visitor that day, your arrival at many smaller museums will

BAIKAL'S TOP FIVE MUSEUMS

1 Taltsy Open-air Museum of Wooden Architecture, Taltsy (see page 96)
2 Buryat History Museum, Ulan-Ude (see page 126)
3 Regional Museum, Kyakhta (see page 135)
4 Ethnographical Museum, Ulan-Ude (see page 127)
5 Volkonsky House Museum, Irkutsk (see page 87)

awaken a troop of pensioners from their slumber, one of whom will take on the task of following you suspiciously through the museum, switching lights on in rooms as you enter, off again as you leave. Many museums have a prescribed route which you must follow, and deviating from this will bring the wrath of the elderly custodians upon your disrespectful Western head. Some museums are visited primarily by groups, and individual visitors are viewed with mild mistrust. Laughter, irreverent behaviour and fashioning your own tour route will earn you a ticking off. With a few rare exceptions (such as the Taltsy Open-air Museum) labelling, explanatory texts and other information are usually in Russian only.

THEATRE, OPERA AND BALLET Irkutsk is one of the best cities in all of eastern Siberia for high-brow culture and upmarket entertainment. The city's list of cultural institutions includes the Okhlopkov Theatre (the first theatre to be built in Siberia), the Philharmonia, a puppet theatre and a musical theatre where ballets are staged. Russian ballet in particular is a cultural treat not to be missed, especially Tchaikovsky's Swan Lake or the Nutcracker, often performed for children around New Year. Also ballet, unlike other performance art, doesn't require a command of the language. Ulan-Ude's grand old opera house has been undergoing much needed renovation for a number of years, but once reopened should return to staging Buryat-themed productions. All of the above venues close over the summer.

MUSIC Irkutsk hosts an annual jazz festival called Jazz by the Angara (see *Public holidays and festivals*), and rock and pop concerts by touring Russian stars take place in the stadium and other large venues. Your best opportunity to hear traditional Russian and Buryat music is at the two open-air museums and more upmarket restaurants, though these are meagre pickings and rather hit-and-miss. Irkutsk's Polish Church stages regular organ concerts, and classical music is the bread and butter of the city's musical theatre.

NIGHTLIFE Nightlife in most Baikal towns and villages means downing a few wet ones at the local watering hole, or a meal at a café or restaurant. The big exception to this is Irkutsk where several large nightclub complexes serve up anything from 1980s nostalgia discos and DJ nights to hardcore striptease acts and wet T-shirt competitions. Most such establishments operate what the Russians call 'face control', bouncers to you and me, who are under strict instructions about who to allow in and who does not fit the bill. If you find yourself at a loose end out in the cuds, it's worth checking out the local village club if there is one. These are mostly run by young people and sometimes double up as cinema and pop disco. Unless you speak Russian, cinema is a nonstarter as foreign-language films are invariably dubbed.

MEDIA AND COMMUNICATIONS

NEWSPAPERS The biggest national Russian dailies are *Kommersant, Izvestiya, Novaya Gazeta, Komsomolskaya Pravda* and *Argumenty i Fakty*. All are owned by state-owned concerns, banks or oligarchs, with a biased agenda too complicated to discuss here. If you don't read Russian it makes little difference anyway. If you do, you'll find a much wider range of views in print than on TV, with some broadsheets taking a blatantly anti-Kremlin line. There are many other smaller publications to be found on newsstands in addition to the above, but Russia's English-language newspapers, the *Moscow Times* and *St Petersburg Times*, are not available in Siberia.

TELEPHONE Pay phones (*taksofon*, таксофон) are still widespread in Russian cities, but you'll need to buy a prepaid card from a newsstand or kiosk to use one. Cards from one city may not work in another. Call centres can be found in both Irkutsk and Ulan-Ude.

Dialling codes The country code for Russia is +7. To ring a number from abroad, dial the local exit code, then 7, then the city code followed by the subscriber number. To make an international call from Russia, dial 8, wait for a second tone, then dial 10 plus the country code, local code and subscriber number. This rather complicated way of calling abroad may be changing slightly in 2010, when the 8 and 10 are expected to be replaced by 0 and 00.

Mobile phones Your mobile phone probably won't work in Siberia, though this may depend on the type of SIM card/phone you have. If you *can* make and receive calls, you will be hit with extortionate roaming charges by your provider. Should you be planning to stay in Russia for a long period of time, consider purchasing a local SIM card from a Russian operator such as MTS (*www.mts.ru*), Beeline (*www.beeline.ru*) or Megafon (*www.megafonsib.ru*), though be aware that not all SIM cards work everywhere (hence the Russian custom of owning several mobile phones and/or SIM cards). Although the mobile signal is now available in large cities, towns and even the majority of villages, it's patchy on the roads between them. Call charges within Russia are reasonable, but calling home may cost you around US$3 or more per minute, and you will also be charged for incoming international calls.

POST The post office is run by *Pochta Rossii* (*www.russianpost.ru*) and branches are easily recognisable by the dark blue sign bearing the words почта россии and the Russian double-headed eagle holding a post horn in each talon. You'll pay RUB19 to send a postcard airmail to another country and RUB22.50 for a letter weighing less than 20g. Letters and postcards take around three weeks to the UK and up to a month to reach addresses on other continents. The Russian postal system has seen huge improvement in recent years and your postcards home are now very unlikely to go astray (unlike much incoming mail).

INTERNET Internet access in Irkutsk is served up by classic internet cafés but in Ulan-Ude they are very thin on the ground. In other smaller towns and villages you could try the post office, or ask around as some schools and youth clubs may let you check emails and browse. Wherever you access the web, expect to pay around RUB40–50 per hour, though some hostels may allow their guests to use a

PC for free or a nominal charge. Wi-Fi is yet to take off in Siberia, though a few places such as Irkutsk's Baikaler Hostel and the Marco Polo Café in Ulan-Ude launched the service a couple of years ago.

The Russian internet suffix is .ru, but many Russian websites use the .com ending. Very occasionally you will come across the now disappearing .su suffix, which Russia inherited from the old Soviet Union. There are numerous sites devoted to Lake Baikal and the communities around it, but the information on them cannot always be relied upon. Surprisingly enough, quite a few Siberian websites are translated into passable English.

RADIO Though the BBC World Service (*www.bbc.co.uk/worldservice*) is no longer the well-funded broadcaster of yore, it can still be heard loud and clear in Russia's eastern cities. Frequencies change throughout the day (check the website) so you'll need to keep retuning. Early morning and late evening/night are the best times for clear reception. Out in the sticks you may have trouble finding anything, even on short-wave, save for a few shrieking Chinese stations.

As in most countries around the world, local commercial FM channels have cleaned up as far as radio is concerned, with several stations pumping out Western and Russian pop around the clock in both Irkutsk and Ulan-Ude. Radio Russia (www.radiorus.ru) is the national station broadcasting on long-wave; The Voice of Russia (www.ruvr.ru) is the state short-wave station, broadcasting in English and myriad foreign languages to other countries, but usually still picked up within Russia.

TV Russian TV is dire, and even if you understand Russian there's seldom anything worth watching. Russians, who watch TV as much as any nation, are spoon-fed a diet of playback pop shows featuring overdressed 'stars' miming bland lyrics, news shows toeing the Kremlin line and recycled Western series and soap operas (or even worse, their own brutal brand of TV drama). If you're lucky you may catch a classic film or cartoon from the Soviet days when TV seemed mildly more watchable than it is today.

There are three mainstream channels which any TV set can receive: *Channel One* (**Первый канал**; *www.1tv.ru*), *Rossiya* (**Телеканал Россия**; *www.rutv.ru*) and *NTV* (**НТВ**; *www.ntv.ru*). Channel One and Rossiya are state-owned, NTV is a private channel. In addition to these big players there are several smaller channels such as MTV Russia, REN TV, Vesti and TNT. Rossiya broadcasts regional news and current affairs several times a day – in Ulan-Ude these programmes are in Buryat.

Upmarket hotel rooms and lobbies usually have TVs with satellite hook-up providing at least some respite from post-Soviet TV. The tens of German satellite stations plus CNN, Eurosport and, if you're very lucky, Sky News and BBC World are the normal fare. Lower down the hotel food chain you'll be thankful just for the full range of Russian channels.

CULTURAL ETIQUETTE

GREETINGS A Russian woman meets an Englishman for the first time:

> Russian woman: 'Hello, my name is Tatiana Sergeyevna, very pleased to make your acquaintance.' (*Enthusiastically presents her guest with a rosy cheek to kiss and a delicate hand to shake.*)
> Englishman: (*Managing a nervous and half-hearted wave of the hand as if to say 'Don't come any nearer!'*) 'Bob.'

Typical urban Russians maintain a certain level of formality when meeting strangers for the first time, far from the immediate first-name terms of Anglo-Saxon countries. When introduced to a woman, kiss her on both cheeks and pronounce your first name clearly. Give males a confident, bone-crushing shake of the hand.

VISITING A RUSSIAN HOME A visit to a Siberian home can be the highlight of any trip, as Russians pride themselves on their famous hospitality. Visits are conducted in an atmosphere of cordial politeness and occasionally almost Chekhovian civility, so you may need a few tips to ensure you don't commit etiquette hara-kiri. Not sticking to the prescribed way of doing things, especially if you hail from that fabled bastion of good manners, Great Britain, will make you seem uneducated and badly brought up, despite being from a different culture.

Arriving late is perfectly acceptable in Russia – about 15 minutes should do it. Arrive bang on time (or early) and you may catch your hosts unprepared, mum still with her rollers in, vacuum cleaner still in action. Russians love to dress up, so you should do likewise if you're invited to dinner, but don't overdo it. Make sure you don't have holes in your socks when you are invited to a Siberian home as the first thing arriving guests do on entering the hall is to take off their shoes. You will normally be handed a pair of slippers (*tapki*, тапки) which you should don immediately. There may be a slight fuss around the *tapki* as the entire family hunts around for a pair that will fit your size-12 foot. Occasionally your host will implore you not to remove your footwear as the floor is cold, they do not have slippers in your size, or it is inconvenient for you. This is just politeness, and marching beshod into your host's spotless apartment will not go down very well.

When paying a visit, take a small gift such as a bottle of wine, a box of chocolates or similar neutral gift as a small token of friendship. Men bearing flowers is a common sight in Siberia's streets and a bouquet makes an easily purchasable gesture of appreciation. Russians would never dream of paying even a close friend a visit without something to hand over just before or after the shoe removal ritual. Presenting something obviously brought from the country where you live will really impress. Never give a present for an unborn baby or a bouquet containing an even number of flowers.

Russians conduct much of their home lives around the kitchen or dining table and, beslippered and degifted, this is where you will doubtlessly find yourself sooner or later. Though the setting may be casual, table manners are quite formal – you should never start to eat before your hosts, rest your elbows on the table or leave the table before your hosts. Vodka is not for sipping but to be downed in one following a toast; foreigners are rarely requested to make a toast unless their Russian is up to it. Stopping the flow of food, which is quite often piled before you despite your protests, is difficult, but leaving a small amount on your plate usually does the trick. Pickiness about certain dishes will probably result in your being given that very thing so that you can discover just how delicious it is. After the meal, it's polite to offer to help clear the table or wash up – this will be registered as good manners and politely refused. Russians have no subtle way of telling guests when it's time to go home (after-meal coffee doesn't mean it's time to get your coat) and the onus is on the guest to know when enough is enough.

TRAVELLING POSITIVELY

Local organisations are always on the lookout for volunteers. Contact the following groups directly to see how you can help. There's usually someone around who speaks English, if you decide to give them a call.

ORTHODOX CHURCH DOS AND DON'TS

Even in tourist hotspots such as Moscow, St Petersburg and the Golden Ring, Orthodox churches are working places of worship and not tourist attractions. Priests, monks and caretakers are not overly keen on tourists milling around in their churches, and you should keep a low profile whenever possible. Out of respect, you should observe the following rules when visiting Orthodox churches and chapels – the head-scarved *baboushki* on duty will soon tick you off if you don't.

- Turn off your mobile phone.
- Men should take off their hats.
- Women should cover their heads with a scarf or shawl.
- No shorts or skimpy attire should be worn by either sex.
- Whisper or keep your voice as hushed as possible.
- Resist the temptation to take photographs.
- Never consume food in a church.
- No holding hands, kissing or affectionate touching.
- Icons, statues, candlesticks are not hands-on exhibits for you to fondle.

Despite this strict list of dos and don'ts, Orthodox churches are wonderfully genuine places to visit. While there, feel free to light a candle, breathe in the incense-perfumed atmosphere, listen to a service, admire the artwork of the iconostasis and wonder at the colours of the intricately painted walls and ceilings.

GREAT BAIKAL TRAIL VOLUNTEERS A superb way to see Lake Baikal's remoter locations and make new friends is by volunteering to build or repair a piece of the Great Baikal Trail (GBT, *Bolshaya Baikalskaya Tropa*, BBT in Russian). The GBT is a non-profit organisation that works to develop, maintain and protect 1,800km of hiking paths around Lake Baikal. Apply online to join one of the cosmopolitan teams creating pathways, building footbridges, clearing rubbish from the shores or promoting the GBT through participation in seminars and conferences. Needless to say, the vast majority of the outdoor physical work takes place in summer. Apply online (*www.greatbaikaltrail.org*), or contact Baikalplan (*www.baikalinfo.com*) in Dresden, a company closely involved with the project.

BAIKAL WAVE This Irkutsk-based non-governmental organisation (*www.baikalwave.eu.org*) runs various environmental projects in the region as well as staffing an information centre in the city and organising rallies and protests. Contact staff directly to find out about volunteer opportunities.

FIRNCLUB According to their website, Firnclub (*www.firnclub.ru*) is a 'non-profit organisation whose mission is to promote the development of civil society in order to help solve social, economic, and ecological problems in the Republic of Buryatia'. Ask what you can do to help.

STUFF YOUR RUCKSACK This simple idea is the brainchild of UK TV presenter, Kate Humble, and basically consists of a website (*www.stuffyourrucksack.com*) where travellers can look up schools, charities and other organisations which may need items that can easily be stuffed into a rucksack. Those arriving back from a destination where schools need books, orphanages need toys or charities need cash can register this on the website. There are plenty of such institutions around Lake Baikal, especially in remote villages.

Part Two

THE GUIDE

3

Irkutsk (ИРКУТСК)

Telephone code: 3952

Described in the late 19th century as the 'Paris of Siberia', Irkutsk is the unofficial capital of the Baikal region and a major halt on the Trans-Siberian Railway. Here many travellers take a much-needed break from the rails for a few days to stretch their legs, visit Lake Baikal and take on supplies to see them through to Moscow, China or Mongolia. The city they encounter is one of very few of this size in Siberia to have kept its historical character pretty much intact; unexpected rows of rickety – but still inhabited – timber houses line entire streets in the city centre, several original church buildings still dot the skyline despite 70 years of Communist rule, and many examples of grand 19th-century architecture stand proudly on its wide thoroughfares and boulevards.

Almost 600,000 inhabitants call this city on the mighty Angara River home, though the low-rise city centre is small enough to be explored on foot. Irkutsk's tourist infrastructure and services make it the natural base for exploring the west and south of the region.

HISTORY

Irkutsk was a relative latecomer on the Siberian landscape, first appearing properly on the map in 1661 when Russian Cossacks raised a fort next to the Angara River to replace a small winter refuge. Just a couple of decades later, the small town which had sprouted around the stockade was granted a charter and over the next 50 years grew relatively prosperous on the fur trade.

Straddling the road to Moscow (the infamous *trakt*) Irkutsk flourished when trade was decentralised from the monarchy in the mid 17th century. In one direction went furs, gold, timber, silk and tea from China, in the other direction came the finer things of life from European Russia such as books, musical instruments, porcelain, artwork and fine furniture to fill rich merchants' villas. In 1805 the Khamar-Daban road to Kyakhta on the border with Manchuria was completed and this brought even more business to Irkutsk, especially in the shape of tea caravans. Every 18th-century Russian expedition to explore the Far East, Yakutiya, Mongolia, China or Alaska was organised and set out from Irkutsk, and the town bustled with gentlemen explorers and the businesses which supplied their forays into the unknown. The most famous of these adventurers was Gregory Shelikhov, often called the Russian Columbus (see box on page 13).

By the 19th century Irkutsk had grown into one of the most important cities in Russia and the administrative centre of a huge chunk of the globe from the Yenisey River in the west to the Pacific in the east. A measure of its status was its 13 churches, the most of any city in Siberia at the time. Irkutsk was a place of exile for groups like the Decembrists (see box on page 88) as well as countless artists, intellectuals, thinkers and anyone else out of favour with the tsar of the day. These groups contributed greatly to the city's cultural life and were key players in

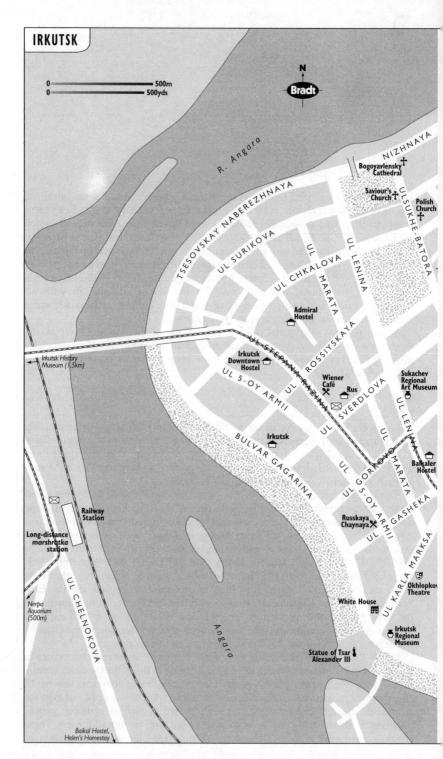

IRKUTSK

0 ———————— 500m
0 ———————— 500yds

N
Bradt

R. Angara

NIZHNAYA

Bogoyavlensky Cathedral †

Saviour's Church †

Polish Church †

TSESOVSKAY NABEREZHNAYA

UL SURIKOVA

UL CHKALOVA

UL MARATA

UL LENINA

UL SUKHE-BATORA

Admiral Hostel

Irkutsk Downtown Hostel

UL STEPANA RAZINA

UL ROSSIYSKAYA

Wiener Café

Rus

UL SVERDLOVA

Sukachev Regional Art Museum

UL LENINA

UL 5-OY ARMII

Irkutsk History Museum (1.5km)

BULVAR GAGARINA

Irkutsk

UL GORKOVO

UL MARATA

Baikaler Hostel

UL 5-OY ARMII

Railway Station

Long-distance marshratka station

Nerpa Aquarium (500m)

UL CHELNOKOVA

Russkaya Chaynaya

UL GASHEKA

Angara

UL KARLA MARKSA

Okhlopkov Theatre

White House

Irkutsk Regional Museum

Statue of Tsar Alexander III

Baikal Hostel, Helen's Homestay

80

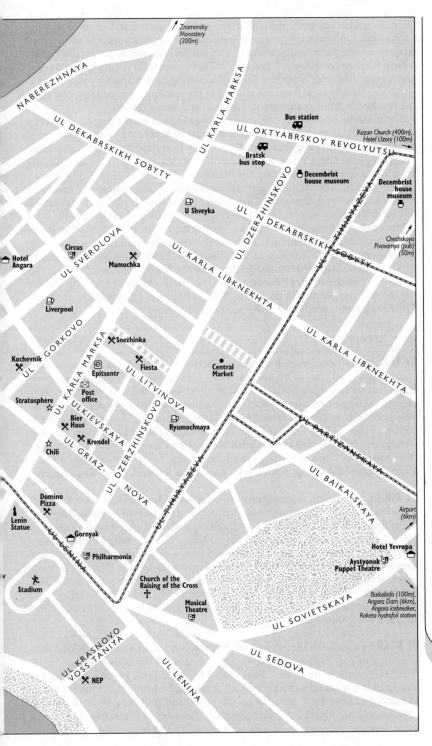

Znamensky
Monastery
(200m)

NABEREZHNAYA

UL DEKABRSKIKH SOBYTY

UL KARLA MARKSA

UL OKTYABRSKOY REVOLYUTSII

Bus station

Kazan Church (400m),
Hotel Uzory (100m)

Bratsk
bus stop

Decembrist
house museum

Decembrist
house
museum

U Shveyka

UL DZERZHINSKOVO

UL DEKABRSKIKH SOBYTY

Cheshskaya
Pivovarnya (pub)
(50m)

Circus

UL SVERDLOVA

Mamochka

Hotel
Angara

UL KARLA LIBKNEKHTA

Liverpool

UL GORKOVO

UL KARLA LIBKNEKHTA

Snezhinka

UL KARLA MARKSA

Kochevnik

UL

Fiesta

Epitsentr

UL LITVINOVA

Central
Market

Post
office

Stratosphere

ULKIEVSKAYA

Bier
Haus

UL DZERZHINSKOVO

Ryumochnaya

Krendel

UL PARTIZANSKAYA

Chili

UL GRIAZ.

UL BAIKALSKAYA

Domino
Pizza

UL NOVA

Airport
(6km)

Lenin
Statue

UL TIMIRYAZEVA

Gornyak

Hotel Yevropa

UL LENINA

Philharmonia

Aystyonok
Puppet Theatre

Stadium

Church of the
Raising of the Cross

Baikalinfo (100m),
Angara Dam (6km),
Angara icebreaker,
Raketa hydrofoil station

Musical
Theatre

UL SOVIETSKAYA

UL KRASNOVO
VOSS TANIYA

UL LENINA

UL SEDOVA

NEP

Irkutsk's golden era when many theatres, schools, galleries and institutions were established. Unfortunately, some 90% of the city's architecture was constructed from wood, the most readily available material, and this was to prove costly when a huge blaze swept through Irkutsk in 1879, destroying three-quarters of the city and leaving thousands homeless. But within a decade a new Irkutsk constructed in stone had literally risen from the ashes, and the spanking new buildings included the first hotels, banks, many grand mansions and even a cinema.

Up until the end of the 19th century all goods had been transported west by road, a journey of several months to Moscow. In 1898 came the momentous arrival of the Trans-Siberian Railway which brought heavy industry and many more people into the city. Despite the Bolshevik Revolution of 1917 and the ongoing Civil War, a university was opened in Irkutsk in 1918.

The wealthy, educated city resisted the Bolshevik Revolution and became a bloody battleground during the Civil War between Red and White forces which followed. The Reds only emerged victorious in this neck of the taiga after the great White admiral, Alexander Kolchak, was shot in the city in 1920. World War II saw entire factories hauled along the Trans-Siberian from European Russia to Irkutsk, and industrialisation continued unabated until the 1980s as the Soviets looked to exploit Siberia's natural resources. In the 1950s the Angara hydro-electric dam was constructed to the south of the city, providing cheap electricity and stopping the riverbanks from flooding in the spring. Today's Irkutsk is a young city with almost 170,000 students attending over 40 faculties and colleges.

GETTING THERE

BY RAIL As a principal stop on the Trans-Siberian Railway, Irkutsk enjoys excellent connections to all parts of the former Soviet Union, Mongolia and China. Direct trains run to and from Moscow (*departs: daily; journey time: 70–100hrs*), Beijing (*departs: weekly; journey time: 47hrs*), Ulaanbaatar (*departs: every other day; journey time: 40hrs*), Ulan-Ude (*departs: up to 11 times daily; journey time: 8–9hrs*), Krasnoyarsk (*departs: 8 times daily; journey time:18hrs*) and Severobaikalsk (*departs: every other day; journey time: 36hrs*), as well as most other major cities across the country. In summer there are direct through carriages from Berlin and Warsaw (*journey time:100hrs*). Irkutsk's grand old railway station is located on the left bank of the River Angara.

BY AIR Located 6½km from the city centre near the Angara Dam, Irkutsk airport (✆ 544191) was receiving a much-needed facelift at the time of research. There are direct flight connections to many towns and cities across Russia including Moscow (*departures: up to 3 daily; journey time: 5hrs 40mins*), St Petersburg (*departs: 3 times/ week; journey time: 6hrs*), Ulan-Ude (*departs: 3 times/week*), Nizhneangarsk (*departs: 3 times/week*) and many others. International destinations include Ulaanbaatar (*twice weekly with Mongolian Airlines; www.miat.com*), Shenyang (*twice weekly with China Southern Airlines; www.csair.com*), Beijing (*twice weekly with S7; www.s7.ru*) and Bangkok (*once or twice weekly with S7*), though check the schedules as these services are particularly unstable.

BY ROAD Few arrive in Irkutsk by road, but if you do, chances are you'll take your first steps in the 'Paris of Siberia' in a bus station (*ul Oktyabrskoy Revolyutsii 11;* ✆ 209411) which is more West Bank than Left Bank! Look beyond the mayhem and dirt and you'll find a functioning coach terminal where you can catch services to Listvyanka (*four daily*), Khuzhir on Olkhon Island (*four daily, all in the morning, summer only*), Slyudyanka (*five daily*), Arshan (*twice daily*), Bratsk (*one daily, from a special stop near the station – see map on pages 80–1*) and many other less popular destinations. The chaos at the station is caused in part by the many *marshrutki* parked here waiting to fill up. These supplement infrequent buses to popular destinations and only depart when passengers are packed in like sardines. For scheduled services buy tickets from the windows inside the building; for *marshrutki* pay the driver. Be aware that no service of either type leaves for Olkhon Island after 12.00. Tram 4 stops near the station. The only other major departure point for *marshrutki* is from in front of the railway station. Services from here leave for Ulan-Ude and several other destinations, but never Olkhon.

GETTING AROUND

Irkutsk has a system of trams, trolleybuses and *marshrutki*, and visitors staying in the city for any length of time will probably need to use some form of public transport sooner or later. Trams are the most user-friendly city transport; buy RUB10 tickets from a kiosk or conductor on board and stamp them as soon as you get on. Trams 1 and 2 run between the railway station on the left bank of the Angara River and the city centre on the other side; tram 4 trundles its way from the Central Market to the bus station. Tram 5 can be used to reach the Angara Dam and the *Raketa* hydrofoil quay, but it's quite a walk from the final stop. Public transport runs from around 06.00 until midnight.

TO AND FROM THE AIRPORT The cheapest way of making good your escape from Irkutsk airport is by clambering aboard bus 90 (RUB10, pay the driver) which runs past the Central Market and along ul Lenina. A taxi should cost RUB150–200. Agree the total price before you get in and make sure the fare quoted is not per kilometre.

ORIENTATION

Irkutsk has no real focal point, no central square or interchange. Ul Karla Marksa, the main thoroughfare, slices the city centre in two, running from the statue of Tsar Alexander III on the Angara embankment in the south until it peters out at the junction with ul Oktyabrskoy Revolyutsii. Ul Lenina is another busy road running from wide ploshchad Kirova (Kirov Square) past several attractions and places to stay to the Church of the Raising of the Cross. The railway station is on the other side of the river and linked to the centre by just one bridge (for now). The Angara Dam provides another crossing point around 6km to the south.

TOURIST INFORMATION

Baikalinfo (*ul Krasnykh Madyar 50;* \ *406 706; www.baikalinfo.ru*) is a commercial tour company masquerading as a tourist information point. Once located just off ul

---

A BRIDGE TOO FAR?

Sometime in 2009 or 2010, a spanking new bridge across the Angara, linking the two halves of Irkutsk, will be complete and open for business. Situated around 3½km south of the railway station, it should take some traffic out of the city centre. However, the authorities, in their wisdom, have decided to close the existing bridge for repairs expected to last years. As all trams and buses between the city centre and the railway station use this bridge, the work is expected to throw the entire city transport system into disarray.

Karla Marksa, they've lost a lot of business by moving to cheaper premises southeast of the city centre. Staff may help you find a hotel or give you directions, but they've no free information to hand out (they'll kindly tell you where you can *buy* a city map!). For assistance, see *Local tour companies and helpers* in *Chapter 2*, page 39.

⌂ WHERE TO STAY

Irkutsk's four backpacker hostels are the best places to stay in town and ideal for meeting fellow travellers, exchanging stories and getting tips on what to expect further down the line, wherever you are headed. The remainder of accommodation can be divided into somewhat overpriced upmarket business hotels and the cheaper sleeps where standards can fluctuate wildly from room to room.

HOTELS

⌂ **Hotel Yevropa** (66 rooms) ul Baikalskaya 69; ☏ 291 515; www.europehotel.ru. Flawless rooms at this 4-star newcomer are surprisingly good value for money. Location in the southeast corner of the centre near the central park is OK for sightseeing, but bad for reaching the stations without a taxi ride. Reception staff speak very good English & the Western-style b/fast buffet is the best you'll be served in Irkutsk. $$$$

⌂ **Irkutsk** (245 rooms) bulvar Gagarina 44; ☏ 250 162, 250 167; f 250 285; e info@baikal-hotel.ru; www.baikal-hotel.ru. This renovated former Inturist block on the banks of the Angara is the city's biggest hotel & almost certainly the place you would have stayed had you arrived here 20 years ago. Ask for one of the renovated rooms, which are much more comfortable. $$$$

⌂ **Rus** (56 rooms) ul Sverdlova 19; ☏ 243 818; f 240 733; e rus@baikal.ru; www.rus.baikal.ru. Not one of Irkutsk's friendliest hotels, but rooms are clean & fairly comfortable, rates inc b/fast & there's a decent restaurant on site. The company also runs another hotel across town, so staff can usually find you a room if you turn up unannounced. $$$$

⌂ **Hotel Angara** (475 beds) ul Sukhe-Batora 7; ☏ 255 105; f 255 103; e info@angarahotel.ru; www.angarahotel.ru. The central location, myriad facilities (inc 5 bars & restaurants) & almost-with-a-smile service make this a sound choice for those on bigger budgets. Rooms on the 5th–7th floors are newly renovated to European standards but cost more. $$$–$$$$

⌂ **Gornyak** ul Lenina 21; ☏ 243 754. The unexciting en-suite rooms with tea- & coffee-making facilities & TV serve their purpose, though tall guests may have problems squeezing their frames into the tiny beds. B/fast not inc, & you should ask for a room away from noisy Lenin St. $$$

⌂ **Hotel Uzory** (25 rooms) ul Oktyabrskoy Revolyutsii 17; ☏ 209 239, 209 220; e yozera@irk.ru. The characterless but popular Uzory, near the bus station, has clean, basic rooms with TV & shared bathrooms, a large fitness centre & a handy bar-cum-café. B/fast is an extra RUB50. $$

HOSTELS

⌂ **Admiral Hostel** Apt 1, ul Cheremkhovsky 6; ☏ 742 440; www.irkutskhostel.irk.ru. The newest addition to Irkutsk's hostel scene enjoys an excellent location in a quiet city-centre street, uncramped dorms & a well equipped kitchen. The downside is that there is no member of staff on duty & guests are more or less left to their own devices. This also means turning up off the train at 04.00 looking for a bed is out of the question. Bookable through Hostelworld (www.hostelworld.com) or directly via the hostel website. $$

⌂ **Baikal Hostel** ul Lermontova 136, apt 1; ☏ 52 57 42; www.baikalinfo.com. This low-cost hostel is run by Baikalplan, a German association heavily involved in the creation of hiking trails around Lake Baikal & promoting tourism & ecology in the region as a whole. The staff provide free daytime pick-ups & facilities are excellent, but the downside is the location several km south of the railway station on the 'wrong' side of the river. Buses 1, 3, 7, 10, 24, 84, 90A, 72, 45, 80, 94 & 99 all run along Lermontova St where you should alight at the 'Mikrochirugia Glaza' stop. It's much simpler to take a taxi or get the hostel to pick you up. $$

⌂ **Baikaler Hostel** (9 beds) ul Lenina 9, apt 11; ☏ 336 240; e info@baikaler.com; www.baikaler.com. Quite possibly Russia's top hostel, Baikaler is run by Baikal expert & tour leader Jack (Yevgeniy) Sheremetoff. Despite its central location, the well-kept modern rooms are very quiet, &

thanks to the low number of beds in each there's ample space to unpack. Many a traveller's tale is exchanged over the kitchen table & there's a washing machine & small library. In 2008 Jack introduced free internet access & Wi-Fi, a feature no other Irkutsk hostel can boast. The staff are mines of information on all aspects of travel in the area & are always eager to help. Best to book ahead here, especially in summer when it's usually chock-full. Enter from the back of the building. $$

🏠 **Irkutsk Downtown Hostel** ul Stepana Razina 12, apt 12; ✆ 334597; e irkutskhostel@yahoo.com; www.hostel.irkutsk.ru. Another very centrally located, clean but sometimes cramped hostel just a short tram ride from the railway station. B/fast inc. The helpful staff can register visas for a fee. We were told this hostel may be moving to a more central location in 2009 so keep an eye on the website. $$

HOMESTAY

🏠 **Helen's Homestay** Yubileyny rayon; ✆ 468 559 or 8 950 130 8362; www.helenpot.com. This cosy apartment homestay has the advantage of an online

service for booking before you leave home. Charming Helen will gladly pick you up from the station or airport for free. $$

✕ WHERE TO EAT

RESTAURANTS

✕ **NEP** ul Krasnovo Vosstaniya 20; ✆ 202 117; ⏰ 12.00–05.00. Soviet-era propaganda posters, waitresses in strangely sexy Red Army uniforms & heaps of Communist regalia make this theme restaurant an interesting place to eat. The extensive menu of Russian & international dishes is in Cyrillic only, but some of the staff speak English. $$$$

✕ **Kochevnik** ul Gorkovo 19; ✆ 200 459; www.modernnomads.ru; ⏰ 11.30–midnight. If you're en route to Mongolia, this very welcoming restaurant is a great introduction to the country's much maligned cuisine. Having been shown to your table in one of the 2 halls by a pretty Mongolian (probably Buryat) waitress, choose from large salads, filling soups, mutton & lamb dishes or beef steaks from the English menu. Large portions, highly recommended. $$$–$$$$

✕ **Bier Haus** ul Gryaznova 1 (main entrance on ul Karla Marksa); ✆ 550 555; www.bier-haus.ru; ⏰ 12.00–02.00 Mon–Thu, 12.00–04.00 Fri & Sat, 12.00–midnight Sun. Czech & German beer for

London prices in Siberia! This mock Bavarian beer hall with its long timber benches & waitresses trussed up as alpine milkmaids is the place to come if you're already pining for a Newkie Brown 5 days into a 3-month RTW trip! The hearty Mitteleuropa-style food is reasonably priced & there's a friendly, almost family atmosphere. $$$

✕ **Snezhinka** Litvinova 2; ✆ 344 862; ⏰ 11.00–midnight. Faded French-style cream furniture, reasonably priced food, good service & a café society ambience make this a very pleasant place for a coffee & cake stop or evening dinner. $$$

✕ **Russkaya Chaynaya** ul Karla Marksa 3; ✆ 201 676; ⏰ 10.00–23.00. The 'Russian Tea Room' is one of the most characterful Russian places in town to eat. Themed as a 19th-century parlour, the gold & plush maroon wallpaper, antique samovars & primly laid tables, complete with matrioshka salt & pepper shakers, create a welcoming atmosphere, & the menu is in English! Meals are reasonably priced but the beers & coffees are a tad steep. $$–$$$

CAFÉS

✕ **Wiener Café** ul Stepana Razina 19; ✆ 202 116; ⏰ 10.00–23.00. This popular, but slightly overpriced, café has a large range of coffees, teas, soft drinks, salads, desserts & spirits to choose from.

The Viennese b/fast sounds tempting, but you may prefer a bowl of steaming porridge when the mercury goes south. Staff speak English. $$$

FAST FOOD

✕ **Krendel** ul Gryaznova 1; ✆ 706 156; ⏰ 10.00–02.00 Mon–Fri, 11.00–02.00 Sat & Sun. Situated just off ul Karla Marksa, this friendly self-service place has cheap grub in a kitsch faux-rural setting. The RUB45 pancakes washed down with a

RUB30 coffee make a sound b/fast, or come here the wrong side of midnight for a few shots & a skewer of shashlyk. $$–$$$

✕ **Domino Pizza** ul Lenina 13A; ⏰ 24hrs. Occupied by day by Western hostel dwellers filling up on cheap grub, Siberian teenagers on low-cost first dates & lunching office workers, at night by clubbers with the munchies & 'I didn't realise that meant Moscow time' Trans-Sibbers, this is a convenient self-service refuelling stop. Though billed as a pizza place, the Italian speciality bears only a passing likeness (taste-wise) to the real thing, so go instead for the *bliny* (pancakes) with a choice of sweet or savoury fillings. Staff get flustered when they don't understand the English menu, but it's all part of the fun. **$$**

✕ **Fiesta** ul Uritskovo; ⊕ 12.00–23.00. This large & noisy fast-food place is in the pedestrian area near the Central Market. Snacks & drinks fuel the feeding frenzy & there's Wi-Fi connection. Upstairs you'll discover the quite upmarket & altogether more subdued Arbatski Dvornik restaurant. **$$**

✕ **Mamochka** ul Karla Marksa 41; ⊕ 09.00–22.00. If it's cheap no-frills Russian grub you are after, look no further than this very popular self-service canteen on one of Irkutsk's main streets. All the mainstays of Russian cuisine are on offer to fill you up on freezing winter days. Décor is basic, service criminal, but the food is hearty & filling. Point, pay, eat, get out. **$$**

ENTERTAINMENT AND NIGHTLIFE

PUBS

🍺 **Cheshskaya Pivovarnya** ul Krasnogvardeyskaya 29; ☎ 538 482; ⊕ 12.00–midnight. Czech pub aficionados will recognise this as an attempt at a Bohemian microbrewery that doesn't quite hit the mark. The Czech-style lager is brewed on the premises & there are gimmicky Czech touches such as soup in a round loaf & beer taps on the tables for you to pull your own. Meal helpings are generous but the beer is a touch overpriced.

🍺 **Liverpool** ul Sverdlova 28; ☎ 202 512; ⊕ 12.00–03.00. This Beatles theme pub in a backstreet basement just off ul Karla Marksa is popular with Western travellers & locals alike. The beer menu is long but overpriced, the food very average but the atmosphere is superb when the place fills up. Dishes are named after Beatles hits, but just how the Norwegian Wood or Rubber Soul tastes we're not sure. There's sometimes live music at w/ends.

🍺 **U Shveyka** ul Karla Marksa 34; ☎ 242 687; ⊕ 12.00–midnight. Schweik restaurants back in the land of beer & Škodas are always touristy affairs & this one is no different. However, the beer is superb (they even have *řezané* – dark & light beer separated in one glass), portions are substantial & there's a summer beer garden. A plaque on the pub wall claims that Jaroslav Hašek, the author of the *Good Soldier Schweik*, lived in the building from 1918 to 1920.

🍺 **Ryumochnaya** ul Litvinova 16; ⊕ 24hrs. Serving perhaps the cheapest beer & vodka in the city centre, this smoky, 2-level bar is predictably well liked among those seeking low-cost inebriation around the clock. There's plenty of soak-up material on the menu for around RUB100 a plate.

THEATRE, MUSIC & CIRCUS

🎭 **Aystyonok Puppet Theatre** ul Sovietskaya; ☎ 290 666. In the unlikely event you have kids in tow, this marionette theatre provides traditional Russian entertainment, with no need to understand the language.

🎭 **Circus** ul Proletarskaya 13; ☎ 240 535. Circuses are very popular in Russia & Irkutsk is no exception. Forget the big top, this is a permanent fixture in the centre of the city.

🎭 **Musical Theatre** ul Sedova; ☎ 277 795. Check out the programme between September & June at this huge ferro-concrete venue, especially good for high-quality performances of Russian ballets.

🎭 **Okhlopkov Theatre** Karla Marksa 14; ☎ 200 477; e teatr@irk.ru; www.dramteatr.ru. If you understand Russian, enjoy a performance at the first theatre to be built in Siberia (1897). Constructed using donations from the city folk of Irkutsk, the first production to be staged was Gogol's *The Government Inspector*.

🎭 **Philharmonia** ul Dzerzhinskovo 2; ☎ 334 777. All kinds of music are performed here, though it has been reported that classical pieces can be spoilt by the noise of trams passing by on the street outside.

NIGHTSPOTS

☆ **Akula** bulvar Gagarina 9; ☎ 336 336; www.akula-club.ru. 'The Shark' is by far Irkutsk's wildest night out, with 24hr bowling, an entertainment centre, & top DJs, occasionally from

Europe, keeping the crowds happy till the wee hours in the ultra-modern nightclub. W/end striptease shows & 'boobs of the year' competitions give way to tamer weeknight 1980s nostalgia discos & quality dance music nights.

☆ **Chili** ul Karla Marksa 26; ✆ 332 190; ⊕ 24hrs. You probably didn't come all the way to Siberia to lounge on trendy couches sipping overpriced cocktails with the beautiful people, but if you did, do it here.

☆ **Megapolis** ul Ulan-Batorskaya 4; ✆ 426 410; www.megaclub.ru; ⊕ 22.00–06.00 Tue–Sun. This is the biggest nightclub in Irkutsk, with 3 dance floors capable of holding 1,000 party people, 5 bars & a local celebrity guest list. Summer outdoor dance floor on the roof!

☆ **Stratosfera** Karla Marksa 15; ✆ 243 436; www.strata-club.ru; ⊕ 18.00–06.00. Irkutsk's most central late night spot has a bowling alley, a pizzeria & a thumping dance floor.

SHOPPING

Irkutsk's modern **Central Market** (*between ul Dzerzhinskovo and ul Timiryazeva;* ⊕ *08.00–20.00*) was only opened in 1997 and is still surprisingly clean, orderly and cheap. Food stalls are located on the lower floor and spill out on to the adjacent streets and square; inedibles (as in what you don't eat) are on the first floor. The fruit and veg, meat, vodka and dried fruit stalls are particularly impressive, and you can also buy tasty ready-cooked meals, ideal for taking on long Trans-Siberian rides or bus journeys. Prices of some goods are a fraction of what you'll pay for lower quality supplies in Irkutsk's supermarkets, and you can also practise your Russian asking for them.

Irkutsk is generally not the best place for picking up souvenirs – save your money for Taltsy, Listvyanka and/or Buryatiya.

OTHER PRACTICALITIES

POST Post offices can be found at ul Karla Marksa 28, ul Stepana Razina 23 and ul Chelnikova 3 (near the railway station).

INTERNET

🖳 **Epitsentr** ul Bogdana Khmelnickovo 1; ✆ 720 708; ⊕ 24hrs (possibly). The staff at this modern, clean, no-nonsense internet café, popular with foreigners, assured us that they would begin to open round the clock in the near future. It's the only one left in town after the authorities closed all the others down.

WHAT TO SEE AND DO

The vast majority of attractions can be found in the city centre within the curve of the Angara River. Exceptions are the Angara Dam, the *Angara* icebreaker and the Znamensky Monastery.

MUSEUMS

Decembrist house museums (*Trubetskoy Hse – closed until 2010. Volkonsky Hse; ul Volkonskovo 10;* ✆ *207532, 208818; adult/student/child RUB90/30/20;* ⊕ *10.00–18.00 Tue–Sun*) The two most famous mansion houses, belonging to the Decembrists Volkonsky and Trubetskoy (see box on page 88), can be found near the bus station. At time of research the Trubetskoy mansion had been completely dismantled and carted off for renovation – workmen were just carefully sledge-hammering the 19th-century brick chimney chutes into oblivion. The house should reappear in 2010, but don't be surprised if takes a lot longer. That just leaves the Volkonsky House, a modest lilac and white affair dating from 1838, set in a scruffy courtyard. Though hard to imagine these days, according to period sources this was once the

THE DECEMBRISTS

Since 1816, two groups of liberal aristocrats, inspired by the ideals of the French Revolution, had been secretly plotting against the monarchy in the hope of creating a constitutional monarchy or full-blown republic. Following the death of Tsar Alexander I and the renunciation of the throne by his brother Constantine in December 1825, the youngest brother Nicholas I stepped forward and was sworn in as tsar. But on 14 December 1825 on St Petersburg's Senate Square, reformist military officers belonging to these revolutionary movements attempted to force the adoption of a constitutional monarchy by preventing the accession. The officers persuaded 3,000 soldiers to reject an oath of allegiance to the new monarch, but when support from St Petersburg's garrisons was not forthcoming, the revolt was doomed. Some 60 people died in the fighting, which lasted just a few hours.

The main protagonists were quickly sentenced to death, but 120 others of high military rank were exiled to Siberia where they became known as the Decembrists (Декабристы in Russian). At first the officers, princes and assorted aristocrats were treated as any other political exiles and sent to work the silver mines of Nerchinsk, but later they were permitted to disperse across Siberia to live a 'normal' life. Many of their devoted spouses followed them selflessly into the unknown wilderness, the most famous of these 'Decembrist wives' being Maria Volkonskaya, often called the 'Princess of Siberia'. The Volkonsky and Trubetskoy families built mansions in Irkutsk and were the focus of the city's cultural life in the mid 19th century, while others washed up in settlements such as Barguzin, Novoselenginsk and Kyakhta. However, despite their 'civilising' influence on the region, few remained true to Siberia, and when Alexander II declared an amnesty in 1855, most returned to their country estates near the capital. Their legacy lives on across Siberia to this day in the form of museums, theatres and street names.

centre of social life in Irkutsk, where the Volkonsky family would hold literary, musical and theatre evenings as well as balls and other parties. With a distrustful member of museum staff and light switch monitor on your tail, browse the various rooms full of period furniture, musical instruments, portraits of the Decembrists and their wives and items the families used in everyday life.

Irkutsk Regional Museum (*ul Karla Marksa 2;* ✆ *333 449; http://museum.irkutsk.ru;* ☉ *10.00–18.00 Tue–Sun; admission RUB100*) Housed in the ornate brick building of the former Siberian Geographical Society headquarters, this is an engaging little museum popular with tour groups. On the ground floor you'll discover glass display cases packed with shaggy shaman costumes and drums, Buddhist artefacts, household items from 19th-century Irkutsk, Evenk clothing and mammoth bones. The second floor hosts an exhibition on the symbols of Russia and Siberia as well as a fascinating section of archaic Soviet-era junk such as TVs, record players, sewing machines, posters and austere-looking clothing. Out in the sticks you'll still see some of these items in use!

Irkutsk History Museum (*ul Chaykovskovo 5;* ✆ *381 020; http://mus.irk.ru;* ☉ *10.00–18.00 Thu–Tue; admission RUB50*) This undervisited museum around 1½km west of the railway station traces the history of Irkutsk from the 17th century and hosts the odd temporary exhibition. Round off your visit with a stroll in the leafy grounds of the Angara spa. Buses 8, 11, 23 and 25 or trolleybuses 8 and 10K will take you to the 'Muzey' stop.

Sukachev Regional Art Museum (*ul Lenina 5;* ✆ *340 146;* ⊕ *10.00–17.30 Wed–Mon; admission RUB100*) Set back from busy Lenin Street, the grand old building of the Sukachev Regional Art Museum boasts the richest art collection in eastern Siberia. The exhibition began life as a private collection belonging to Irkutsk merchant and art lover Vladimir Sukachev (1849–1920), and includes 250 works by Russian and western European artists as well as a section of Chinese and Japanese *thangkas* and porcelain collected by the Siberian Geographical Society on its expeditions. The creaky parquet floors, dimly lit rooms and keen-eyed *babushkas* guarding every door just add to the experience.

CHURCHES

Saviour's Church (Spasskaya tserkov) (*ul Sukhe-Batora 2;* ⊕ *08.00–20.00*) This is the city's oldest surviving place of worship and dates from 1706. Shut down by the Bolsheviks in the 1930s, the building served as a museum from 1982 until 2006 when it once again began to welcome worshippers. Its long closure and almost 2½ decades of secular use explain its bare interior. Until the 1930s it was overshadowed by one of the largest cathedrals in Russia, which stood on the site of today's regional administration building. This was demolished on Stalin's orders after suffering considerable damage in the Civil War. Next to the church flickers the Eternal Flame war memorial, a popular place for wedding photographs.

Bogoyavlensky Cathedral (*Nizhnyaya naberezhnaya 2*) Located near the Saviour's Church, the Bogoyavlensky Cathedral dates from 1726, and is a prettier affair with a wonderfully ornate interior and newly painted façades and spire.

Polish Church (Polski kostyol) (*ul Sukhe-Batora*) Often overlooked, this neo-Gothic church was built in 1881 to replace a wooden structure that had occupied the site. Closed for much of the Soviet period, it reopened in 1978 after extensive restoration and the installation of an organ. Used by Irkutsk's Polish community (descendants of 19th-century Polish exiles) it also hosts regular organ concerts.

Church of the Raising of the Cross (Krestovozdvizhenskaya tserkov) (*ul Sedova 1*) Located across town, on a piece of raised ground at the end of Lenin Street, is this salmon-pink-and-cream church. The nave is filled with icons and the smell of incense. Built in 1758, it is an almost unique example of Siberian Baroque and the only church in Irkutsk to stay open during the Soviet era.

Kazan Church (Kazanskaya tserkov) (*ul Barrikad 34*) On the other side of the Ushakovka Stream from the bus station, the Kazan Church is possibly the city's prettiest place of worship. Built between 1885 and 1892, the recently renovated exterior glows a deep pink and blue while the interior was, at time of research, being transformed into Irkutsk's finest, with walls and ceilings decorated in intricate patterns of blood red, pine green, gold and white. To reach the church, take tram 4 from the Central Market to the 'Fuchika' stop.

OTHER PLACES OF INTEREST

White House (*bulvar Gagarina 24*) Located on the corner of Gagarin Boulevard and Karl Marx Street, the White House was built in 1804 by Sibiryakov, a rich Irkutsk merchant, but later served as the residence of the governor of East Siberia. It now houses a branch of the university library.

Statue of Tsar Alexander III On the nearby riverfront you will find this bearded statue erected in 1908 in gratitude for his decision to build the Trans-Siberian

Railway. An obelisk stood here from 1920 until 2003 when the statue made a reappearance. A fearsome double-headed eagle guards the base of the plinth, but the tsar himself looks as though he's holding a balloon on a string that's long since drifted way.

Lenin statue (*ul Lenina, opposite Domino Pizza*) If you've been in Russia for a long time you'll have got used to them, but first-timers may be fascinated to see Irkutsk's great-coated and waist-coated statue of Lenin. Behind the statue extends some pleasant parkland where young Irkutskites gather of a summer eve.

Across the Angara Crossing to the opposite bank of the River Angara, the main sight is Irkutsk's grand **old railway station** (*ul Chelnokova*). Its long turquoise, custard and white façade was first raised in 1898 and enlarged a decade later. It's still one of the most impressive on the entire 9,000km line.

Those who've fallen in love with the doe-eyed Nerpa seals (see box on page 31), or are yet to make their acquaintance, can get up close and personal with the lovely creatures at the **Nerpa Aquarium** (*ul 2-Zheleznodorozhnaya 66;* ❧ *435047;* ☉ *11.00–18.30 Wed–Sun*). To get there take tram 1 to the 'Chayka' stop.

OUTSIDE THE CITY CENTRE
Znamensky Monastery (*ul Angarskaya 14; free admission*)Though getting there involves a tricky approach along busy roads and across a huge chaotic roundabout, the Znamensky Monastery is well worth the trouble. At the gates you are greeted

---

ST INOKENT OF SIBERIA

Siberia's patron saint was born in around 1680 in faraway Chernihiv (in what is now Ukraine). Rising up through the Orthodox Church hierarchy, he spent all but the last ten years of his life living in relative comfort as a monk, priest and church administrator in the Orthodox hotspots of Kiev, Moscow and St Petersburg. In the early 18th century he was the star turn at top theological seminaries and cathedrals across European Russia, and could have lived a long life in similar fashion. But in 1721 Peter the Great dispatched him to Asia as Bishop of China, and after a year of gruelling travel along the *Trakt* from Moscow, he arrived at the border with what is now Mongolia. The Chinese, suspicious of this Orthodox missionary, refused him entry and Inokent fell on hard times in Irkutsk. In the five years from his arrival until becoming Bishop of Irkutsk in 1727, he was engaged in intense missionary work across the Baikal region, converting Buryats to Christianity and improving the general moral climate of the debauched capital of Russia's wild east (Irkutsk). He's even said to have learnt Buryat in order to pass on God's message to the locals in their native tongue.

Inokent died in 1731, but that's where the story really begins. Buried beneath the Ascension Monastery in Irkutsk, his remains were discovered after a fire, his body untouched, the flesh still intact. Between 1766 and 1800 many a miracle was attributed to him, and he was eventually beatified in 1804 after appeals from the pious folk of Irkutsk. Following the 1917 Revolution, his 'mummy' was held in storage or displayed as a curio by the Soviets until 1990, when it was returned to the Church. St Inokent was laid to rest again within the Znamensky Monastery that same year, and today his sarcophagus attracts hundreds of worshippers a day, most hoping for some of his miracle-working powers to rub off on them.

St Inokent of Siberia is often confused with the American St Innocent of Alaska who was, to confuse things even further, born near Irkutsk.

by the controversial **statue of Admiral Kolchak**, White-Russian commander and explorer (see page 15), erected in 2004. He was shot by the Reds nearby and his body thrown into the Ushakovka Stream towards the end of the Civil War. Inside the monastery you will find Irkutsk's most atmospheric **Orthodox church**, with its aromatic, mysterious interior, wonderful muralled vaulting, a large iconostasis and, most importantly, a gilt casket containing the relics of St Inokent (see box on page 90). The church is always quietly busy with women young and old, their hair concealed under flowery headscarves, reverently lighting candles, crossing themselves and touching the floor with their foreheads before kissing the saint's tomb. Back outside, the grounds are the final resting place for two of Irkutsk's most famous personalities. The grave of Decembrist wife Yekaterina Trubetskaya is a surprisingly humble affair, while the more flamboyant theme-tomb of celebrated explorer Gregory Shelikov, with its sextants, masts and anchors, leaves visitors in no doubt what the 'Russian Columbus' did for a living.

Angara Dam area Some 6km south of the city centre the Angara hydro-electric dam holds back the Angara River, the only waterway to drain Lake Baikal. This was a Soviet project of monumental proportions, and the length (2km) and size (44m high) of the dam's structure are impressive. When it was completed in 1958 and the valley behind it flooded, the water level in Lake Baikal 70km upstream rose by 1m. The only real tourist sight here is the *Angara* **icebreaker** (✎ *358 551;* ⊕ *09.00–22.00*) which was built on the River Tyne in 1899 and shipped to Siberia in sections. The steamer was used to transport Trans-Siberian passengers over Lake Baikal before the Circumbaikal section was constructed. The carriages travelled on her sister, the *Baikal*, which was also built in Newcastle but has long since lain on the lake's deep bottom. The Angara is now a museum reached by a permanent gangway. Opposite the ship there are several summer shashlyk cafés. Around 500m across the headland lies the *Raketa* hydrofoil station where boats depart in summer for Listvyanka, Olkhon Island and Severobaikalsk.

To reach this part of town, take trolleybus 1, 5, 7, 8 or 10, all of which cross to the other side of the river via the dam.

Irkutsk WHAT TO SEE AND DO

3

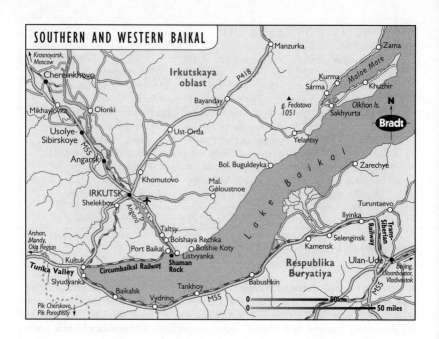

SOUTHERN AND WESTERN BAIKAL

Krasnoyarsk, Moscow
Cherenkhovo
Mikhaylovka
Olonki
Usolye-Sibirskoye
Angarsk
M55
Khomutovo
IRKUTSK
Shelekhov
Angara
Taltsy
Bolshaya Rechka
Port Baikal
Bolshie Koty
Listvyanka
Circumbaikal Railway
Shaman Rock
Kultuk
Tunka Valley
Slyudyanka
Pik Cherskovo
Pik Poroshisty
Baikalsk
Vydrino
Tankhoy
M55

Irkutskaya oblast
Manzurka
Zama
P418
Bayanday
Kurma
Sarma
Maloe More
Khuzhir
g. Fedotova 1051
Olkhon Is.
Sakhyurta
Yelantsy
N
Bradt
Ust-Orda
Bol. Buguldeyka
Zarechye
Mal. Goloustnoe
Lake Baikal
Turuntaevo
Ilyinka
Trans-Siberian Railway
Selenginsk
Kamensk
Ulan-Ude
Beijing, Ulaanbaatar, Vladivostok
Babushkin
Respublika Buryatiya
M55

Arshan, Mondy, Oka Region

0   50km
0   50 miles

4

Southern and Western Baikal

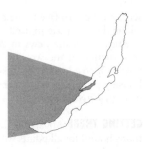

The southern and western shores are where most travellers get their first glimpse of the shimmering waters or glistening ice of Lake Baikal. The stretch of shoreline from Olkhon Island, 200km to the north of Irkutsk, to Slyudyanka, 80km to the south, forms the main tourist area, with more hotels, restaurants and services than any other lakeside location. A mere 70km southeast of Irkutsk, Listvyanka is a summer tourist hotspot and a popular place for city dwellers to build their multi-storey *dachi* (weekend cottages). It's also the most convenient stretch of Lake Baikal for time-pressed Trans-Siberian travellers, though the village is wholly unrepresentative of the rest of the lake's 2,000km of shoreline. The Circumbaikal Railway is another popular attraction here, as are watersports in summer and ice fun in the winter months.

The Tunka Valley takes visitors away from the lake into the Sayan mountain range in the west, the focal point of which is the small spa town of Arshan. This is officially Buryatiya, and somewhere on the road between lakeside Kultuk and mountainside Arshan the locals' facial features change from Slavic to Asian, and the local religion alters from Orthodox Christianity to Buddhism. The wide Tunka Valley, defined by the saw-tooth peaks of the Eastern Sayan range in the north and the Khamar Daban range to the south, is a superb place for wilderness trekking, though you'll need the right equipment and a local guide to venture far.

GETTING AROUND

The Trans-Siberian Railway runs from Irkutsk south to Kultuk from where it hugs the shoreline of Lake Baikal almost until it reaches the Selenga Delta on the opposite side. The Circumbaikal Railway from Port Baikal to Slyudyanka is more tourist attraction than working rail service, but it can be used as such with a little patience and good timing. Summer hydrofoils ply the Angara reservoir between Irkutsk, Listvyanka and Olkhon Island, while bus is the only option for reaching anywhere in the Tunka Valley. Note that you cannot cross the border from Russia into Mongolia at the western end of the Tunka Valley, though this situation may change in coming years. This is frustrating for those wishing to visit Baikal's sister lake Khövsgöl just a short distance beyond the frontier.

ANGARSK (АНГАРСК) *Telephone code: 3955*

Very (very) few Baikal visitors take the time to call at this huge petrochemicals town, 35km northwest along the Trans-Siberian towards Moscow. Although not an unpleasant place, with its large flowery parks and heaps of quite attractive 1950s Neoclassical architecture, there's little to see here unless you have a passion for clocks. However, in contrast to Irkutsk, the citizens of Angarsk will be surprised to see your Western face in their wholly off-the-beaten-track town, a good reason for taking the short trip in itself.

Angarsk hit the news in 2006 when the Russian government announced the construction of the world's first international uranium enrichment plant in the town. Opposition has been strong, and in July 2007 an environmentalists' camp housing protestors was attacked by 15 baseball-bat-wielding thugs. One protestor died. (*www.gorodangarsk.ru*)

GETTING THERE Angarsk is the first or sometimes second stop for Trans-Siberian trains bound for all points west of Irkutsk. However, it's much less hassle to make the trip by bus, with large coaches (RUB43.50) leaving at 20-minute intervals from Irkutsk bus station, or by regular *elektrichka* from the railway station.

✕ **WHERE TO EAT** Prospekt Karla Marksa is the place to go for a cheap café meal. Self-caterers and snackers will find sufficient supermarkets and food shops, or why not try the **Central Market** (*ul O. Koshevovo*).

🍴 **Bier Haus** 75 Kvartal; ☏ 521 414; ⏰ 12.00–02.00 Mon–Thu, 12.00–04.00 Fri & Sat, 12.00–midnight Sun. The Angarsk branch of Irkutsk's Bier Haus can be found near Lenin Square. It serves the same beer & food as its Irkutsk big sister, but you'll definitely be the only foreign guest. It's the best place to eat in town. **$$$**

WHAT TO SEE AND DO Having wandered Angarsk's carefully laid out grid of streets, wondering why you came, it's time to head for the town's only tourist attraction, the surprisingly impressive **Clock Museum** (*ul Karla Marksa 31;* ☏ *523 345;* ⏰ *10.00–17.00 Tue–Sat*) situated just off Lenin Sq. The exhibition features a once private collection of over 1,100 timepieces from Russia, Japan and most of Europe, some almost 300 years old. If you're around at noon the cacophony of chimes is deafening.

UST-ORDA (УСТЬ-ОРДА) *Telephone code: 39541*

Until 2006 this ramshackle Wild East town of 14,000 souls, some 70km northeast of Irkutsk, was the administrative capital of the Ust-Ordynsky Buryat Autonomous Region within the Irkutsk oblast – that is until it voted itself into the dustbin of history in a referendum. Now re-consigned to provincial anonymity, this almost entirely Buryat town is worth visiting for its regional museum where at least a brief encounter with Buryat culture can be had, should you not be planning a stop on the lake's eastern shore.

The entire town extends on all sides off ul Lenina, the main thoroughfare where you'll quickly locate the bus station, the museum, shops, the hotel and places to eat. The only sights away from here are the local datsan, 20 minutes' walk back towards Irkutsk, and the handicraft centre, a short walk northwest.

GETTING THERE *Marshrutki (journey time: 30mins; tickets: RUB68.50)* leave Irkutsk bus station for Ust-Orda every 30 minutes. They generally return when full, but you won't normally wait long.

 WHERE TO STAY

🏠 **Hotel Baikal** (12 rooms) ul Lenina 24; ☏ 32236. This surprisingly smart hotel (the only place to stay) wouldn't look out of place in rural Poland or the Czech Republic, with clean, well maintained if bland en-suite & TV/fridge-equipped rooms. Staff are relatively pleasant & even more incredibly there's a vegetarian b/fast option! **$$$**

WHERE TO EAT

✕ Baikal Hotel Restaurant Ground floor, Hotel Baikal, ul Lenina 24; ⏱ 12.00–02.00. This is the only classic sit-down meal stop in Ust-Orda & the focus of its tiny nightlife scene. The extensive menu features many signature Buryat dishes, the vast majority of which you won't know. They also do a good line in Russian staples, & you can enjoy your meal in the cosy hotel forecourt yurt if you call ahead. **$$$**

✕ Poznaya Odon Cnr ul Lenina & ul Kalinina; ⏱ 11.00–20.00. Always busy with locals slurping & munching their *pozy* at RUB20 a shot, this basic

but clean dumpling bar fills the belly without emptying the wallet. **$**

✕ Stolovaya Anna ul Kalandarashvili, next to the bus station; ⏱ 08.00–20.00. This Soviet-era classic is an absolute gem & worth travelling from Irkutsk to see on its own. Unchanged since the collapse of the Soviet Union, you'll have the feeling you've been transported back in time, & the prices are pretty retro too. Filling Siberian staples are first paid for at the *kassa* then collected from the frilly dinner ladies in the kitchen. Pure, unadulterated Soviet vintage. **$**

OTHER PRACTICALITIES

✉ **Post office** ul Lenina 26; ⏱ 08.00–21.00 Mon–Fri, 09.00–18.00 Sat & Sun. Offers internet access (09.00–12.00 & 14.00–18.00 Mon–Fri).

WHAT TO SEE AND DO

Ethnographical Museum (*ul Lenina 6;* ☎ *31402;* ⏱ *09.00–13.00 & 14.00–17.00 Mon–Fri; admission RUB100*) The main reason for making the trip to Ust-Orda is to wander the four halls of the local museum, which focuses on the culture of the western Buryats. Although you may feel like the only foreigner ever to have set foot in the town, don't be surprised to open the door of the museum and be confronted by a horde of camera-toting French or Germans, as this is a regular tour-bus stop. Nor are the staff that used to individuals turning up off the street unannounced, and you may be followed round with suspicion.

Exhibits with Russian-only labels range from dusty petroglyphs from the surrounding hills to full-blown folk costume, and from early 20th-century photos of shaggy shamans to a sorry-looking, rather threadbare deer. There's Buryat folk art, iron agricultural implements, wooden kitchen utensils, ornately embroidered silk robes, and silver-and-coral jewellery, and even if you don't fully understand what you're seeing, the exhibits still give a picture of the rich traditional cultural life of the western Buryats before the modern world intruded.

If you're really organised and phone ahead, or if a tour group have stumped up the cash, you might be able to watch a shaman performance or ethnic Buryat musicians and taste a few local specialities out in the courtyard or in the wooden yurt outside.

Datsan (*ul Kalandarashvili*) The splayed eaves of Ust-Orda's Buddhist place of worship are barely visible from the road, despite standing just a few metres away from it. Inside the tiny temple there are just a handful of butter lamps, a few bits of silk, offerings of rice and coins and a couple of *thangkas*. This datsan's size and out-of-the-way location may be a reflection of the dominance shamanism enjoys over Buddhism west of Lake Baikal. The building is open for anyone to wander in and take a peak, but the effect is spoilt slightly by the plastic windows.

If arriving by *marshrutka* from Irkutsk, ask the driver to stop at the datsan to save yourself a 20-minute walk back along the road from the bus station.

Other places of interest As you enter the village, look out for the huge and impressive silver **statue of a Buryat horseman**, the symbol of the town. A mounted and freshly painted **tank** at the bus station end of ul Lenina has its gun aimed squarely at the museum's roof. Further up ul Lenina behind the cinema, the immaculate **Trinity Church** dating from 2007 is worth a look for its beautifully carved iconostasis and icons peering out of wall-mounted glass display cases. The inevitable **Lenin statue** rises near the Hotel Baikal and surveys the scene from a black granite plinth. The hit-and-miss **Buryat Traditional Handicraft Centre** (*ul Budennovo*) 1km northwest of ul Lenina has displays of Buryat national costume, wedding clobber, hunting gear, traditional warrior garb, musical instruments and other ceremonial items. However, there wasn't a whole lot happening when we were there, and you'll be lucky to find the place open.

TALTSY OPEN-AIR MUSEUM OF WOODEN ARCHITECTURE (АРХИТЕКТУРНО-ЭТНОГРАФИЧЕСКИЙ МУЗЕЙ 'ТАЛЬЦЫ')

Not much of the village of Taltsy, 47km southeast of Irkutsk, remained after the valley in which it stood was flooded in the 1950s as part of the Angara hydro-electric project. Once famous for its glassworks, Taltsy now draws day trippers from Irkutsk and Listvyanka to its alfresco museum where various farmsteads, churches, Cossack houses and mills, mostly from the areas around Bratsk and Ust-Ilimsk, were hauled and reassembled during the 1970s. Many of the 40 buildings occupying the site were saved from a watery fate when the villages where they stood were submerged by another dam project further up the Angara. Some of the timber structures are well over 300 years old and give an insight into the way the first settlers in Siberia lived, worked and worshipped.

The museum is set in 67ha of woodland on the banks of the Angara Reservoir, and the tour route is a relaxing and pleasant walk. Most of the explanations are in English (a rarity in these parts) and the whole place has a laidback but well organised feel with no unofficial guides touting their services or hard sell at the souvenir stalls. No matter what day you turn up, you're likely to find something going on here such as a wedding celebration, festivities to mark Easter, Shrovetide or other national holiday, or a folk festival.

GETTING THERE
By bus Unless you take a tour from Irkutsk (which is, frankly, quite unnecessary), a bus or *marshrutka* (*departs: four times daily; journey time: 40–60mins; tickets: RUB70*) from Irkutsk or Listvyanka is the only way to reach Taltsy. Buses don't stop here automatically, so be sure to keep reminding the driver that you want to get off there. The entrance is marked with a sign; walk a short way through the forest to find the ticket office.

By *marshrutka* Another alternative is the odd *marshrutka* (*journey time: 40mins; tickets: RUB70, different service from above marshrutka*) from Irkutsk that terminates at Taltsy and which leaves from the right-hand side of Irkutsk bus station.

✖ WHERE TO EAT
There's a restaurant and café behind the souvenir stalls, or bring a picnic to enjoy in the woods or by the river.

SHOPPING
Taltsy has one of the best ranges of souvenirs you'll find anywhere in the Baikal region with stall after stall selling birch items such as boxes, shoes, table mats, *matrioshka* dolls, wooden toys and semi-precious polished stones, as well as books, DVDs and postcards. Prices are reasonable, though only some of what you see here has been made locally.

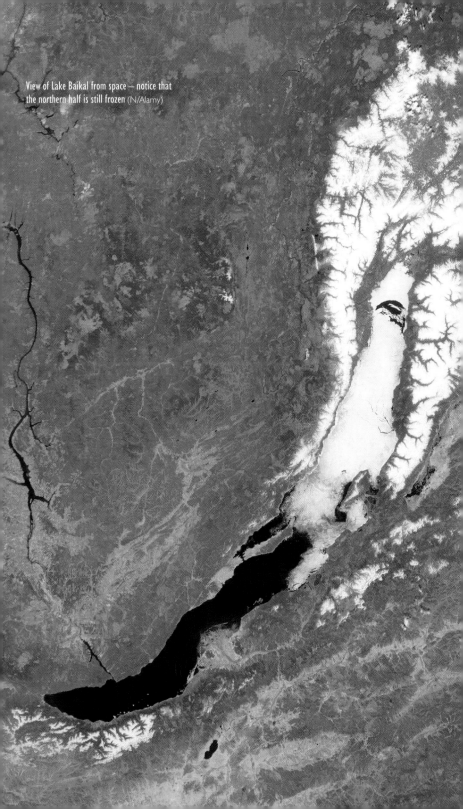
View of Lake Baikal from space – notice that the northern half is still frozen (N/Alamy)

The magnificently remote Barguzin Valley; punctuated only by flower meadows and the occasional timber village (B/Alamy) page 141

above   Plenty of hiking opportunities, especially inside Baikal Biosphere Reserve
(IM/Alamy) page 32

right   Marker on the Great Baikal Trail. Volunteer to expand or repair the route which aims to create a hiking path that encircles the entire lake
(MDD) page 105

below   Explore the lake on two wheels
(FF/W/Alamy)

above   Trans-Siberian train running
         along Lake Baikal's shoreline
         (WK/Alamy) page 43

right   Smoked *omul* fish on sale at
         Listvyanka market
         (MDD) page 101

below   Enjoy the views while soaking
         in a hot-spring tub
         (KO/N/Alamy) page 155

above left   The white-tailed eagle — also known as the sea eagle — can live to be over 25 years old (DD/FLPA)

above right   Muskrat. These semi-aquatic rodents are named after the two scent glands, located at the base of their tail, that secrete a musky odour (DMJ/MP/FLPA)

left   The Siberian lemming. The myth of mass suicide among lemmings was first suggested by the 1955 Disney cartoon *The Lemming with the Locket* (WW/FLPA)

below right   White Baikal Anemone (I/FLPA)

below left   Gray marmot. Individuals use loud whistles to communicate with each other (NB/FLPA)

above left	Male Siberian roe deer (I/FLPA)
above right	The sable is a species of marten; their fur is highly prized (I/FLPA)
right	Pasque flower (KW/MP/FLPA)
below	Pallas's cat — also known as the Manul — was named after the naturalist Peter Simon Pallas, who first described the species in 1776 (TW/FLPA)

Lake Baikal shoreline on a summer's day (A/D)

WHAT TO SEE AND DO

The Museum (*Kilometre 47, Baikalsky trakt;* ☎ *145 249; adult/child RUB120/60;* ⊕ *winter 10.00–16.00, summer 10.00–17.00*) If there's one thing you find an abundance of in Siberia, it's wood, so it can come as no surprise that Siberia's first buildings and those constructed in rural areas to this day were, and are, built from the stuff, often without nails and covered with timber slat roofs. However, the first structures visitors encounter on entering the museum predate the arrival of Russian Cossacks to the Baikal region and belong to the Evenk people. The Evenk burial site illustrates how this native people used to lay their dead to rest above ground.

A short way through the birch forest brings you to the **Greater Village (Volostnoe selo)** where the Spasskaya Tower (1667) from the Ilimsk Fortress faces a row of Cossack farmsteads with the Kazan Chapel (1679) in the middle. Most of the weather-silvered houses and the fort can be explored and inside you'll discover various 18th- and 19th-century household items, themed exhibitions and 'locals' in period costume.

Continuing along the track, visitors arrive at the next section of the exhibition, the **Lesser Village (Derevnya malodvorka)**, where the substantial onion-domed Trinity Church (Troitskaya tserkov) dominates a large settlement of houses, yards and outhouses, and where row upon row of stalls tempt passers-by with interesting if sometimes rather quirky souvenirs.

The final part of the museum, the **Buryat Settlement (Buryatsky ulus)** is perhaps the most interesting with its wooden yurts housing exhibitions on Buryat shamanism, family life and national costumes.

LISTVYANKA (ЛИСТВЯНКА) *Telephone code: 3952*

If you're short of time and only have one chance to admire the beauty of Lake Baikal on a RTW or Trans-Siberian trip, it's likely to be from Listvyanka's touristy foreshore. This sprawling village some 70km southeast of Irkutsk is the most popular and most easily accessible Baikal resort from Irkutsk and it knows it. Sometimes called the Baikal Riviera, no other lakeside settlement flaunts so many hotels, guesthouses and activities, or receives so many visitors, especially in July and August when it's overrun with Russians and foreigners alike. Most come here from Irkutsk for the day, but staying longer allows further exploration of the hinterland and the surrounding forested hills. On quieter days outside of the season enjoy the hazy views of the Khamar Daban mountain range on the opposite shore in peace while picnicking on the pebbly beach.

Listvyanka is a rambling settlement with no real centre. The walk from the mouth of the Angara River to the souvenir market at the far eastern end measures almost four kilometres. Add to that the three valleys which cut inland and make up the bulk of the village, and you have yourself a considerable amount of legwork if you want to explore the village in full.

If you notice that the road south from Irkutsk to Listvyanka (the only road) is in surprisingly good condition, there's an explanation. It was built specially for the visit of US president Eisenhower in 1960, but just as the asphalt was hardening in the May sunshine, the Soviets shot down a U-2 spy plane over their territory and the visit was cancelled. During most of the Soviet era the Irkutsk Region on the western shores of Lake Baikal was open to tourists while Buryatiya on the eastern side was not. In this zone permitted to receive foreign visitors, most tourists were funnelled down this fine stretch of asphalt to the lake's showpiece resort, Listvyanka. Old habits die hard and the vast majority of Trans-Siberian transit tourists passing along the southern shores of Lake Baikal see little more than Irkutsk and Listvyanka, not because some bureaucracy faraway in Moscow has

4

decided so, but thanks to Eisenhower's road and other infrastructure inherited from the Inturist days.

Thankfully, plans to transform Listvyanka into a glittering, high-rise, five-star mega-resort for New Russians and their petrodollars were recently shelved, though this fate may simply be thrust upon the tiny fishing hamlet of Bolshoe Goloustnoe further north instead.

GETTING THERE Four buses (*journey time:1¼hrs; tickets: RUB63*) and countless *marshrutki* (*journey time: 1hr*) hurtle along the smooth road between Irkutsk and Listvyanka every day. Services stop at the Baikal Museum (near the ferry quay for Port Baikal) and the information centre. In summer you have the additional option of taking the hydrofoil from near the Angara Dam (see *Getting around* page 60). Some travellers may also arrive by ferry from Port Baikal after getting off the Circumbaikal Railway.

TOURIST INFORMATION Listvyanka boasts a fairly helpful tourist information booth (*Hydrofoil quay, ul Gorkovo;* ✆ *496 987; www.baikalvisa.ru;* ⊕ *10.00–13.00 & 14.00–18.00*) operated by the Baikal Visa tour company. Staff can assist with accommodation, tickets and tours and there is internet access for RUB2 a minute. Open year-round, but hours are unpredictable.

 WHERE TO STAY If arriving in July or August be sure to book as early as possible. Outside of these months you should have no difficulty getting a bed.

FULL STEAM AHEAD – THE RUSSIAN BANYA

You can't really say you've had the complete Russian experience until you've spent an hour or two in a traditional Siberian *banya*. The closest translation of the word would be sauna or Turkish baths, but the Russian version is quite different and provides a wholly unforgettable experience.

Usually a hut constructed of pine logs, a real *banya* has to be fired up about an hour before you enter. After stripping off in the *predbannik* (pre-*banya* reception room) 'bathers' then gather in the *parilka* (steam room) where stones have been heated in a special wood-burning stove. Water is thrown on to the red-hot rocks creating a cloud of steam, the cue for people to take it in turns to whip each other with birch switches (*veniki*), a somewhat painful but cleansing experience. Thus steamed and whipped, the next stage is to dive into the cold tub, which at the wrong end of the year in eastern Siberia can contain water just above freezing point, before rushing back into the steam room. This invigorating and allegedly rejuvenating process is repeated five to ten times over the course of 60–90 minutes. Tea, beer and vodka are consumed during the process and many men like to play chess. *Banya* is a male dominated affair, though women do visit occasionally for special female-only sessions.

Today you'll find just one type of *banya* described above, but at the Banya Museum in Ust-Barguzin (see page 139) you can inspect a so-called 'black *banya*', the original type used for over a millennium, in which the smoke from the furnace escapes through a hole in the roof. This stains the interior with soot and gives it a strange smoke- and sap-infused fragrance.

For some reason the local *banya* in towns and villages around Lake Baikal is usually a well-kept secret, but ask around at hotels and travel companies to locate the nearest one. Apart from Ust-Barguzin's Banya Museum, the Baikal Guesthouse in Listvyanka has a great *banya*, as do several others listed in this book. At Nikita's on Olkhon Island it's virtually the only way of getting clean!

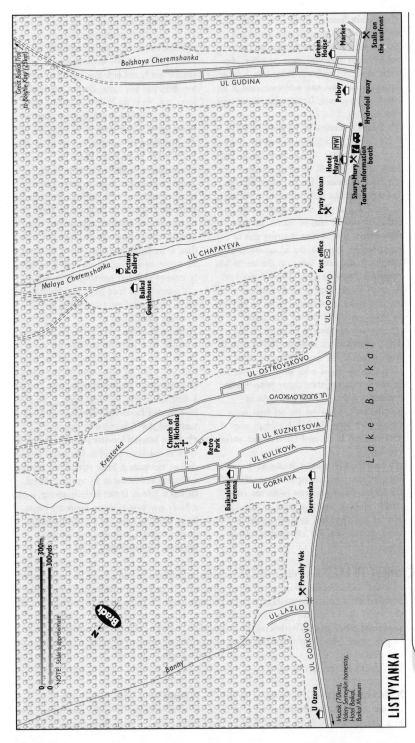

LISTVYANKA

Great Baikal Trail
to Bolshie Koty (25km)

Bolshaya Cheremshanka

UL GUDINA

Green
House

Market

Stalls on
the seafront

Priboy

Hydrofoil quay

Pyaty Okean

Hotel
Mayak

Shury-Mury

Tourist information
booth

Malaya Cheremshanka

Picture
Gallery

UL CHAPAYEVA

Baikal
Guesthouse

Post office

UL GORKOVO

L a k e   B a i k a l

UL OSTROVSKOVO

UL SUDZILOVSKOVO

Krestovka

Church of
St Nicholas

Retro
Park

UL KUZNETSOVA

UL KULIKOVA

UL GORNAYA

Baikalskie
Terema

Derevenka

Proshly Vek

300m

300yds

NOTE: Scale is approximate

Black!

N

Banny

UL LAZLO

UL GORKOVO

U Ozera

Irkutsk (70km),
Valery Semeykin homestay,
Hotel Baikal,
Baikal Museum

🏠 **Baikalskie Terema** ul Gornaya 16; 📞 780 120; www.gotobaikal.ru. One of the most upmarket & pleasant places to stay in Listvyanka, this chunky timber complex on a ridge above the village offers timber rooms (dbl only) with timber beds & timber furniture. Some rooms have wide-screen views of the lake & all are en suite. The somewhat inflated room rates inc b/fast. $$$$

🏠 **U Ozera** ul Suvorova 2; 📞 250 444, 496 777; f 204 367; e yozera@irk.ru. A small new timber hotel on the lakefront with panoramic Baikal views. Rooms are on the small side. $$$–$$$$

🏠 **Baikal Guesthouse** ul Chapaeva 69; 📞 496 758. This large guesthouse, recognisable only by the street number, is a great place to stay thanks to the enthusiastic owner & excellent facilities. There are many different types of room of varying sizes to choose from inc large dbls, tiny loft conversions & summer-only shed-rooms. Guests can also use the fully equipped kitchen & the comfy communal area. Rates inc hearty Siberian b/fast prepared by the owner who also loves to fire up his *banya* (see box on page 98) for foreign guests (RUB1,200 for 2hrs). $$$

🏠 **Derevenka** (7 cabins) ul Gornaya 1; 📞 250 459; e fligel@mail.ru; www.village2002.narod.ru. Go rough & rural at this cosy, family-run log cabin complex on the side of a hill where each room has its own wood-burning stove, chunky timber furniture & bathroom (but no shower). There's also an intimate dining room where you can order dinner (though you'd better like fish!) & a *banya* which at RUB250/hr may be the most expensive wash you've ever had. $$$

🏠 **Green House** (5 rooms) ul Shtorkmana 3; 📞 496 707. With some rooms costing as little as RUB1,000, this intimate timber guesthouse (which now rather cheekily advertises itself as a hostel) set 50m back from the lake offers value for money as well as a *banya*, common room & a fully equipped kitchen. $$$

🏠 **Hotel Baikal** ul Akademicheskaya 13; 📞 250 391; f 250 162; e incoming@baikal-hotel.ru; www.baikal-hotel.ru. Just like its sister hotel in Irkutsk (the Angara), this former Inturist establishment located high above the village would have been your only option 20 years ago. Despite its Soviet past, this is one of the most civilised places to stay, if you can afford it, with upgraded rooms, a Russian *banya*, a posh restaurant & a bar. $$$

🏠 **Hotel Mayak** (66 rooms) ul Gorkovo 85; 📞 496 910, 496 911; e mayakhotel@mail.ru; www.mayakhotel.ru. The 'Lighthouse' is, by all accounts, the shape of things to come as far as tourism around the lake is concerned. If the Russian authorities have anything to do with it, whole stretches of Lake Baikal will soon be lined with upmarket establishments like this. Rooms are shiny & clean, & the Baikal views from some of the rooms & the terrace are excellent, but the hotel is occupied by members of Russia's nouveau riche, lending it a rigid atmosphere of faked luxury & pomposity. Despite its upmarket appearance, rooms are reasonably priced. $$$

🏠 **Priboy** ul Gorkovo 101; 📞 496 725. Housed in a building which looks like something left over from the space race, the chintzy Priboy stands on the main road just a few metres from the lake. Rooms are comfortable if hideously done out, most have TV & some are en suite. The larger rooms at the front enjoy excellent Baikal views. Downstairs you'll find a handy food shop & fancy-looking restaurant. $$$

🏠 **Valery Semeykin homestay** ul Akademicheskaya 2, apt 8; e baikal-inform@irk.ru. Experienced English-speaking tour guide & Baikal expert Valery Semeykin rents cheap, basic rooms in his apartment behind the Baikal Museum. Contact Valery in advance as he is hardly ever there to receive unexpected guests. Hearty b/fast inc. Valery can also arrange hiking, canoeing, rafting & horseriding trips around Listvyanka & further afield. $–$$

✕ **WHERE TO EAT** For a village that receives thousands of visitors a day in the summer months, eating options are surprisingly limited. Most visitors are content to pick at a smoked *omul* from the market, washed down with a Baltika beer. If you can't stand the sight of yet another greasy inhabitant of Baikal's depths, try the **stalls on the seafront** where locals barbecue meat (*shashlyk*) over wood grills and keep huge woks of pilau rice (*plov*) warm for hungry tourists. There are usually tables and chairs set out nearby but there's a hefty charge for those who want to sit out on the beach. Listvyanka has plenty of grocery stores and bakeries for self-caterers and picnickers.

✕ **Shury-Mury** 📞 250 452; ⏲ 10.00–11.00. This café next to the tourist information office is ideal for a proper, indoors, knife-&-fork meal. $$

✕ **Proshly Vek** ul Lazlo 1; 📞 496 984; ⏲ 12.00–midnight. The English menu features *omul* in many guises, & cheap, filling pancakes. $$$

✘ **Pyaty Okean** ul Gorkovo 59A; ↘ 496 726; ⊕ 11.00–22.00. Friendly place that serves meat dishes & salads at glass-top tables inside, or outside by the gurgling Cheremshanka Stream. **$$–$$$**

SHOPPING The range of souvenirs on sale at Listvyanka's daily **market** at the end of ul Gorkovo is second to none. One half of the marketplace is packed with stalls selling anything from typical birch bark and cedar items, mineral jewellery and shaman masks to plastic seals, carved spoons and Baikal DVDs; the other half is occupied by a fragrant fish market where locals keep smoked *omul* warm in large padded boxes to sell to tourists. Fish are splayed out with toothpicks to allow the smoky taste to penetrate the oily flesh from the inside.

WHAT TO SEE AND DO
Baikal Museum (Limnological Institute) *(Akademicheskaya 1; ⊕ 09.00–19.00; adult RUB80 or RUB150 depending on whether you are charged the foreigner or local price (it's the luck of the draw here)* Most people setting out to visit Listvyanka's Limnological Institute are probably clueless as to what the word 'limnological' means. The dictionary defines it as 'the scientific study of conditions in bodies of fresh water'. This just about sums up this antiquated, unimaginative museum near the Port Baikal ferry quay, whose only saving grace is the aquaria containing many species of fish (including some *omul* who can count themselves fortunate not be in a hotbox at the market) and two adorable nerpa seals who perform 'aquabatics' in two huge tanks.

Other sights Listvyanka is divided into three valleys packed with typical single-storey Siberian timber houses with their light-blue carved window frames and ramshackle vegetable gardens. Heading into the village from Irkutsk, the first valley is of greatest interest as here stands Listvyanka's oldest building, the **Church of St Nicholas**. It was built in 1846 using funds left by a local merchant, Ksenofont Sibiryakov, who claimed he had been rescued in a storm on Lake Baikal by St Nicholas himself. Since its construction this simple timber church with its yellow and pink plank walls and two tiny onion domes has had a vagrant existence. It originally adorned the nearby village of Nikola with its presence, but was moved to the lakefront in Listvyanka, from where it was shifted inland in the 1950s when the Angara Dam raised the water level in the lake. A short distance along the Krestovka Stream (exactly 157m if the pedantic sign is to be believed) you may stumble across the bizarre **Retro Park** *(admission RUB15)*, which at first resembles a junkyard. On closer inspection the junk turns out to be several pieces of sculpture fashioned from old Soviet cars, motorbikes and truck parts.

At the end of the road in the second valley, lined with a mixture of ramshackle timber dwellings and posh *dachas*, a small **Picture Gallery** *(ul Chapeyeva 76; ↘ 496 752)* founded by local poet and architect Vladimir Plamenevsky, is worth the walk. All the works by local artists portraying Baikal landscapes, Irkutsk churches and other subjects are for sale.

ACTIVITIES Listvyanka is one of the region's liveliest activity centres where diving, horseriding, hiking, yachting, angling, snow scooter riding, snowmobiling, dogsledding and much more can be enjoyed. Ask Valery Semeykin (see *Where to stay* opposite), any Irkutsk tour company or at the information centre about tours and equipment hire. Believe it or not, Listvyanka also has a small ski resort! The slopes are located on the side of the Kamen Cherskovo Mountain rising up from behind the Baikal Museum.

4

When crossing the mouth of the Angara from Listvyanka to Port Baikal, look out for the so-called Shaman Rock which sticks up out of the water mid-river. Every schoolchild in the region knows the legend surrounding the rock:

In times of yore, mighty Baikal was jovial and kindly. All of his heart was devoted to his only daughter, the beautiful Angara. By day she was bright – brighter than the sky, by night she was dark – darker than a storm-cloud. Whoever passed by her, marvelled at her beauty, and heaped praise upon her. Old Man Baikal cared less for his own soul than for his daughter. Once, while he was resting, Angara ran away to young Yenisey. Her father grew angry, sending out huge waves in rage. A great storm broke, the mountains reverberated, the forests bent, the heavens turned black, animals scattered across the face of the Earth in horror, fish took refuge at the very bottom of the lake, and birds hid behind the sun. The wind wailed and the mighty sea raged. Powerful Baikal grasped a mountain, broke a huge rock away and hurled it after his fleeing daughter, but the boulder landed on her throat. The blue-eyed Angara pleaded, choking and weeping: 'Father, forgive me and give me a single drop of water, for I am dying of thirst'... Baikal cried out in fury: 'I have nothing to give you but my tears!' For millennia, the Angara brought these tears to the Yenisey, while the heartbroken Baikal turned gloomy and ominous. People dubbed the boulder that Baikal cast after his daughter the 'Shaman Rock'. Sacrifices were once offered to Baikal there and people used to think that if Baikal became angry, he would tear the Shaman Rock up and water would flood the Earth.

PORT BAIKAL (ПОРТ БАЙКАЛ)

When in 1900 the Trans-Siberian Railway ran up against its biggest obstacle in the shape of Lake Baikal, engineers had to solve the problem of how to transport trains across the lake to Mysovaya (where the tracks started again) while the technically challenging route around the lake's southern shore was being constructed. The stopgap solution was to load carriages on to one icebreaker (the *Baikal*, sunk during the Russian Civil War) and passengers on to another (the *Angara*, now anchored near the Angara Dam in Irkutsk), both of which were built in Newcastle-upon-Tyne. The settlement which sprouted around the harbour created for this purpose became known as Port Baikal. Even after the chiselling and tunnelling had ended on the so-called Circumbaikal line in 1904, over the next decade the icebreakers were very often called into action due to frequent derailments. Trans-Siberian trains plied this romantic lakeside route until the 1950s when, due to the flooding of the Angara Valley, new tracks were laid from Irkutsk to Kultuk, thus stranding Port Baikal at the end of what became a little used, dead-end branch line from Kultuk.

From Listvyanka on the other side of the Angara, Port Baikal looks little more than a rusty stain on the pristine lake shore. Today it's hard to imagine the hustle and bustle the now decaying port once witnessed as 24-carriage transcontinental trains were shunted on to the *Baikal* icebreaker, and passengers hauled their trunks and suitcases on to the *Angara* for the four-hour crossing. The initial impression is, however, misleading as a few hundred metres along the track lies a tranquil Siberian village with prettily carved window frames and farm animals wandering the streets. While Listvyanka buckles under the pressure of summer visitors in their thousands, Port Baikal, in contrast, leads a drowsy existence which attracts visitors from the other side of the river looking to escape the crowds. The only time the village comes alive these days is when a train travelling on the Circumbaikal Railway rumbles to its final halt at the newly renovated railway station, and then only fleetingly.

GETTING THERE Three or four times a day a rusty old **car ferry** (*journey time: 20mins*) chugs its way slowly across the mouth of the Angara from one crumbling quay near the Baikal Museum to another at Port Baikal, battling against the strong currents sucking it inland all the way – somehow it always seems to make it. Buy tickets on board. Once a day in summer, a hydrofoil service links the village with Irkutsk and Listvyanka. The only other way to reach Port Baikal is by infrequent **train** from Slyudyanka.

WHERE TO STAY

⌂ **Hotel Yakhont** (4 rooms) ul Naberezhnaya 3; ☎ 250 496, 117 819; e yahont@baikalrest.ru. Port Baikal's only classic place to stay is this inviting timber & stone guesthouse at the opposite end of the village to the ferry quay. Comfortable rooms furnished with cedar beds & chairs are built into the hillside, & guests can make use of a sunny terrace with beautiful lake views, a Russian banya higher up the hill & a pleasant communal area. At time of research the owners were constructing a large restaurant below the guesthouse. A virtual monopoly on accommodation in the village means rooms are not cheap. $$$$

Homestays If the Yakhont is full or overstretches your budget, consider crossing the Angara to Listvyanka (as most do) or try asking around for a homestay. There aren't a huge number of villagers willing to put people up, but it's never hard to find a bed somewhere.

WHERE TO EAT
Apart from a couple of grocery stores selling basic foodstuffs, vodka and cigarettes, there's little sustenance on this side of the Angara. The situation is set to change when the restaurant at the Yakhont opens for business. In the meantime, bring your own picnic.

WHAT TO SEE AND DO If you arrive by ferry, Port Baikal's first attraction is a clumsy-looking **steam locomotive**, parked up on the old tracks which once led along the Angara to Irkutsk and still sporting a large red star on its nose. Follow the tracks round to reach the recently renovated **railway station**. When there is no service departing, the building is locked, though there is often a policeman around who may let you in to see the otherwise closed **museum**. Here you'll find an interesting scale model illustrating how carriages were shunted on to the *Baikal* icebreaker, bits of old railway machinery, model trains and large photos of tunnels and other scenes from the Circumbaikal line.

If you haven't come to ride the Circumbaikal Railway, you can at least **walk along the tracks**. Many summer hikers cover the entire 84km route from Port Baikal to Kultuk on foot, camping and bathing in Lake Baikal as they go. Day trippers usually manage around 4km before turning back. Admire the views across the lake, venture into the musty tunnels and walk tightrope along wide-set rails hugging the shoreline, before breaking for a picnic lunch on one of the thin strips of pebbly beach, and perhaps taking a refreshing dip in Baikal. The infrequency of services on the line means you're unlikely to be disturbed by a train.

BOLSHIE KOTY (БОЛШИЕ КОТЫ)

From its current state of torpor, it's hard to imagine that late 19th-century Bolshie Koty on the shores of Lake Baikal was a thriving gold-rush settlement with glass, soap and candle factories, schools and a church. These days, if it weren't for the summertime hydrofoils disgorging their human cargo on the scrap-littered foreshore a couple of times a day, Koty, home now to less than 50 people, would perish as a community and end its days as a deserted collection of *dachas* belonging to Irkutsk's nouveau riche. The village makes for a pleasant stroll or can be used as a base for hikes into the hinterland or along Lake Baikal. The best way to take in the village is to arrive here at the end or beginning of a walk along a section of the Great Baikal Trail between Bolshie Koty and Listvyanka (described below), as a day trip from Listvyanka may see you kicking your heels in the timeless silence sooner than you think, waiting eagerly for the buzz of the hydrofoil in the distance.

GETTING THERE With no road from Irkutsk suitable for buses, the only way to reach the village is by boat or on foot from Listvyanka. The summer hydrofoil service takes around 20 minutes; the hike is a five-hour affair along the Great Baikal Trail. From January to May, when the lake freezes, an ice road replaces the hydrofoil and transport links improve slightly.

 WHERE TO STAY For the few who decide to stay in Bolshie Koty or get stranded here, there are a couple of homestays available. Ask around or look out for signs reading сдаётся комната (room for rent).

⌂ Priyut Staratelyey 2½km along the Great Baikal Trail at Pad Chornaya; www.gotobaikal.ru. Set back 200m from the shore a 20min walk back towards Listvyanka, this simple log cabin camp has 5 small huts, a dining room & *banya*. $

✗ WHERE TO EAT In summer, small kiosks appear near the hydrofoil jetty to cater for tourists. At all other times of the year you're pretty much at the mercy of the poorly stocked village shop. If you intend to embark on the long hike back to Listvyanka, it's best to bring supplies with you as there is no food available *en route*.

WHAT TO SEE AND DO
Baikal Museum and Biological Research Station (⏲ *mid-Jun–late Sep*) Koty's tiny
but lovingly maintained museum housing collections of pickled fish, crustaceans and insects constitutes only a minor diversion. It's part of the Biological Research Station where in the early part of the 20th century many breakthroughs in the study of Baikal's flora and fauna were made. Students from Irkutsk University still travel here on field trips.

Great Baikal Trail from Bolshie Koty to Listvyanka Armed with a stout pair of
walking boots or trainers, a water bottle and a picnic lunch, you are ready to take on the scenic 20km hike from Bolshie Koty to Listvyanka, which mostly follows the deserted shores of Lake Baikal. Most manage the hike in a long afternoon but the route could be broken into two sections with an overnight camp on the beach halfway.

From the Baikal Museum, take the lakeside dirt track through pine forest with cliffs to your left. After around two hours of walking, the track dips down to a stony beach scattered with the remnants of campfires, an excellent place to cool off in the lake, take on water and break for lunch (or even camp). The forest then changes from pine to birch and descends once again to another deserted pebbly beach. After around 2½ hours, be prepared for a tricky section on a narrow loose gravel path hugging the very edge of a sheer drop. The trail then climbs and zigzags inland before returning to the lake where a small stream flows into Baikal. From here many are inclined to keep to the (allegedly quite dangerous) path along the shore, but you should instead head along a red-marked trail which climbs inland through a fern-carpeted valley. Follow the red spots and rags tied to branches to the most difficult section of the hike, a steep 45-minute zig-zagging climb which precedes the gentle descent into Listvyanka's third valley. For a relatively fit hiker the whole route should not take more than five hours.

OLKHON ISLAND AND KHUZHIR (ОСТРОВ ОЛЬХОН & ХУЖИР)

Of Lake Baikal's 26 islands, Olkhon, around halfway up the western shore, is by far the biggest. Peaceful and sparsely populated (only around 1,800 people across 730km²), Olkhon is the perfect place to escape the clutches of civilisation, swim in the warm waters of the Maloe More, sunbathe on the golden sandy beaches, enjoy some wilderness trekking and camping or just hang out with other travellers over a beer in Khuzhir, the island's tumbledown 'capital'.

The island has particular significance for the shamanist Buryats of Baikal's western shoreline and many sacred locations can be found around the island's rocky coast. Almost every rock, hill, cave and cape on the island has an ancient legend attached to it, and dotted around the island are countless *obos* and cairns, places the Buryats believe to be inhabited by spirits. Drivers can be seen tossing ten-kopeck coins from the side window of their vehicles as they pass these sites, and some may even get out to perform the ritual and ask for a safe journey. You can recognise an *obo* by the rags and ribbons tied to tree branches or posts, beneath which the ground is literally carpeted in coins and cigarettes. Many gods and celestial beings mentioned in the Mongol epic *Geser* (see box on page 107) are believed to inhabit Olkhon.

Measuring a mere 72km by 15km, Olkhon packs in a diverse range of landscapes. The island is divided into bare flat steppe in the west and south and forested hills in the north and east. The highest peak, Mount Zhima (1,274m), is situated near the deepest part of Lake Baikal (1,637m), an incredible height difference of almost 3,000m in just a few kilometres. The east coast is lined with

OLKHON ISLAND AND MALOE MORE

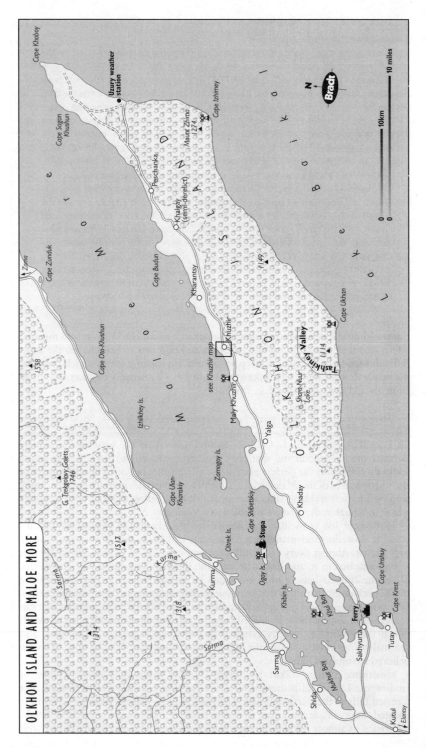

Cape Khoboy

Uzury weather station

Cape Sagan Khushun

Cape Zunduk

Zama

Cape Oto-Khushun

Izhilkhey Is.

1538

G. Trekgolovy Golets
1746

Sarma

1517

1318

1314

Sarma

Sarma

Shida

Mukhur Bay

Kutul

Elantsy

Tutay

Sakhyurta

Ferry

Cape Krest

Cape Unshuy

Khaday

Yalga

Maly Khuzhir

Zamogoy Is.

Cape Ulan-Khanskiy

Kurma

Kurma

Olrek Is.

Cape Shibetskiy · **Stupa**

Ogoy Is.

Khibin Is.

Khul Boy

Peschanka

Khalgay (semi-derelict)

Cape Budun

Kharantsy

Kharantsy

Khuzhir

see Khuzhir map

Mount Zhima
1274

Cape Izhimey

1149

Tashkiney Valley
1114

Shara-Nuur Lake

Cape Ukhan

O L K H O N   I S L A N D

M a l o e   M o r e

L a k e   B a i k a l

N

Bradt

10km

10 miles

high cliffs, while in the west golden beaches gently slope into the balmy shallow waters of the Maloe More. The island receives only very small amounts of rainfall per year and precious little grows here, meaning the population survive on a repetitive diet of *omul* and dairy products.

Olkhon was only connected to the national grid in 2005 and there are still no land-line telephones, although Khuzhir is now covered by the mobile phone signal. There's no running water, sewerage system or any flush toilets on the entire island, and not one metre of road is paved (despite what maps would have you believe). Since the collapse of the Soviet Union, life has been hard on the island and several villages have been deserted as population numbers have tumbled. With the recent influx of Russian and foreign visitors, many have come to rely on tourism to eke out a living.

Although 4x4 van tours of the island's north and south leave Khuzhir every morning, the island is best seen unhurried from the seat of a mountain bike or on foot. With a tent you can strike out to explore the island for weeks on end, should you wish, building campfires on the beach each evening and taking cold baths in Lake Baikal as you go, though you'll need to call in at Khuzhir now and then to take on supplies.

HISTORY From prehistory to the present day, humans have been attracted to Olkhon Island thanks to its sunny climate, easily accessible fish stocks in the shallow Maloe More, and spiritual lure. Between the 5th and 10th centuries AD the mysterious Turkic Kurykan tribes who inhabited many sites along the shore of the Maloe More and the Svyatoy Nos Peninsula dotted the island with walls and burial mounds and decorated cliffs and caves with their matchstick petroglyphs. In the 11th and 12th centuries AD the Buryats arrived on Olkhon, gradually absorbing the local tribes into their culture over the next two centuries. During the rise of the Mongol Empire in the 13th century, legend has it that Genghis Khan himself stayed on the island, though there is no hard evidence to prove this.

Russian Cossacks made it to Olkhon in 1643 and although they forced the native islanders to pay tribute, the European invaders had little effect on everyday life, with the population remaining 100% Buryat until the early 20th century. Despite the Civil War and collectivisation, living standards were lifted during the early Soviet decades with the construction of a new fish processing factory in

GESER – AN EPIC TALE

The *Geser Epic* is the most famous epic poem in central Asia, with the Buryats, Mongols and Tibetans all claiming it as their national classic. Believed to be approximately 1,000 years old, it's possibly the longest work of literature in the world, and at 20 million words it makes *War and Peace* look like a recipe for boiled eggs. With countless different adaptations of the tale circulating in the region, a single English-language edition would probably prove impossible to compile, though a couple of considerably abbreviated translations do exist. No-one has, as yet, put in the considerable effort it would require to translate the full version into English.

The blockbuster tale essentially relates the adventures of fearless King Geser, ruler of the legendary Kingdom of Ling, who is born to crush evil kings, demons and monsters on Earth. With a cast of thousands and more plot twists than the complete works of Agatha Christie, it's truly incredible how ballad singers could memorise the entire tale. They would retell the epic in installments to enraptured audiences who would gather around the yurt's central fireplace to listen on moonlit winter nights on the endless steppe.

Khuzhir, a small hospital and a post office, though the island was also home to a Stalinist penal colony. During World War II a number of Lithuanians were banished to Olkhon where they could live and work freely, and a handful even stayed after they were amnestied in the 1960s. The 1990s were a hard time as Khuzhir's fish factory was privatised and people were laid off, the electricity supply was cut and direct flights from Irkutsk were axed. Things have improved slightly in recent years with the arrival of tourists from all over the world seeking Olkhon's beaches, forests and general otherworldliness.

GETTING THERE Getting to Olkhon is half the fun – the asphalt runs out just after Yelantsy, the Buryat settlements become more and more ramshackle and the views turn increasingly dramatic as the road meanders among bare hills and mountains until you reach the ferry crossing to the island.

In summer and autumn, four buses a day (*departs: all before 12.00; journey time: up to 7hrs; tickets: RUB290*) leave Irkutsk bus station and bounce their way to the MRS ferry quay, take the ferry to the island and continue on to Khuzhir. Tickets should be bought a couple of days in advance as these services fill up quickly. A daily minibus also runs between Irkutsk and Nikita's Homestead (see *Where to stay* below) and is a much quicker option (ask at Irkutsk's hostels).

In winter, an ice road replaces the ferry but, for several weeks in spring and winter when the ice between the island and the mainland is either melting or not yet fully formed, Olkhon is completely cut off, though it may still be possible to make the crossing using an ad hoc mini-hovercraft service operated by enterprising locals. From mid-June until mid-September a twice weekly hydrofoil links Olkhon with Irkutsk, Severobaikalsk and Nizhneangarsk (see the *Getting around* page 60).

GETTING AROUND Apart from the buses to the ferry and on to Irkutsk, there's no public transport on the island. The only way to get to attractive locations in the east and west is to hike and camp or take one of the jeep tours which leave on a daily basis from spring through to autumn from Khuzhir's guesthouses.

WHERE TO STAY With the sheer volume of tourists descending on the village, it is no surprise that the locals have started to cash in on Khuzhir's unlikely popularity by putting people up in spare rooms in their log cabins. These homestays can be found in almost every street – just look for сдаются комнаты (rooms for rent) signs. Prices start at around RUB500–600 per bed, though you may be able to negotiate this down outside of the summer months.

🏠 **Baikalsky Priboy** ul Baikalskaya 48; m 3952 200 777. Yet another selection of log cabins & other timber structures on Khuzhir's main drag. $$
🏠 **Hotel Olkhon** ul Baikalskaya 64; m 03952 708 885; www.alphatour.ru. This brick-built hotel at the northern edge of Khuzhir with an adjoining complex of 2-storey timber Monopoly houses has a more upmarket feel, though it lacks the atmosphere of Nikita's. Cabins of varying standards are simple but all have great views of the mountains on the opposite shore. Less backpacker scene but more comfort (showers, en-suite facilities). $$
🏠 **Nikita's Homestead** ul Kirpichnaya 8, Khuzhir; m 8 0914 937 4820 ; e nikita@olkhon.info;

www.olkhon.info. This complex of timber bungalows, cabins, houses & yurts run by Nikita & Natasha Bencharov is the place to stay in Khuzhir & has become firmly established in backpacker legend. Accommodation is in dbl rooms within traditional Siberian log buildings, still fragrant with pine & cedar sap, equipped with their own wood stoves, chunky timber furniture, shamanist décor & shared pit lavs. Price inc 3 filling meals a day served in the busy canteen. Nikita runs various jeep tours to the north & south of the island, hires boats & bicycles & can even register your visa. Book early in summer as this place is overwhelmed with visitors from July until September. $$

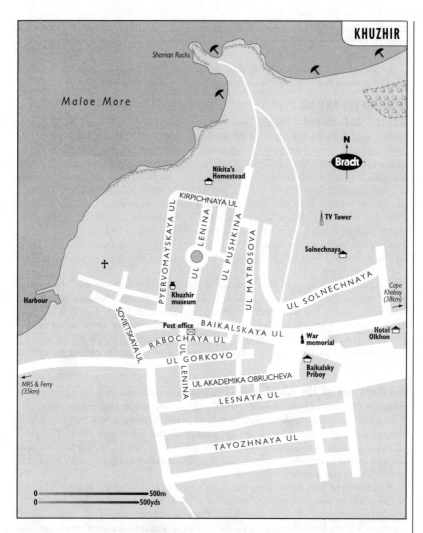

Maloe More

Shaman Rocks

Nikita's Homestead

KIRPICHNAYA UL

PYERVOMAYSKAYA UL

UL LENINA

UL PUSHKINA

UL MATROSOVA

Khuzhir museum

Harbour

SOVIETSKAYA UL

Post office

BAIKALSKAYA UL

RABOCHAYA UL

UL GORKOVO

UL LENINA

UL AKADEMIKA OBRUCHEVA

LESNAYA UL

MRS & Ferry (35km)

TAYOZHNAYA UL

N

Bradt

TV Tower

Solnechnaya

UL SOLNECHNAYA

Cape Khoboy (38km)

War memorial

Hotel Olkhon

Baikalsky Priboy

0 ————— 500m
0 ————— 500yds

Solnechnaya ul Solnechnaya 14; **m** 8 0908 661 6519; **e** info-irk@yandex.ru; www.olkhon.com. A similar set-up to Nikita's but with a fraction of the charm & atmosphere. The log cabins & timber houses range in size from no bigger than a garden shed to cottages with balconies. Meals inc, taken in a large yurt near the reception. $$

✗ WHERE TO EAT When staying at Nikita's Homestead you won't have to worry too much about food (unless you don't eat fish) as three hearty, rustic meals a day are served up in the busy dining room. Some of the other complexes also provide full or half board. Self-caterers have several relatively well-stocked food shops to choose from, but if you are leaving the 'capital' on a hike or cycle ride, be sure to buy all the provisions you need before you depart as there is no food anywhere else on the island.

The local staple diet consists of fish, dairy products and perhaps the odd piece of beef or pork. The *omul*-heavy menu at some of the log cabin complexes can become very monotonous, though the cooks do their best to prepare it in a variety of ways to keep diners interested. If you don't eat fish things can get tricky, and it may be better to request a vegetarian menu to avoid going hungry and to savour a bit of variety.

In the summer season a handful of simple cafés and a bar on dusty Baikalskaya ul do a roaring trade in Buryat dishes, grilled fish, shashlyks and beer.

WHAT TO SEE AND DO

Khuzhir and around If Kuzhir were in rural Belarus or Ukraine, you'd hardly notice such a fly-blown smudge of rambling shacks and crooked homesteads as you sped past it on your way elsewhere. It is, therefore, almost surreal to see so many Western travellers strolling its sandy, litter-strewn streets and crowding into the village shops to buy bottled beer and biscuits. As the island's largest community it's the obvious place to stay but has precious few attractions of its own. The one exception is the somewhat fuzzy **museum** (*ul Pervomayskaya 24; ⊕ 12.00–19.00 Mon–Fri; adults RUB50*) which is cluttered with a mishmash of interesting junk from stuffed animals in a sorry state, an old Buryat hut and Soviet-era knick-knackery to art by local youngsters, a 1992 wine bottle (?) and the personal effects of the museum's founder, Nikolay Revyakin, who taught at the school next door for half a century.

Olkhon's real attraction is its wonderful natural beauty and you don't have to go far from Khuzhir to find some. A short walk to the shore from Nikita's Homestead will bring you to the wonderfully photogenic **Shaman Rock** (see box on page 102), a tower of crumbling lichen-coated stone at the end of a tiny arc of pebble beach. Scramble among the boulders or take a swim from the beach before heading a few hundred metres north to the huge stretch of sandy **shoreline** backed by inviting cedar forest.

Northern end of the island Tours of Olkhon, which can pick up from any of Khuzhir's hotels and guesthouses, usually divide the island into north and south. The most common mode of transport here is the Soviet-era 4x4 minibus which throws passengers around a bit on the sand roads but never gets stuck. The price of the tour almost always includes a picnic lunch of fish soup, tea and biscuits cooked by the driver over an open fire. The drivers double up as guides but speak only Russian and Buryat.

The northern tour heads along the coast via a couple of deserted villages, a former Stalinist labour camp, shamanist ritual sites, sandy beaches and rocky capes to the northernmost point of Olkhon Island, **Cape Khaboy**, one of the most sacred locations for the local Buryats. From the end an almost 360-degree view of the Lake opens up, with the Maloe More to the left and Lake Baikal proper to the right. If you are really lucky you might just catch some nerpa seals basking on the rocks below. The tour winds its way back to Khuzhir via the lonely weather station at **Uzury**, where a shallow valley meets the lake, and along very rough sand tracks through the forest.

Where the north tour won't take you is **Mount Zhima**, as Buryats are forbidden to climb it. A three- or four-day expedition on foot through the forest to the highest point on the island can feel like a real adventure.

Southern end of the island The flatter, treeless landscape of the south lends itself to mountain biking and hiking, but is less popular with tours. One highlight of the south is warm **Shara-Nuur** (Yellow Lake) around 15km south of Khuzhir. The water is said to possess curative properties and dyes the skin red if you bathe too long. Another is the cool **Tashkiney Valley** which slopes gradually down to Lake Baikal. Both of these places can be reached on foot or by bicycle on a day trip out of Khuzhir.

MALOE MORE (МАЛОЕ МОРЕ)

Wedged between the mainland and Olkhon Island, the shallow waters of the Maloe More or Small Sea are warmed through by the summer Siberian sun. The tepid water plus sandy beaches hemming its southern shores make this a much-loved holiday spot among Russian sun-seekers, while remaining firmly off the beaten track when it comes to overseas visitors. The beaches are lined with relatively cheap holiday camps and guesthouses, meaning there's usually a bed waiting for anyone who makes it this far. Bookings can only be made through Irkutsk tour agencies.

No towns pollute the Maloe More and the villages are one-road one-shop deals. Outside of the main July/August season, the road which traces the shore falls silent and very often it's quieter here than on Olkhon Island. When baking on the sands loses its appeal, there are plenty of walks into the hills behind, and occasional boat trips run to tiny uninhabited islands just offshore. Otherwise there are no sights as such, just 150km of empty Baikal vistas, unspoilt countryside and a lonely rough road along which everything is strung.

GETTING THERE The effort required to reach the Maloe More is possibly the reason its beaches are not lined with German and French backpackers. From June through to August a single daily bus or *marshrutka* leaves, for some unknown reason, from in front of the Hotel Angara in Irkutsk, stopping at the villages of Sarma (*tickets: RUB380*) and Kurma (*tickets: RUB500*). The bus returns the same day and may be complemented by unofficial minibuses at the height of demand.

Another option is to catch the Olkhon bus, ask to be let off well before MRS ferry quay, then hike along the road to Sarma (around 15km) or hitch a (paid) lift. In summer you may just be able to persuade a boat owner in Khuzhir (Olkhon Island) to take you across, though this is likely to drain your rouble fund significantly. In winter the shallow Maloe More freezes earlier than the rest of Lake Baikal and basically becomes joined to Olkhon by thick ice, crossable in cars and vans.

GETTING AROUND If you want to move from beach to beach, bay to bay, camp to camp, you'll have to either walk or hitch a lift.

WHERE TO STAY There are numerous lakeside *turbazy* along the shores of the Maloe More and you should have no difficulty finding a bed. Many are open year-round making a magical winter trip possible. The villages of MRS (at the ferry quay), Mukhur, Sarma and Zama all have ample beds, or you could take a tent and wild camp by the lake. If camping, be aware that water quality in the lake (not in the rivers) drops during July and August. In late spring bears can be seen on the shores, usually looking for food after months of hibernation.

SLYUDYANKA (СЛЮДЯНКА) *Telephone code: 39544*

In the hazy light of early autumn, this gritty railway town at the southern extremity of Lake Baikal is everything you want a halt on the Trans-Siberian to be. Time seems to have stopped here sometime in 1985 – men in oily overalls and uniforms carrying flask and sandwiches can still be seen heading off to work their shift on the railway; grandmothers push babies in prams through overgrown parks and children in uniform still dawdle home from school in mid-afternoon, the girls with ridiculously oversize flowers in their hair, the boys in ill-fitting blazers, scuffing their shoes. The town's refreshingly uncommercial, almost Soviet feel makes this an interesting stop at the beginning or end of the Circumbaikal Railway or *en route* from Irkutsk to Buryatiya. It's also a launch-pad for trips into the Tunka Valley and the Khamar-Daban mountain range.

Slyudyanka (*www.sludyanka.ru*) not only lies on the Trans-Siberian Railway but the Moscow–Vladivostok highway also forms its main street (ul Lenina). One very post-Soviet sight you may witness on this road is the convoys of used right-hand-drive Japanese cars being driven from Vladivostok to be sold on in Irkutsk and points west. Siberia's roads are now full of such vehicles with the steering wheel on the 'wrong side'.

One of the biggest settlements on Baikal's entire shoreline, Slyudyanka has no real centre and most activity focuses on the scruffy bus station just off Lenin Street. Residential districts extend inland while the railway station stands on the other side of the main thoroughfare, just a few hundred metres short of Baikal itself.

HISTORY Slyudyanka shares its name with the fast-flowing river on which it stands and which once used to wash glittering flakes of mica (слюда, *slyuda*) into Lake Baikal. Although established as early as 1640, the town didn't really spring to life until the building of the Circumbaikal section of the Trans-Siberian Railway in 1904, and by 1930 had almost reached its current size. In the 1950s, a unique kind of marble began to be quarried nearby, and mica was mined until the 1970s. The mines along the Slyudyanka valley now lie idle, though the surrounding area is paradise for mineral collectors.

GETTING THERE Straddling both the Trans-Siberian and the main trans-Russia highway (M-55), Slyudyanka is very easy to reach from all points east and west. All Trans-Siberian trains *en route* to or from Moscow, Beijing, Ulan-Ude, Vladivostok and Ulaanbaatar stop here, and Circumbaikal services from Port Baikal begin and terminate in front of the gleaming marble façade of the town's architecturally pleasing station. From Irkutsk there are also three slow local trains (*tickets: RUB43.60*) a day and five buses (*tickets: RUB90*). Arshan and other communities in the Tunka Valley are also served by bus and *marshrutka*.

🏠 WHERE TO STAY

🏠 **Hotel Chayka** (20 rooms) ul Frunze 8A; 📞 54073. Slyudyanka's only hotel is a long hike north along the main road heading towards Kultuk or a 10min taxi ride. The no-frills rooms are brutally basic & the design of the lino changes every 2m throughout, but the staff are friendly & accommodating, & it's fairly clean. You are certain to encounter other foreign travellers here as it's virtually the only place to stay in town. The residential district 'where time stood still' in which the hotel is situated is serviced by an adequate number of grocery shops & cafés. 💲💲

🏠 **Hostel Slyudyanka** (6 beds) ul Shcholnaya 10, Apt 7. A 6-bed dorm in an apt around 3km from Lake Baikal. Really just a homestay, but with the advantage of advance bookings through Hostelworld. Arrange to be picked up from the station (RUB200) by the owners as you'll never find it on your own. 💲

🏠 **Komnaty otdykha** (station resting rooms) The newly refurbished resting rooms at the railway station charge an unbelievably cheap RUB15/hr for a dorm bed. 💲

🏠 **Mineral Museum homestay** ul Slyudyanaya 36; 📞 53440. The owner of the mineral museum rents out a simple room in the grounds of the museum, May–Oct. 💲

✖ WHERE TO EAT

✖ **Kafe-Gril** ul Lenina 118; ⏰ 10.00–21.00. Throw-away plastic plates, cups & cutlery but belly-filling Russian stodge such as pelmeni or meatballs & mash for a handful of roubles. Service with a glower but who cares when you're hungry. Just about the only option in town. 💲

✖ **Bonus Supermarket** ul Lenina 116; ⏰ 09.00–22.00. Somewhat surprisingly perhaps, Slyudyanka has a small Western-style self-service supermarket where you can stock up on enough instant noodles, cheese, bread & tea to keep you going all the way to Beijing should you wish. Opposite the bus station, next door to the Kafe-Gril.

WHAT TO SEE AND DO If you're arriving by train, your first sight of the town will be Slyudyanka's finest piece of architecture, namely the pretty white marble **railway station** built in 1904. The building recently received a serious sandblasting and was renovated inside and out. The ticket window is one of the few sales-points along the Trans-Siberian where *bilety* are always available and come with a smile.

Leaving the station, head towards the lake, passing a small, colourfully painted **timber church** on the way. Unfortunately, the shore is a messy stretch of patchy woodland with an ugly concrete wall keeping Baikal's larger waves out of the town. Where there could be cafés, a marina and an attractive promenade you will find only beer bottles and washed-up detritus. Nevertheless, the views of the lake are impressive and it's quite a good place for a swim (though we don't recommend you drink the water here). According to the Russian Railways timetable, some trains wait up to 30 minutes at Slyudyanka station, ample time to leg it to the shore, take a welcome dip and make it back in time for departure. Be sure to check with the *provodnitsa* first so you don't get duffilled (left behind).

Back at the railway station, cross the footbridge on to ul Zheleznodorozhnaya, lined with railway administration buildings and workers' canteens. Continuing to the end you will reach the low timber building of the semi-interesting **Regional Museum** (*ul Zheleznodorozhnaya 22; ↘ 2351; ⊕ 11.00–17.00 Wed–Sun; adult RUB50*) with exhibitions dedicated mostly to the railway. If you have a lot of time between trains and a particular interest in minerals, Slyudyanka's owner-run **Mineral Museum** (*ul Slyudyanaya 36; ↘ 53440; ⊕ 08.00–20.00; adult RUB100*) is a 1½km slog up ul Slyudyanskikh Krasnogvardyeytsev or a short *marshrutka* ride. The owner-curator claims to possess over 9,000 specimens representing every mineral known to man.

A 4km walk along the pebbly shores of Lake Baikal towards Kultuk will bring you to a rocky peninsular known as **Cape Shaman**. Bronze Age and Stone Age finds have been made in the area, a popular excursion from Slyudyanka. With considerably more time, **Pik Cherskovo** in the Khamar-Daban range is a 2,090m-high mountain at the end of the Slyudyanka Valley and a superb two-day hike

---

THE CIRCUMBAIKAL RAILWAY

Anyone with a nerdy soft spot for the clickety-clack of wheel on rail will get huge enjoyment from a ride on the Circumbaikal. Blasted and chiselled from the solid rock of Lake Baikal's southern cliffs in the early years of the 20th century, the line packs in 59 tunnels and 24 bridges between Slyudyanka and Port Baikal, a distance of 89km. The journey is a picturesque jaunt at almost walking pace, providing ample time to admire this amazing feat of engineering as well the Baikal vistas which open up by the tracks.

It's possible to simply take a ride from Slyudyanka to Port Baikal as a side trip off the main Trans-Siberian line; another option is to take a trip from Irkutsk via Slyudyanka, spending the night in Port Baikal. There are only four trains a week in either direction, meaning you'll have to plan well ahead. Be aware that the service from Port Baikal to Slyudyanka travels during the night.

Schedules (and heaps of other fascinating information) can be found at http://kbzd.irk.ru/Eng/shedule.htm and are not likely to change very much in the coming years. Arrivals and departures are listed in local rather than Moscow time. Any Irkutsk tour company can arrange an outing on the Circumbaikal, but one of the best is Kruglobaikalsky Ekspress (*www.turexpres.ru*) who specialise in trips on the railway. Every year hundreds of walkers hike the route.

south from the town. With the right equipment and enough food and water the route can be tackled in summer without a guide, though it may be safer to hire one in Irkutsk or Slyudyanka for the trip.

BAIKALSK (БАЙКАЛЬСК) *Telephone code: 39542*

Pollution and skiing are an odd double act which draw and repel visitors from Baikalsk in equal measure. No other lakeside settlement attracts as much controversy as Baikalsk, thanks to its huge cellulose factory, the largest polluter on the shores of Lake Baikal. Discharging 120,000m^3 of contaminated industrial waste into the lake a day, the concern was under pressure from UNESCO, protestors and environmentalists for years to clean up its act, but to little avail. However, in late 2008 the plant – incidentally part of the Oleg Deripaska empire – temporarily halted production and looked like it might be on the brink of bankruptcy, which had local eco-activists high-fiving and punching the air with glee. In the end it may be the global economic downturn which saves Baikal's crystal clear waters, but the likely closure is bad news for the town's economic prospects as it employs about a quarter of the population.

The only sane reasons to stop here are to enjoy a bit of skiing or to rejoin the Trans-Siberian after a scenic *elektrichka* ride from Slyudyanka. Thanks to the large amount of snow which falls each winter on nearby Gora Sobolinaya (Sobolinaya Mountain) the town boasts the largest ski and snowboarding resort in the region. Anyone you speak to in the town will, within five minutes of conversation, remind you that President Putin spent a skiing holiday here back in 2002.

GETTING THERE The simplest way to reach Baikalsk from Slyudyanka is by *marshrutka* – services leave from the bus station when full. A more interesting way is to take one of the twice-daily *elektrichki* which follow a scenic route along the shoreline. Trans-Siberian trains pull in at the Baikalsk station 8km from the centre; *elektrichki* halt at the much more convenient Baikalsk Passazhirsky station.

WHERE TO STAY

🏠 **Hotel Baikal** (86 beds) ul Gagarina 169; ☎ 34898. The imaginatively named Baikal is virtually the only place to stay in the town proper. Newly renovated rooms are modern & comfortable & there's a small café. The price is about right outside the skiing season but inflated during it (Dec–Apr). $$$

🏠 **Hotel Sobolinaya** (90 beds) Gora Sobolinaya ski resort; ☎ 32455. The super-modern hotel at the ski resort. Once & future President Putin stayed

here in 2002 during his much publicised skiing holiday. Good location if you're enjoying a bit of piste fun, bad if you want to visit the town or have an early train to catch. $$$

🏠 **Hotel Uyut** (26 rooms) ul Stroitelnaya 13; ☎ 37312; www.baikaltur.ru. Situated down by the lake, this complex has comfortable if slightly cramped rooms with stomach-churning décor, a decent café & a sauna. $$

WHAT TO SEE AND DO

Gora Sobolinaya ski resort (☎ *32596; www.baikalski.com*) Baikalsk's main draw is the ski resort , which sits at the foot of Mount Sobolinaya, a RUB70 taxi ride from the railway station. There are 12km of piste, the colour-coded slopes designed for skiers of varying levels of ability. Those who have skied here say the mountains and views across Baikalsk and Lake Baikal are simply awe-inspiring. Snow is more or less guaranteed from December through to April and there are snow cannons at the ready should the heavens not deliver. A day pass in high season costs RUB1,300 at weekends, RUB750 weekdays.

Around Baikalsk The shallow water in the bays lining the shore near Baikalsk warms up in summer and is ideal for **bathing**. Autumn is the best time to head into the surrounding taiga, where the floor is carpeted in berries and mushrooms. Locals will point the way to the best trails into the forest. The more adventurous can strike out on a three-day return **hike to the top of Pik Poroshisty** (2,025m). Base camp is only six hours' walk out of town, and the mountain can be climbed by virtually anyone from June through to early September.

ARSHAN (АРШАН) *Telephone code: 30147*

The focal point of the wide Tunka Valley is the small spa town of Arshan, some 130km west of Lake Baikal in the foothills of the Eastern Sayan Mountains. At almost 900m above sea level this settlement, whose name in Buryat means 'holy water', stands astride the fast-flowing River Kyngarga which tumbles down from a dramatic backdrop of saw-toothed, cloud-ripping peaks. The main draws for Russians are the two large health resorts at either end of the town, between which extend unpaved streets lined with traditional timber houses and ramshackle gardens. Most westerners visit Arshan as a two-day trip from the Trans-Siberian or from Irkutsk, or use the town as a base for hikes into the wild and rugged terrain to the north and west.

Health-giving mineral water splutters out of the ground and the air is pure and fresh, but many locals seem to prefer a nicotine and vodka-based cure to ease their ills, and don't care a kopeck piece about their surroundings. In fact, this corner of Buryatiya is a schizophrenic place, with snow-capped peaks, pine forests and Milka Chocolate advert cows with jangling neck bells roaming alpine meadows, standing in stark contrast with beer bottles bobbing in pristine rock pools, muddy litter-plagued streets and Buryat drunks in flat caps snoozing among trees and boulders. Sometimes it is difficult to prise Arshan's two identities apart.

The town is simple to navigate; the road which enters from the southeast becomes the main (and only paved) street, ul Traktovaya. This slopes gently uphill in a straight line before taking a sharp left at the spa. Streets sprouting off Traktovaya lead to a tangle of unsurfaced lanes and paths where the local Buryats dwell.

HISTORY Judging from the name, local Buryats had known about the medicinal qualities of the local spring water long before a Russian missionary mentioned Arshan's aqua mineralis in a report to Tomsk University in 1894. By 1920 it had become a state health resort and the first sanatorium (The Arshan) was built for particularly deserving workers in 1928. The Sayany sanatorium was begun in 1974.

GETTING THERE Buses run to and from Irkutsk (*departs: twice a day; tickets: RUB194*), Slyudyanka (*departs: twice a day; tickets: RUB110*) and Ulan-Ude (*departs: three times a week; tickets: RUB500*). Services are backed up or replaced by quicker *marshrutki*. Other less frequented destinations include Kyren and Mondy further along the Tunka Valley. Tickets for most services can be bought at the 'bus station' ticket kiosk in the centre of town.

WHERE TO STAY

Zamok Gornovo Korolya (13 rooms) ul Gagarina 18; ☏ 92384. The grandly named 'Castle of the Mountain King', which with its naff green turrets & rough brickwork looks like a badly built McMansion, should only be used as a last resort as it's overpriced & the staff don't give a monkey's. $$$$

Priyut Alpinista ul Bratiev Domyshevykh; ☏ 97697; e irkutsk@iwf.ru; www.iwf.ru. The best place in the Tunka Valley to kip & meet other Western travellers & hikers. The en-suite rooms are basic & a mite overpriced, but the communal atmosphere in the summer season is more like a backpacker hostel. The pleasant staff can help with maps, tour guides & cycle hire, & they also organise 10-day adventure treks into the Sayan Mountains. $$$–$$$$

Homestays Almost every second house in Arshan offers rooms to rent. Standards vary wildly so shop around. Expect to pay RUB200–500 a night without breakfast. Buryat kids often board buses as they arrive in the town to offer accommodation – though cheap, these rooms are of the lowest standard and house facilities are, quite frankly, pretty unsanitary (see box *Choosing a homestay* on page 63).

✘ WHERE TO EAT

✘ **Novy Vek** ul Traktovaya 4; ☏ 97330; ⏰ 10.00–midnight. This brand new eatery is a welcome addition to Arshan's 'dining scene' & the only real restaurant in town. Enjoy Buryat & Russian dishes & a large selection of wines & beer in clean Western-style surroundings. The restaurant's flush toilet may be a more welcome sight than you could ever have imagined! $$–$$$

✘ **Zakusochnaya Khamar-Daban** ul Traktovaya; ⏰ 10.00–04.00. An unsophisticated but handy café on the main drag opposite the gates to the Sayany Spa. Wooden picnic tables inside & out, & an indecipherable hand-written menu of *pozy* & other simple meat dishes. $–$$

✘ **Stolovaya** ul Traktovaya 13; ⏰ 09.00–19.00. Enjoy your meal with a generous dollop of Soviet nostalgia at this spartan self-service canteen near the post office. $

✘ **24hr grocery store** ul Traktovaya 71. Arshan has several small grocery stores but this one is open round the clock.

OTHER PRACTICALITIES Arshan's busy **post office** is located at ul Traktovaya 32.

WHAT TO SEE AND DO

Arshan and Sayany Spas Located at the top of ul Traktovaya the 1920s Arshan Spa is naturally the grander of the two spas as it was built much earlier. The shady grounds are a perfect place to take a relaxing stroll while sipping the mildly sulphurous, lukewarm mineral water which, it must be said, is an acquired taste. The second spa, at the far southern end of town, is a less attractive 1970s affair, and even the public drinking 'fountain' resembles a leaky sewer someone forgot to repair *circa* 1980. The trees around are draped in weather-worn ribbons marking this as a sacred shamanist site.

Datsans Arshan has two dinky *datsans* (Buddhist temples) which can be visited free of charge. The **Bodkhi Dkharma Datsan** around 1½km out of Arshan is the bigger and strikes an incredibly photogenic pose, set as it is against a backdrop of soaring snow-dusted peaks, the ideal location for working on your *vipassana* and *samatha* (Buddhist meditation). The temple was only re-established in 1991 and the simple building is kept company by prayer wheels and two small stupas. Services take place here every day at 10.00 and 15.00, though the doors may be unlocked at other times. To get there, follow ul Traktovaya until it peters out at the river, cross the bridge and follow the dirt track through the forest.

The **Dechen Ravzhalin Datsan** can be found behind a low fence on Traktovaya, and here too the grounds are home to more spanking new prayer wheels and a miniature stupa. The interior is a riot of Technicolor prayer flags, icons, Buddhas, silk streamers, cushions and various trinkets left as offerings by local worshippers. The temple only opened in 2002 and is the more popular of the two thanks to its roadside location.

Walks around Arshan Having sampled the waters and spun the prayer wheels at the temples, it's time to don walking boots and explore the pristine alpine landscape around Arshan. Most walkers head straight along the left bank of the ice-cold, boulder-strewn Kyngarga for an easygoing stroll to a **waterfall** around half an hour away. More adventurous walkers continue along the river to another set of waterfalls, beyond which around 2½ hours of further legwork brings you to the **confluence of the left and right Kyngarga rivers**, a great place to camp. It's feasible to do this hike as a day trip but be sure to take enough food along. Another day-trek destination is the **Arshan Pass**, five to six hours away. Follow the riverside path as far as the confluence, as above, then take a trail to the right in the direction of the Kitoi River. The path to the pass is easy to find and the views are simply breathtaking. Another popular day-walk is the ascent of Pik Lyubvi or **Love Mountain**, though for this you may need a local guide to show you the route (ask at the Priyut Alpinista guesthouse). From the summit the panoramic views of the Tunka Valley and the Sayan Mountains are unforgettable.

MONDY (МОНДЫ)

At the far western end of the Tunka Valley the village of Mondy lies just a few kilometres from the border with Mongolia, beyond which Khövsgöl Lake, Baikal's little sister, shimmers temptingly. Sadly the crossing here is closed to foreigners though this may change in 2010, potentially opening up what will surely become a popular route overland between Siberia and Mongolia. Some foreigners and large tour companies do make it through to Mongolia by prearranging the crossing with the Russian and Mongolian authorities, a complicated, expensive process to say the least.

GETTING THERE Buses or *marshrutki* make the journey to Mondy a couple of times a day from Arshan and Slyudyanka, usually early in the morning.

WHERE TO STAY Your choice of places to stay is limited to a few homestays. Ask around.

WHAT TO SEE AND DO Some 20km west of Mondy, the main attraction in this distant corner of Siberia is **Munku Sardyk**, the highest peak in the Eastern Sayan Mountains at 3,491m. It stands on the border between Russia and Mongolia and in early May attracts hundreds of climbers who make an annual ascent of the mountain. This traditionally marks the beginning of the summer climbing season.

OKA REGION

Beyond Mondy a fork in the road sends traffic either towards the border or north into the exceptionally remote and mountainous Oka Region. The asphalt runs out soon after, and from there you set out on a dramatic drive following the twists and turns of the Oka River as it snakes its way between the peaks of the Eastern Sayan Mountains. The end of the road is the low-rise regional centre, **Orlik**, 187km from Mondy and as far-flung a place as you're ever likely to visit. The tiny museum, Buddhist temple, shop and café are minor diversions from the main activity in these parts – hiking. The virtually uninhabited Oka Region, with its mountains, valleys, natural springs and impenetrable forests steeped in local legend, is ideal for wilderness trekking, but decent maps are scarce and it's best to hire a guide to take you into a region some have dubbed 'Tibet in miniature'. A good place to start is **BARS** (*ul Sovietskaya 29*), a tour company that organises treks and horseriding trips into the surrounding back country, some lasting up to a week. Tour companies in Ulan-Ude can also help find accommodation and arrange transfers. There's no public transport beyond Mondy, though you may track down the odd minibus or supply truck heading from Slyudyanka along the Tunka Valley and into the mountains, but it's very hit-and-miss.

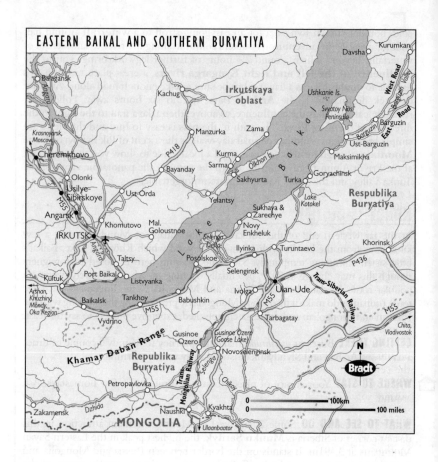

EASTERN BAIKAL AND SOUTHERN BURYATIYA

Kurumkan

Davsha

Balagansk

Kachug

Irkutskaya oblast

Ushkanie Is.

Svyatoy Nos Peninsula

West Road

Barguzin Valley

East Road

Barguzin

Angara

Krasnoyarsk, Moscow

Manzurka

Zama

Ust-Barguzin

Cheremkhovo

Olonki

Kurma

Sarma

Olkhon Is.

Maksimikha

Usilye-Sibirskoye

Ust-Orda

Bayanday

Sakhyurta

Turka

Goryachinsk

Angarsk

Yelantsy

Respublika Buryatiya

Khomutovo

Mal. Goloustnoe

Sukhaya & Zarechye

Lake Kotokel

IRKUTSK

Selenga Delta

Novy Enkheluk

Khorinsk

Taltsy

Posolskoe

Ilyinka

Turuntaevo

P436

Kultuk

Port Baikal

Listvyanka

Selenginsk

Arshan, Khuzhiry, Mondy, Oka Region

Baikalsk

Tankhoy

Babushkin

Ivolga

Ulan-Ude

Trans-Siberian Railway

M55

Vydrino

Tarbagatay

Chita, Vladivostok

Khamar Daban Range

Gusinoe Ozero

Gusinoe Ozero (Goose Lake)

Novoselenginsk

Republika Buryatiya

Trans-Mongolian Railway

Selenga

Chikoy

N

Bradt

Petropavlovka

0   100km

0   100 miles

Zakamensk

Dzhida

Naushki

Kyakhta

MONGOLIA

Ulaanbaatar

5

Eastern Baikal and Southern Buryatiya

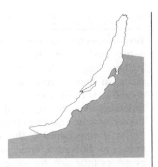

Less visited by foreign travellers than the western shore, Lake Baikal's eastern shore falls entirely within Buryatiya, an autonomous republic within the Russian Federation. On this side of the water you will find some of the lake's most striking features, such as the wide delta of the River Selenga in the south and the Svyatoy Nos Peninsula further north, as well as countless picturesque bays, beaches and headlands. From the Selenga Delta northwards, the untouched shoreline is thinly inhabited, stunningly beautiful but impossibly remote.

Away from the lake's chilly waters, Buryatiya is a fascinating country in its own right. The capital, Ulan-Ude, sports the world's largest Lenin head, which from its plinth on the main square has been forced to witness the switch from Communism to capitalism. As Buryatiya's only city, this is naturally the best base for plotting your escape to the countless places of interest and natural beauty the republic offers. First stop for most is the Ivolginsky Buddhist temple, the centre of Russian Buddhism, though the republic is now dotted with the upturned eaves of this revived religion. A day excursion to the Old Believers' villages south of Ulan-Ude gives an insight into Russia's troubled religious past, while a trip to Kyakhta on the Mongolian border illustrates just what riches were once up for grabs when the Tea Road from China cut through the region. To the north, the Barguzin Valley, legendary birthplace of Genghis Khan's mother, is as stunningly remote and peaceful as the Khamar Daban mountain range in the south is dramatic. Shamanism and Buddhism intertwine throughout Buryatiya, with holy sites, springs, rocks and rivers revered by both. Remnants of ancient civilisations in the form of standing stones and Scythian-era *kurgans* (burial sites) pockmark the landscape, especially in the dry plains of the far south.

Buryatiya is an intriguing but virtually unknown part of the world, and one whose culture and beauty is well worth exploring at length. However, the basic low-cost resorts which line the shore between the Selenga Delta and Ust-Barguzin are ideal for those who just want to relax, feel the sand between their toes and enjoy a barbecue on the beach. Trekking and horseriding opportunities are almost unlimited in the mountainous terrain, but local guides are needed to see you safe.

GETTING AROUND

Despite its size most journeys in Buryatiya start and finish in Ulan-Ude. The city is a major stop on the Trans-Siberian Railway and the last before Mongolia-bound (and some Beijing-bound) services peel off to head south along the Trans-Mongolian Railway. From the railway station forecourt and the two disordered bus stations *marshrutki* and buses scuttle out across the republic with most destinations served by at least one service a day.

Few visitors take the time to explore Baikal's coastline south of the Selenga Delta as they push on for Ulan-Ude and points north. However, with the Trans-Siberian Railway hugging the shingle line and the M-55 Moscow–Vladivostok highway taking an identical route all the way to the Buryat capital, this section of the lake's shoreline is easily accessible and worth exploring if you have enough time. The following route description also provides a bit of background if you are just taking the scenic train ride from Irkutsk to Ulan-Ude during the day.

On leaving Baikalsk, the next settlement you arrive at is **Vydrino**, the first village in Buryatiya, lying just beyond the administrative border. The village possesses little save for some superb Baikal views and the **Teplye Lakes** to the south, a short hike along the valley of the Snezhnaya River. The lakes' name translates as 'warm', as the water temperature here is higher than in Baikal. Vydrino is also the launch-pad for trips into the **Baikal Biosphere Reserve** (see *Natural history*, page 30), but you'll need to arrange a guide to visit. From Vydrino the road and railway line clutch the edge of the shore, and before long reach the village of **Tankhoy**, where the headquarters of the biosphere reserve (*ul Krasnogvardeyskaya 34;* \ *30138 93710*) are located. Ask here about guided walks into the mountains of the reserve for a spot of indigenous animal spotting.

Leaving Tankhoy, the tarmac and trains continue to hug the lake's shore for dear life, the high Khamar Daban mountain range to the right, the deep waters of Baikal to the left. Tiny fishing communities punctuate this stretch as far as the town of **Babushkin**, a place of particular interest to Trans-Siberian fans. Formerly called Mysovaya, it was here from 1900 until 1904 that the icebreakers *Baikal* and *Angara*, both built on Tyneside, would disgorge their human and rail-carriage cargoes at the end of the crossing from Port Baikal. The *Baikal* found its final resting place in 1918 on the bottom of the lake not far offshore from here; the *Angara* is now a museum in Irkutsk (see page 91). In the 1940s the town was renamed after Ivan Babushkin, a comrade of Lenin's, who was executed here in 1906, but the railway station still bears the old name, Mysovaya. This is also the place where many of the 18th- and 19th-century Europe-bound tea caravans from China would get their first glimpse of Lake Baikal after traversing the lonely passes of the Khamar Daban range.

Continuing on our journey east, the road and tracks part for a short while, reuniting at Bolshaya Rechka from where a 7km-long road leads to the lakeside village of **Posolskoe**. Here you'll find the impressive and newly renovated **Posolsky Monastery**, established as early as 1681 on the orders of Tsar Feodor III. The church was built by a well-to-do tea merchant by the name of Oskolkovy and

TRANS-MONGOLIAN RAILWAY

This branch line of the better known Trans-Siberian Railway links Ulan-Ude with Ulaanbaatar, the Gobi Desert and China, and was only built in the 1950s. The line leaves the main Trans-Siberian tracks at a set of points to the east of Ulan-Ude and follows the Selenga as far as Tarbagatay (no stop). It then skirts Gusinoe Ozero (Goose Lake) before barrelling down to the border at Naushki. The line is used primarily for freight and only two or three passenger trains rattle its tracks in each direction a day – the daily 362 Irkutsk–Naushki, the daily Ulan-Ude–Naushki *elektrichka* and the weekly Moscow–Peking express. Railroad devotees will undoubtedly enjoy the bum-numbing six-hour ride through the parched hills of southern Buryatiya.

the village snowballed around the complex. The monastery was closed down when the Bolsheviks seized power in 1917, but the monks returned in 2000, albeit to a set of crumbling ruins. It's now possible to stay at the monastery in the 23-bed dormitory (✆ *30138 91094*).

Russia's two principal transport arteries say farewell to Lake Baikal at the Selenga Delta (see page 136) and head inland to the sizeable, but wholly uninteresting, industrial town of **Selenginsk**.

The blacktop and the Trans-Siberian now follow the twisting and island-snagged Selenga River to **Tataurovo** where, apart from the rail bridge, a tiny car ferry is the only link on the route between Baikal and Ulan-Ude (a road bridge was under construction at the time of research). From here the steel traces the north side of the valley, the M-55 the south side until the two meet again in Ulan-Ude.

ULAN-UDE (УЛАН-УДЭ) *Telephone code: 3012*

For those stepping off overnight trains at Ulan-Ude's Trans-Siberian station, the Asiatic features of the city's inhabitants can come as quite a surprise. Ulan-Ude is the capital of the Autonomous Republic of Buryatiya, and although only a quarter of the republic's population possess Mongol features, in its main city this feels like many more. Far fewer travellers take a break from the rails here than in Irkutsk, which is a pity as Ulan-Ude is arguably the more interesting, diverse and exotic of the two, though tourist infrastructure here is less developed than on the western side of the lake.

Ulan-Ude is the gateway to a fascinating and wholly undiscovered land wedged between Lake Baikal and the border with Mongolia. The city is the republic's only major settlement, the seat of government, a place of education and the focal point for Buryat culture. It also serves as a major junction on the Trans-Siberian, where the line divides, one branch heading south to Mongolia and on to China, another continuing east to Vladivostok. Many communities on the eastern shore of Lake Baikal can only be reached from Ulan-Ude by bus, and naturally the city is the best base for exploring southern Buryatiya.

Ulan-Ude (never, by the way, known orally as UU for obvious reasons, unlike the handy UB for Ulaanbaatar) is located to the east of the Selenga River at its confluence with the Uda (from which the city gets its name, which means 'Red Uda'). This is a huge city of 390,000, but most of the population live in self-contained housing projects, leaving a small centre which can be easily explored on foot. The central streets and squares have a quieter feel than Irkutsk, with less traffic, narrower roads and fewer tourists. However, one of the few locations in town which occasionally does become busy with foreigners is the area just below Lenin's goatee, where every visitor likes to pose to have their picture taken.

HISTORY Ulan-Ude's relatively short history began in the same way as the majority of settlements in Siberia, with the establishment of a Cossack fort in 1666. At first called Udinsk, the Cossack stronghold played a major role in bringing peace to the region, which Manchuria saw as within its sphere of influence. A century later, Verkhneudinsk, as it had become known, had grown fat on trade, especially thanks to its position on the Tea Road which entered Siberia to the south at Kyakhta and continued on to European Russia. Merchants' profits largely funded the construction of the Odigitria Cathedral, the first place of worship here to be built in stone, as well as many private villas, a bridge across the Selenga, banks, paved roads and the all-important trading rows which witnessed huge biennial markets. The Trans-Siberian Railway arrived in the city in 1900, leading to another boom in trade, and brought many immigrants into the region. Following the October Revolution and the Russian Civil War, Verkhneudinsk was declared capital of the Buryat-Mongol Autonomous Soviet Republic, and in 1934 the city was renamed Ulan-Ude. The Buryat capital emerged unaffected by World War II and in the early 1950s, in thanks for the Buryat contribution to the war effort, Stalin allowed local Buddhists to build a monastery at nearby Ivolga. The 1950s also saw the construction of one of eastern Siberia's most striking buildings, the Buryat State Theatre of Opera and Ballet, which remains an impressive sight today and still dominates part of the city centre. The city's military-based economy suffered badly in the 1990s following the collapse of the USSR, and recovery is an ongoing process.

GETTING THERE As the republic's capital, Ulan-Ude is a major transport hub for the entire region as well as enjoying excellent international links.

By train Train is the obvious way of arriving in the Buryat metropolis, with services pulling in from Mongolia, China and all points east and west along the Trans-Siberian. There are services to Irkutsk (*departs: up to 11 times daily; journey time: 8–9hrs*), Moscow (*departs: up to 4 times daily; journey time: 3–5 days*), Beijing (*departs: every Friday; journey time: 66hrs*), Ulaanbaatar (*departs: daily during summer, every other day in winter; journey time: 29hrs*) and Vladivostok (*departs: up to 5 times daily; journey time: up to 72hrs*).

By air Ulan-Ude's small Mukhino airport (✆ 227 611) 11km to the west of the city centre handles domestic flights to Moscow and Krasnoyarsk and handy services to Irkutsk and Nizhneangarsk, the only way of reaching the north of Buryatiya which is otherwise completely cut off from the south. There are currently no international services to or from Ulan-Ude, but the airport was recently taken over by an Austrian company who are keen to restart flights to Ulaanbaatar and even begin a direct service to somewhere in western Europe, possibly Frankfurt.

By bus The majority of towns and villages in southern Buryatiya can only be reached by bus or long-distance *marshrutka*. Local and city services depart from Ulan-Ude's Banzarova bus station. For destinations in Buryatiya (Ivolga, Novoselenginsk, Kyakhta, Ust-Barguzin, Petropavlovka and Arshan) head for the main bus station. For long-distance *marshrutki* (Irkutsk, Chita) you'll need to look outside the railway station. To Irkutsk, overnight train is a far more comfortable option than long-distance *marshrutka*; and be aware that *marshrutka* journeys off the main Ulan-Ude–Irkutsk highway can be torturous and uncomfortable ordeals along washboard dirt roads.

GETTING AROUND Ulan-Ude has a system of local trams, buses and *marshrutki*, but the only service you are likely to use is *marshrutka* 8 which runs from the Banzarova bus station via ploshchad Sovietov to Verkhnyaya Berezovka and the Ethnographical Museum. A tram or bus ride costs RUB10 (buy tickets on board) and there is a flat fare of RUB10 for all *marshrutki*. As mentioned previously, the centre is manageable on foot. To reach the airport, take *marshrutka* 77 or bus 10 or 34. If you must take a taxi, call ✆ 222 222 or ✆ 661 111 for reputable companies.

WHERE TO STAY Ulan-Ude recently saw the opening of a backpacker hostel of sorts, providing a pleasant alternative to the city's pricey hotel accommodation, which is tuned primarily to the needs of business travellers. Other options for those on a budget are the Barguzin or a homestay, although in a city the size of Ulan-Ude homestays can be difficult to track down without going through a tour company.

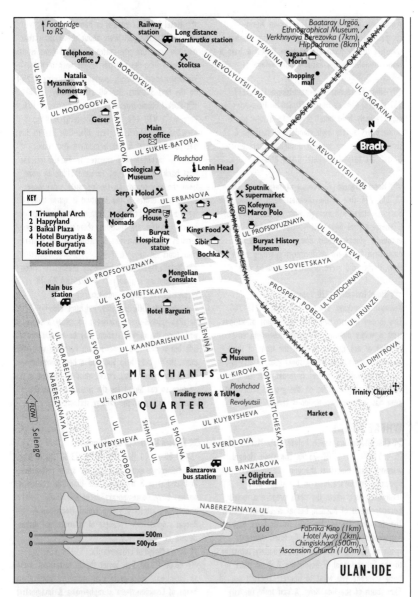

ULAN-UDE

KEY
1 Triumphal Arch
2 Happyland
3 Baikal Plaza
4 Hotel Buryatiya & Hotel Buryatiya Business Centre

🏠 **Baikal Plaza** (68 rooms) ul Erbanova 12; 📞 210 838; f 220 570; e info@baikalplaza.com; www.baikalplaza.com. Transformed from sad Soviet to new Russian crass in the space of a few weeks, this hotel commands an enviable location on ploshchad Sovietov, meaning some guests wake up with a huge Lenin head framed in their windows. Renovation has brought the standard of the rooms up to a European level but rates are high. $$$$

🏠 **Geser** (63 rooms) ul Ranzhurova 11; 📞 215 383; f 216 151; e hotel_geser@mail.ru; www.geser-hotel.ru. From the outside it may look like a 1980s town hall in northern England, but inside things get considerably better with a cosy welcoming atmosphere by Siberian standards & decent if slightly overpriced rooms. $$$$

🏠 **Sagaan Morin** ul Gagarina 25; 📞 443 647; www.morintour.com. Very popular among Trans-Siberian travellers. For the price rooms are of a remarkably good standard. The Sagaan Morin company also runs all kinds of tours, can arrange transfers to any point around Lake Baikal & have a resort complex in the eastern-shore village of Sukhaya. $$$$

🏠 **Sibir** (22 rooms) ul Pochtamtskaya 1; ☎ 297 257; f 218 604; e trksibir@mail.ru. Ulan-Ude's most recently built hotel shines like a new pin, & inside offers a very high standard of facilities & services. Rooms are spotless if slightly characterless & staff are helpful & polite. B/fast RUB130 extra. $$$$

🏠 **Hotel Barguzin** (70 rooms) ul Sovietskaya 28; ☎ 215 746. One of the cheapest deals in town, the Barguzin starts well enough with its clean-cut glass & stainless steel foyer. But venture beyond & you'll encounter gloomy rooms, dodgy plumbing & an omniscient Soviet-era *dezhurnaya* guarding every floor. If they did serve b/fast, it would be dire. $$$

🏠 **Hotel Buryatiya** (220 rooms) ul Kommunisticheskaya 47a; ☎ 211 505; f 211 760. This former Inturist behemoth has rooms of various sizes & wildly differing standards depending on whether or not they've reached the front of the queue for renovation. One distinct plus to staying here is the raft of services (internet, tour companies, souvenir kiosks) on offer on the ground floor — it even has its very own Buddhist temple. $$$

🏠 **Hotel Ayan** (27 rooms) ul Babushkina 164; ☎ 415 141. The bad news about the Ayan is that it's 2km from the city centre. The good news is that it's one of Ulan-Ude's better hotels, with modern, Western-standard rooms, sparkling bathrooms & Wi-Fi on the first 3 floors. Bus 40 stops nearby. $$$

🏠 **Baikal Ethnic Hostel** (8 rooms) Flotskaya 12A, Poselye; ☎ 220 442; e baikalhostel@mail.ru; www.baikalhostel.com. At last! Ulan-Ude has its first backpacker hostel & not a moment too soon. Although inconveniently situated in Poselye on the west bank of the Selenga (around 10km by road from the city centre on the opposite side), buses run to the centre & the location is quite handy for the airport. Contained within a new timber building, dorms are spacious, there's a full range of services such as internet & kitchen, & the owner runs tours on request. $$

🏠 **Natalia Myasnikova's homestay** (Address provided once a booking is made) ☎ 8 9025 64 82 78; e myasnikova_nat@rambler.ru; www.uude.info/ENG/homestay_eng.html. Elderly Natalia's spick-&-span apartment homestay, a short walk from the railway station, may be on the pricey side but it gets rave reviews from everyone who stays there. She'll gladly help you find a bed somewhere else if her place is full. Places must be booked in advance so call ahead for the precise address & directions (it's near the railway station). $$

✖ WHERE TO EAT

✖ **Chingiskhan** Sun Tower, bulvar Karla Marksa 25a; ☎ 415 050; ⏱ 11.00–23.00. Two stout Mongol warriors greet diners at the entrance to this upmarket restaurant built in the shape of a traditional yurt, where the chefs prepare a mixed Eurasian menu of Russian, Buryat & Chinese dishes. The ambience created by clean Asiatic lines, expertly harmonised *feng shui* & skilfully fused dishes is spoilt by waiting staff who most definitely subscribe to the Soviet school of hospitality. A good place to bring someone you want to impress. Located around 4km south of the Uda River. A taxi from the city centre costs around RUB150. $$$$

✖ **Bochka** ul Pochtamtskaya 1; ☎ 222 020; ⏱ 11.00–01.00 Sun–Thu, 11.00–02.00 Fri & Sat. Housed in a purpose-built log structure behind the Sibir Hotel, the Bochka with its hefty timber tables & European pub atmosphere is good for a relaxing night out over a few (pricey) tankards or for a meal of Siberian staples & meat dishes brought to your table by unusually friendly staff. Superb summer beer garden. $$$

✖ **Modern Nomads** ul Ranzhurova 1; ⏱ 11.00–23.00 Mon–Fri, 12.00–23.00 Sat & Sun. This Mongolian eatery has popular sister restaurants in Ulaanbaatar & Irkutsk, & the Ulan-Ude branch is no less busy. Contemporary décor & a lively atmosphere attract a young crowd. Mongolian & Buryat staples with a couple of international dishes thrown in. $$$

✖ **Serp i Molod** ul Erbanova 7a; ☎ 214 114; ⏱ 08.00–23.00. Fun Soviet theme restaurant with an intentional mock-proletariat *stolovaya* atmosphere, heaps of Communist-era paraphernalia & imaginative names for the dishes such as 'Hero of Soviet Labour roast pork' & 'Red Caucasus tongue'. A large bust of Lenin watches over proceedings as he does on the nearby square. Live music every day from 19.00. To get there, just follow the hammer & sickle signs off ploshchad Sovietov. $$$

✖ **Stolitsa** ul Revolyutsii-1905 31; ☎ 552 836; ⏱ 11.00–01.00. Getting into this respected restaurant on the railway station forecourt can be problematic as it operates face control & door staff may not let daypacks & travelling clothes past the front entrance. However, once inside you can savour well-prepared European dishes in the elegant black & red interior for reasonable prices. If you are denied access, retreat to the cheap café & beer garden downstairs, or boycott the place. **$$$**

✕ **Baataray Urgöö** Verkhnyaya Berezovka, *marshrutka* stop 'Yurt'; ✆ 267 810; e dangina@ baikalkhan.ru; ☺ 12.00–23.00. Almost always dubbed the 'yurt restaurant' by foreigners (perhaps as most can't pronounce its Buryat name), this is the most characterful place to eat in Ulan-Ude & well worth the trip out to the Verkhnyaya Berezovka district. Dining spaces are spread through a series of interconnected yurts traditionally decorated with horsehair rugs, silk throws, Buryat folk costumes & bear skins. The compound also contains yurts which you can hire for the night. Food is pure Buryat. Take *marshrutka* 8 from the Banzarova bus station or ploshchad Sovietov. **$$**

✕ **Happyland** ul Lenina 52; ☺ 10.30–23.00. Ulan-Ude's most central self-service cheap eat, almost always full of students & cinema-goers filling up on hot dogs, burgers, chips, rice & pasta for a fistful of roubles. You can also nurse an inexpensive beer here until 23.00. **$–$$**

✕ **Kings Food** ul Kommunisticheskaya 43 (basement); ☺ 11.00–23.00. The gaudy décor & desperate lack of AC are accompanied by cheap-as-chips no-frills dishes, Russian flat-screen MTV & a noisy teenage clientele. Despite all the downsides, it's well-located, clean & ideal if you just need to speedily fill the hole in an informal atmosphere. **$**

✕ **Sputnik supermarket** ul Kommunisticheskaya 48; ☺ 24hrs. The Buryat capital's only centrally located Western-style supermarket, stocking a wide range of (overpriced) foodstuffs not available anywhere else. Ideal for sourcing the smelliest food you can find for a long Trans-Siberian journey (as Russians like to do). Get there early for real, freshly baked croissants & pastries. There are a couple of ATMs in the entrance.

ENTERTAINMENT AND NIGHTLIFE Despite its large student population, Ulan-Ude is not exactly a thumping nightlife hotspot, and you'll probably be limited to the restaurants and bars of an eve. The one place you could try for the disco and cinema (though most films are dubbed) is **Fabrika kino** (*ul Sakhyanovoy 9; www.fabrika-kino.ru*), a modern orange and white building outside of the city centre. The 1980s nostalgia discos can be entertaining.

SHOPPING Unless you are here to buy a military helicopter or some spare parts for your own private fleet of Soviet locomotives, there's not much in the way of shopping in the Buryat capital. Various kiosks in the Hotel Buryatiya sell a selection of souvenirs (books, maps, dolls etc) and there are numerous stalls at the Ivolginsky Datsan selling gaudy made-in-China Buddhas, mini-prayer wheels and the like.

OTHER PRACTICALITIES

✉ **Post office** ul Lenina 61; ☺ 08.00–19.00 Mon–Fri, 9.00–18.00 Sat

e **Hotel Buryatiya Business Centre** ul Kommunisticheskaya 47a (ground floor); ☺ 08.30–12.00 & 13.00–17.30. Ulan-Ude's most central internet place (it's not a café) possesses a meagre 3 PCs & charges RUB50/hr.

e **Kofeynya Marco Polo** ul Kommunisticheskaya 46; ☺ 09.00–22.30. This Western-style coffee house offers Wi-Fi connection for RUB3/MB.

Telephone office ul Borsoyeva; ☺ 09.00–08.00. The minuscule public telephone office near the railway station has 3 PCs & charges RUB35/hr to get online.

WHAT TO SEE AND DO The vast majority of Ulan-Ude's sights can be found in an area defined by the railway tracks, the Uda River and the Selenga River. Ul Lenina links the timber tenements and sandy streets of the former merchants' quarter with the newer ploshchad Sovietov area at the top of the hill, rich in grand Stalinist-era Neoclassical structures. Both parts of the city centre are interesting to explore but the rough and litter-strewn backstreets of the merchants' quarter should perhaps be avoided after dark.

Lenin Head (*ploshchad Sovietov*) Whatever Ulan-Ude may have been famous for in the past, it now has just one claim to fame in most people's eyes, and that is as the custodian of the largest Lenin head in the world (where are all the others with which it so vehemently competes?). The city's most photographed monument was raised in 1970 to celebrate the 100th birthday of Grandfather Lenin, and the bronze bonce weighing 42 tons rises to a height of 7.7m. Locals joke that Buryatiya's bird population chooses not to soil Lenin's pate out of respect for the great man's achievements. Before Lenin's slightly cross-eyed expression extends the cracked and flaking asphalt of Soviet Square, often still used as a military parade ground.

Geological Museum (*ul Lenina 59;* ↘ *218 264;* ⊕ *11.00–17.00 Mon–Fri; free admission*) This small three-room museum exhibits rocks, crystals and ores from the Baikal region, as well as a small exhibition of works of art made entirely out of different coloured sand and grit. Many of the works which depict scenes from Lake Baikal are for sale and make novel souvenirs.

Opera House and around (*ul Lenina 53;* ↘ *214 454*) Ulan-Ude's Buryat State Theatre of Opera and Ballet, dating from the early 1930s, is one of the most attractive buildings in the city. At time of research this grand old lady was receiving a major facelift, but when completed, her stage will once again play host to Russian classics such as *Swan Lake*, and Buryat operas and ballets such as *Enkhe-Bulat-Bator* and *Geser*. Next to the opera house a 2006 copy of the **triumphal arch** built in 1891 to honour the imperial heir, Nicholas II, spans Lenin Street. On the southern side of the opera house stands a **statue** of a woman representing Buryat hospitality. She proudly offers visitors a traditional bowl of milk and a white scarf as she gazes down Lenin Street.

Odigitria Cathedral (*ul Lenina 2*) The principal place of worship for Buryatiya's Orthodox Christians was built between 1741 and 1785, making it the oldest of Ulan-Ude's churches. It was also the first stone building to appear in the city and displays features of the rare Siberian Baroque style. The Communists shut the church down in 1929 and the building was used as a store for the museum for almost 60 years before worshippers returned in 2000. As with most churches that were put to civil use during the Soviet era, the bare whitewashed interior is a disappointment, though the renovated exterior is striking enough. At time of research a new Byzantine-style chapel was being (re)constructed in the weed-plagued grounds. Behind the cathedral lurk Ulan-Ude's only semi-public toilets.

Other city-centre churches The Buryat capital sports two other less grand Orthodox Christian places of worship. The **Trinity Church (Svyato-Troitsky khram)** (*ul Kuybysheva*) to the east of the merchants' quarter dates from the early 19th century and is surrounded by a former cemetery. It should have reopened after long renovation by the time you arrive. The rarely visited **Ascension Church (Svyato-Vosnesensky khram)** (*ul Proizvodstvennaya*) stands on the opposite bank of the Uda River to the cathedral and was built in 1809. Moved several times, it was the only church to remain open from 1945 onwards.

Buryat History Museum (*ul Profsoyuznaya 29;* ↘ *210 653;* ⊕ *10.00–18.00 Tue–Sun; adult RUB150*) One of the top museum collections in the Baikal region is housed in modern, purpose-built premises to the southeast of ploshchad Sovietov. It's the nearest Buryatiya comes to a Western-style museum and is one of the highlights of the Buryat capital for anyone with even a passing interest in the republic's history and religion.

Having bought your ticket, climb up to the second floor where the exhibition starts. The theme of this whole level is Buddhism. The superb collection of *thangkas*, Buddha statues in all kinds of poses, bodhisattvas, mandalas, Tibetan medical diagrams, figures in papier-mâché, wood and bronze, masks, costumes, old photographs and models of temples from across Buryatiya is unmissable, and sheds much light on Buryat Buddhist tradition and its past. Many of the items on display were rescued from monasteries in the 1930s before they were demolished.

The first floor deals with the history of Buryatiya, starting with the migration of the Buryats into the region and continuing with sections on the tea trade, shamanism, folk costumes, the Circumbaikal Railway, Decembrists, Buddhist temples and many other topics relevant to the region. The ground floor is split into three sections devoted to Buddhism, costumes and masks used in the Buddhist *Tsam* dance and Old Believers.

City Museum (*ul Lenina 26;* ☏ *217 990;* ⊕ *10.00–13.00 & 1400–19.00; adult RUB40*) Ulan-Ude's city history museum was only set up recently and is still a work in progress. Exhibits relating to the tea and fur trades, old maps and a collection of samovars provide only a minor diversion, though the ticket also allows access to a small gallery where local artists put on temporary shows of their work.

Ploshchad Revolyutsii Ulan-Ude's second square was once the heart of the merchants' quarter and is home to the **trading rows** from which they proffered their wares in the 19th century. The less glorious Soviet retail past is represented in the centre of the square by the old **TsUM** (*Central Department Store;* ⊕ *10.00–19.00*) where you can pick up some overpriced souvenir material if little else.

Verkhnyaya Berezovka This leafy district 7km northeast of Ulan-Ude's city centre is an area of forested hills dotted with weekend cottages belonging to well-to-do city dwellers. It's also the location of one of Ulan-Ude's most popular tourist attractions, the open-air **Ethnographical Museum** (*Verkhnyaya Berezovka;* ☏ *335 754;* ⊕ *09.00–17.00 Tue–Sun; adult RUB70*). The impressive complex is divided into seven areas, each containing examples of dwellings from a particular time in history and/or region and belonging to different peoples who have inhabited (and, in some cases, still inhabit) Buryatiya. The archaeological section contains Hun standing stones and ancient burial mounds, while a little further along the path rise Evenk tepees or *chums* lined with pine bark. Next come the yurts of the Western Buryats, followed by an Eastern Buryat Buddhist prayer house and more traditional yurts. The next stage in Buryatiya's history was the Russian invasion and in the fifth section you can explore Cossack homesteads to see how the first European settlers lived. From there move on to the Old Believers' complex, cut from larch and spruce trunks. End your tour through the history of Buryat architecture at a complex of timber townhouses and a church moved here from Ulan-Ude. Most of the interiors can be inspected and in many you will encounter 'locals' in period costume and countless pieces of original furniture, tools and everyday domestic items. Allow around two hours to see everything.

Verkhnyaya Berezovka is also home to one of the best restaurants in the city (Baataray Urgöö, see *Where to eat*) which, with its yurts and folk costumes, can be an apt way of rounding off a morning or afternoon at the museum. Other attractions in these parts include the **hippodrome** (☏ *442 254*), which hosts the annual *Surkharban* (see *Festivals and special events*, page 68), and a couple of exotic datsans, both built in the last ten years. You are free to take a peek inside and there is a small souvenir shop in one of the temples.

Marshrutka 8 heads this way regularly throughout the day from the Banzarova bus station and ploshchad Sovietov.

One of the Baikal region's most fascinating ethnic minorities is the so-called Old Believers (in Russian *starovyercy* or *semeyskie*), who inhabit a group of villages to the south of Ulan-Ude. The story of how they came to establish communities far from their homelands is a fascinating one, and their traditions and way of life provide a rare glimpse into European Russia's religious past.

In the mid 17th century the Patriarch Nikon devised a set of reforms to bring the Russian Church into line with Greek Orthodoxy. Having failed to consult priests and congregations prior to imposing these changes, Nikon found his efforts regarded by many conservatives as heretical and unacceptable. By today's measure, crossing oneself with three extended fingers instead of two, or singing two *alleluias* instead of one, may seem like inconsequential matters, but when large groups from many parts of society refused to comply with the new liturgical practices, the autocratic Church authorities launched a campaign of persecution, with those who most vehemently and publicly advocated sticking with the old ways tortured, executed or banished. Some Old Believers even cut off their fingers, rendering themselves incapable of making the sign of the Cross in the new way; others committed suicide, taking their families with them in fires. This split in the Orthodox Church is known in Russian history as the *raskol* or schism, and is said to have torn as many as a quarter of the Russian population away from the mainstream Church.

OLD BELIEVERS IN BURYATIYA The first Old Believers arrived in Buryatiya in the late 18th century and established themselves in the Zabaikalye. They were nicknamed *semeyskie* ('family people') as they usually arrived in large family groups. They soon became known in the region for their love of work, cleanliness, pious nature and sense of order, and even today their single-shuttered houses in laser-straight rows along the village's main street appear much neater than those of other Russians. Their Technicolor clothing, hearty food and centuries-old Bibles also set them apart from their neighbours, and until recently intermarrying was rare. Even young *starovyercy* still keep to the old ways though perhaps not as vehemently as their parents and grandparents. Since the fall of Communism there has been a huge resurgence in Old Believer culture with new churches built, new choirs forming and special venues created where tourists can watch performances and sample Old Believer food.

VISITING OLD BELIEVERS Buryatiya's Old Believers can be found mainly in the town of **Tarbagatay** (around 60km south of Ulan-Ude) and the surrounding villages. There's a new **church** and **museum** in Tarbagatay and a group of Old Believers has set up a kind of **visitors' centre** in a timber house in **Desyatnikovo**. Here they entertain guests with traditional songs and dancing in full costume, and fill them full of irresistible homemade food. As performances and food are only laid on when the Old Believers are expecting company, you'll get a lot more out of a visit to Tarbagatay and Desyatnikovo if you book a tour. Companies in Ulan-Ude such as **Baikal Naran Tour** and **Buryat Intour** (see *Local tour companies and helpers* on page 39) run superb trips out to these villages for individuals and groups.

IVOLGINSKY DATSAN (ИВОЛГИНСКИЙ ДАЦАН)

The Ivolginsky temple complex (*www.datsan.buryatia.ru*) 35km west of Ulan-Ude is a must-see for anyone spending more than a day in Buryatiya. Though not as grand as some temples around Chita further east, this is the official epicentre of Buddhism in Russia and the largest Buddhist place of worship north of Mongolia.

The large compound containing several temples and schools is a working monastery and university, where purple-robed monks scurry among the racks of prayer wheels and stupas, and pilgrims walk clockwise beneath flayed oriental eaves.

Aware that the temple has become a major regional tourist attraction, the lamas also cater to a limited extent for visitors, with gift stalls and other facilities. A visit makes for a fascinating half-day trip out of the Buryat capital, especially when there's a colourful religious festival taking place, or if you can make it in time for morning prayers.

HISTORY It was Stalin, of all people, who gave lamas and monks released from Gulags across Siberia, permission to establish the Ivolginsky Temple in 1945, as an act of gratitude to Buryatiya for its part in the defeat of Hitler. The site selected for the new datsan was a former shamanistic cemetery, and was so marshy that stone had to be brought from Lake Baikal to establish a firm base on which construction could begin. At a meeting of Buddhist bigwigs from the Irkutsk oblast, Tuva, Chita and Buryatiya which took place in Ulan-Ude in 1946, Lubsan Nima Darmayev was selected as the first Pandito Khambo Lama (Russia's head Buddhist). For 45 years this was one of only two working temples in Russia (the other was at Aginskoe near Chita) though few outsiders knew of its existence. The complex was badly damaged by fire in 1972 and the buildings we see today date from rebuilding work which has been ongoing ever since. In 1991 a Buddhist university was founded here, with faculties teaching Buddhist Philosophy, old Buryat literature, iconography, Tibetan medicine and more everyday subjects such as foreign languages and even computer skills. It now boasts over 100 students from across the Russian Federation.

GETTING THERE The town of Ivolga is 28km southwest of Ulan-Ude and the temple complex 7km beyond the town. *Marshrutka* 130 (*tickets: RUB25*) runs frequently from Ulan-Ude's Banzarova bus station to Ivolga from where you must switch to a taxi or hitch a lift. Most tour companies in Ulan-Ude operate guided half-day excursions to the datsan with prices starting around RUB1,500. This is by far the best way to visit as you can arrange to arrive in time for morning prayers and gain access to the monastery library and museum.

WHERE TO STAY AND EAT Thanks to the temple's proximity to Ulan-Ude, hardly anyone stays in the nearby town of Ivolga. Outside of the main summer tourist season you could ask the monks at the temple itself if they can put you up in a dorm for a small donation. The only place to eat is a small *pozy* joint next to the souvenir stalls. Otherwise bring a picnic.

WHAT TO SEE AND DO Having passed through the entrance hemmed in by stalls offering mass-produced made-in-China mini-prayer wheels, plastic laughing Buddha statues and coin-sucking prosperity frogs, visitors find themselves in a large compound ringed by distant mountains. Monastic dwellings, refectories and large, colourful temple buildings are interspersed with prayer wheel racks, whitewashed stupas, brightly painted statues and trees hung with prayer flags. Don't forget to walk in a clockwise direction around the complex, and feel free to spin the prayer wheels and enter the temples unless instructed otherwise by the monks.

The 1972 **main temple** or *tsokchen* (цокчен) is the star attraction and though not as sophisticated in its decoration as other large temples in Russia's east, it more than makes up for it in size. Inside you'll find a huge statue of Buddha accompanied by blue-skinned protector deities and hundreds of small golden Buddhas, as well as the usual offerings of rice, coins and butter lamps, brightly coloured silks and *thangkas*.

In 1956 a cutting of the **Bodhi Tree** under which Buddha attained enlightenment was brought to the temple and encouraged to take root in the grounds. The result is Ivolga's very own Bodhi tree which can be seen growing in the middle of the compound behind glass (to stop overzealous pilgrims taking their own cuttings).

If you come to Ivolga on an organised tour, agencies can arrange a visit to the monastery **library**, custodian of the biggest collection of Buddhists texts in Russia (mostly in Tibetan). Groups are also given access to the small **museum** housing local Buddhist art as well as other precious items from around the Buddhist world. Accessing these places as an independent traveller takes patience and a lot of asking around.

The miraculous **body of the Khambo Lama Itygelov** (see box *The Sleeping Lama* below) is now kept in a brand new temple building under construction at the time of research. It's not yet clear whether this part of the datsan will be freely accessible to the public. There's little chance you'll catch a glimpse of Itygelov's incredibly well preserved body, still seated in the lotus position in which he was buried in 1927, as the sarcophagus is only wheeled out six times a year (including Buddhist New Year in late January/early February and Maidari in late June).

TAMCHINSKY (GUSINOOZERSKY) DATSAN (ТАМЧИНСКИЙ (ГУСИНООЗЕРСКИЙ) ДАЦАН)

Travelling south from Ulan-Ude on the Trans-Mongolian Railway, an interesting place to break the journey is the rarely visited Tamchinsky Buddhist Monastery (sometimes known as Gusinoozersky) in the village of Gusinoe Ozero. Situated on the southern bank of the romantically named Goose Lake (Gusinoe Ozero), the village is a ramshackle, almost derelict affair, but at its heart you'll find a humble compound of Buddhist structures, prayer wheels, fluttering prayer flags and a few pale reminders of Buryatiya's rich Buddhist past.

THE SLEEPING LAMA

Dashi-Dorzho Itygelov, the Khambo Lama at the beginning of the 20th century, is a well-known figure around the Tibetan Buddhist world. He died in 1927, apparently at a time of his own choosing, and was buried in a wooden casket in a seated position as if meditating. His 'grave' was a secret known only to the lamas and it remained so until 2002 when the body was exhumed. To everyone's amazement Itygelov was still intact (very much like St Inokent in Irkutsk) and looked the same as the day he had been buried. Now housed in a special glass case, monks and locals claim the body is warm and soft, that his hair still grows and that he sweats but never loses weight. Even scientists are at a loss to explain the Itygelov phenomenon, and the Dalai Lama claims that the lama didn't die at all, but went into a deep state of meditation and is, therefore, still alive. The Ivolginsky Datsan has since become a destination for thousands of pilgrims from Russia, Mongolia and Tibet who arrive on the six days a year when the body is brought out for display (see the datsan's website – in Russian only). Tibetan Buddhists believe that touching the lama's hand or his clothing can have miraculous effects.

Most visitors' temple visiting ends with the Ivolginsky Monastery, but Buryatiya has many other remote Buddhist datsans which have been built or re-established over the past two decades. The following is a selection of the best; some are impossible to reach without a car and a local to point the way.

TAMCHINSKY DATSAN (Тамчинский дацан) Once the centre of Buddhism for the entire Russian Empire but now a shadow of its former self (see opposite).

ATSAGATSKY DATSAN (Ацагатский дацан) Located by the River Uda, 50km east of Ulan-Ude, this was once one of the greatest temples in Buryatiya and was even visited by Tsarevich Nikolay on his travels around Siberia in 1891. Ulan-Ude tour companies can take you there.

KURUMKANSKY DATSAN (Курумканский дацан) The main place of Buddhist worship in Kurumkan (Barguzin Valley), which attracts Buddhists from all over Russia to meditate in this idyllic mountain-backed setting.

OKINSKY DATSAN (Окинский дацан) Situated in far-flung Orlik, the administrative centre of the Oka region.

SARTUL-GEGETUYSKY DATSAN (Сартул-Гегетуйский дацан) Tucked away at the end of Gegetuy village (Dzhida District) in southern Buryatiya, this remote temple was built in 2001.

BULAG-SARTULSKY DATSAN (Булаг-Сартульский дацан) Were it near any road or village, this tiny and incredibly lonely Buddhist retreat surrounded by the parched hills of southern Buryatiya would receive many more visitors, as locals claim it was the first to be built in Buryatiya (1709). The temple's proximity to the Mongolian border suggests that this may be true.

HISTORY From its diminutive state today, it's hard to imagine that the Tamchinsky Monastery served as the centre of Russian Buddhism from 1741 until 1938 when it was closed by the Soviet authorities. At its height in the early 20th century it housed 1,000–2,000 monks and boasted 22 faculties, which gives an idea of how big and busy the compound must have been. It was the centre of intense Buddhist activity, a place of religious education, philosophy, wood-block printing, icon painting, sculpture, carpentry and traditional Tibetan medicine. It was also the main centre for learning the traditions of the *Tsam* dance. Closed in 1938, it was never completely destroyed and was declared a national monument in 1960. However, the main temple faced a real threat in the late 1940s when it was discovered that the plans for the new Trans-Mongolian Railway routed the tracks straight through the building! In a rare example of Soviet consideration for religious sentiment, the route was diverted around the village, though monks maintain that trains swerving to miss the monastery disturb its energy. The key moment which sealed the monastery's fate was when Stalin gave permission for the centre of Russian Buddhism to be established at Ivolga, and not to be reinstated at Gusinoe Ozero. The Tamchinsky Datsan officially reopened in 1990 and on the monastery's 250th anniversary in 1991 was visited by none other than the Dalai Lama. Since then rebuilding work and renovation have been slow at this once glorious place of Buddhist worship and learning.

GETTING THERE Should you decide to make the trip without assistance from a tour company in Ulan-Ude, the simplest way is to board a train heading south from the Buryat capital towards Naushki and the Mongolian border, alighting at Gusinoe Ozero's unexpectedly attractive timber station. The Irkutsk–Naushki train (No 362) leaves at 06.55 in the morning (*tickets: RUB257*), returning to Ulan-Ude at 17.35. The journey takes a bum-numbing four hours, though the views are stupendous. You can carry on towards the Mongolian border at 21.50.

 WHERE TO STAY AND EAT Visitors are rare here as most tourist interest is focused on the more elaborate and easier-to-reach Ivolga temple near Ulan-Ude. Officially there's nowhere to stay, but the head lama may let genuinely Buddhist-minded visitors kip over in the administrative building. The friendly staff may even feed you soup, bread and milky tea in the tiny refectory – leave a donation. If you've got the gear, you may be permitted to pitch up in the temple grounds, or why not camp by the tranquil and seldom-visited lake (preferably out of sight of the village). The only shop in Gusinoe Ozero is the 24-hour Universam on the awfully bedraggled square.

WHAT TO SEE AND DO Today renovation work is progressing at snail's pace on the building of the former **Philosophy School** which should have been returned to its erstwhile glory in late 2008 (but wasn't). The *tsokchen* (main temple), dating from 1858, is rather bare but still impressive with its forest of steel-hard, pillar-box red larch pillars and astounding acoustics which cling on to the monks' prayers for several seconds before releasing them up into the roof. In front of the main temple stands the *Oleny Kamen*, a standing stone covered in 3,500-year-old petroglyphs. The entire complex is overseen by a mobile-phone-toting lama in purple robes and scratched sunglasses who is happy to show people round. The *Khural* (morning prayers) take place here every day with monks coming in from the surrounding towns and villages. Otherwise things are pretty quiet.

NOVOSELENGINSK (НОВОСЕЛЕНГИНСК) *Telephone code: 8245*

Just off the Kyakhta–Ulan-Ude road among bald, featureless hills lies the small Wild East settlement of Novoselenginsk, little more than a scar of dark timber shacks and wide dusty streets on the crumbling banks of the Selenga River. Though there's not a great deal to see here, a remote chapter of the Decembrists' story and the interesting fate of some 19th-century British missionaries make the ramshackle town a strangely engaging and romantic stop *en route* elsewhere.

From its current unloved state, it's difficult to imagine that Selenginsk (the town's original name) was once a thriving 18th-century town where tea caravans from China would halt on their long journey north. The caravans began bypassing the town in the mid 18th century and a period of decline followed from which the town never recovered. To make matters worse, Selenginsk sat just north of the confluence of two major rivers, the Chikoy and the Selenga, whose combined waters regularly flooded the streets. The townsfolk eventually moved to the opposite bank of the Selenga (hence the present name, which means New Selenginsk) but the white spire of the Saviour church on the opposite shore serves as an eerie reminder of the original community.

GETTING THERE *Marshrutka* from either Kyakhta or Ulan-Ude is the only method of reaching Novoselenginsk. All services plying the main road between the Mongolian border and the Buryat capital stop here and the trip takes around 1½ hours from either place.

WHERE TO STAY AND EAT If for some unimaginable reason you decide to overnight in Novoselenginsk (or you get stuck there), your only option is to ask around for a homestay, though anything you find is likely to be pretty basic and rather grim. Equipped with a tent, you could head off in almost any direction and find a decent camping spot – but be careful of the locals if you plump for a pitch near town. If you bed down next to the Selenga don't use its water for cooking (or anything else for that matter). *En route* to Lake Baikal the river is joined by water which has passed through Mongolia's capital Ulaanbaatar so its purity cannot be guaranteed.

There's no food to speak of in town and you'll probably have to rely on snacks bought in the local general store or your own supplies.

WHAT TO SEE AND DO
Decembrist Museum (*ul Lenina 53;* ✆ *96716;* ⊕ *10.00–18.00 Wed–Sun; adult RUB40*) From 1839 until the 1850s Decembrist brothers Nikolai and Mikhail Bestuzhev, their three sisters and their friend Konstantin Torson lived and worked in Novoselenginsk. As the Decembrists generally did across eastern Siberia, they brought a civilising European influence to the local community by setting up schools, caring for the sick and holding cultural events. They also took an interest in Buryat culture and Buddhism, and Nikolai even befriended the Khambo Lama of the time. The small museum housed in the grandest building in town, the home of Nikolai's son, merchant Alexei Startsev, tells the story of their fate through their drawings, portraits, furniture and other everyday items.

Monument to Scottish missionary An obscure book *Shamans, Lamas and Evangelicals* by C R Bawden printed in 1985, and a short passage in Colin Thubron's *In Siberia* tell the fascinating story of three priests who were sent with their families to Novoselenginsk by the London Missionary Society to convert the local population. Granted land by Tsar Alexander I, from 1819 they spent 22 years by the Selenga translating the bible into Mongolian and trying to convince the local Buryats to give up their Buddhist faith. As Colin Thubron writes, underestimating the Buryats' commitment to Buddhism they failed to win a single soul throughout the two decades they lived by the Selenga.

The only reminder of the missionaries' fruitless efforts in this forgotten corner of Buryatiya is an obelisk raised to Martha Cowie, wife of one of the missionaries, Robert Yuille, which stands around 2km beyond the town below a crumbling mountain known as 'Anglichanka' (Englishwoman) beside the Selenga River. The monument, which bears inscriptions in both Latin and Russian, is surprisingly well looked after by local people.

Though distant from the tranquil shores of Lake Baikal, the busy border town of Kyakhta, where Russia peters out and Mongolia takes over, is a vital piece in the region's historical jigsaw. Here tea caravans once entered Russia from Manchuria, and thanks to this lucrative trade, the town could boast merchant millionaires to rival those of the capital, St Petersburg, very hard to imagine today. Reminders of Kyakhta's golden age dot the town in the form of grand churches, a richly stocked museum, the remnants of merchants' villas and the trading rows. The town is well worth a stop *en route* to or from Mongolia, though the Trans-Mongolian Railway line between Ulaanbaatar and Ulan-Ude crosses the border 36km to the west at Naushki.

HISTORY Founded as Troitskosavsk on the newly created Russo-Manchurian border in 1721, Kyakhta was once one of the main stopping-off points on the famous Tea Road (see box below) between China and Europe, and an eastern gateway to Russia. The town grew rich on the tea trade in the 18th and 19th centuries as bricks of tea on their way to Moscow and Europe passed through. In return, the Russians sent huge quantities of leather, fur, skins and cattle through the town in the opposite direction. Interestingly, many of Kyakhta's tea tasters were English, and some of the tea crossing the border found its way to English tables. By 1800 this far-flung border settlement boasted more millionaires than the imperial capital, St Petersburg, and grand mansions, public buildings and even raised timber pavements appeared along its streets. A number of Decembrists and their families fled here in the 1830s and later many Russian expeditions into the heart of Asia would leave from the town. However, the opening of the Suez Canal in 1869 slowed the flow of caravans along the Tea Road and Kyakhta's golden era came to a juddering end as Europe-bound tea began to bypass the expensive overland route in favour of cheaper sea transport. The construction of the Trans-Siberian in the early 20th century and the routing of the Trans-Mongolian Railway 20km to the west of the town four decades later caused Kyakhta to slide ever further into provincial obscurity, where it has languished ever since.

GETTING THERE Trains travelling the Trans-Mongolian line between Ulaanbaatar and Ulan-Ude make a lengthy halt at the border town of Naushki from where it's

---

THE TEA ROAD

Tea was exported from China to a thirsty Russia from the 17th century onwards and this remained a lucrative trade for at least a century and a half. From the tea-growing regions of southern China tea caravans crossed the Gobi Desert, travelled up to Ulaanbaatar and crossed into Russia at Kyakhta. From there the long lines of heavily laden camels didn't take the route of today's road but crossed the Khamar Daban mountain range and skirted around the southern reaches of Lake Baikal to Irkutsk. From there caravans would make their slow way across Russia, sometimes taking almost a year to reach the tea and fur fair held each winter in the town of Irbit, northwest of Yekaterinburg (the last one was held in 1929). There the tea was sold on to merchants who transported it to the tea rooms of St Petersburg and Europe.

Tea was transported in easy-to-carry bricks, examples of which can be seen in the museum in Kyakhta. To stop the bricks from crumbling, the leaves were mixed with ox blood and left to dry.

Kyakhta lies directly on the frontier with Mongolia, with the crossing point in the Sloboda district. The border is open from 10.00 until 19.00 but cannot be crossed on foot. Either take a taxi from Kyakhta (around RUB350) to Sükhbaatar on the other side of the line, or try to hitch a lift by asking around the front of the queue. Another option is to take the bus 35km west to Naushki where the Trans-Mongolian crosses the border, but this can be risky as it's officially out of bounds to foreigners. Note that most foreign nationals need a visa to enter Mongolia.

If you're planning to cross into Mongolia, be sure to grab a copy of the excellent *Mongolia: The Bradt Travel Guide* (*www.bradtguides.com*).

possible to take a taxi or *marshrutka* (which wait for trains in front of the station) for the short hop to Kyakhta. Occasionally ticket offices will refuse to sell foreigners tickets to Naushki as it is officially closed to outsiders (even Russians need special passes). Otherwise *marshrutki* run to Kyakhta from Ulan-Ude (*journey time: 3½hrs; tickets: RUB250*) via Novosélenginsk. The border crossing (see box *On to Mongolia* above) in the Sloboda district of Kyakhta, 2km to the south of the town proper, is open to foreigners; take a taxi or hitch a lift as you can't cross on foot.

WHERE TO STAY

Hotel Druzhba (11 rooms) ul Krupskaya 8; 91321. Virtually the only civilised place to stay, the basic Druzhba, near the Uspenskaya Church, boasts en-suite rooms & a café. $$–$$$

WHERE TO EAT Kyakhta still awaits its first Michelin star and visitors have very little to choose from. Basic options include the cheap **Sloboda Zakusochnaya**, a few steps from the border post in the Sloboda quarter, where you can fill up on the mainstays of Siberian and Buryat cuisine, and the **Troika Café**, opposite the museum.

WHAT TO SEE AND DO

Regional Museum (*ul Lenina 49;* 92333; ⊕ *10.00–18.00 Tue–Sun; adult RUB100*) Kyakhta's star attraction is a quirky but broad-ranging museum at the northern end of the main Lenin Street. One travel website describes this poorly funded institution as the 'Hermitage of the East', which may be going slightly too far, though it is one of the most interesting and full museums in Siberia. The musty rooms with creaky floors and 19th-century wooden display cabinets are crammed with exhibitions on the tea trade, local flora and fauna, expeditions led by Russian explorers, prehistory, the history of Kyakhta, ethnography (Buryats, Old Believers), Asian art brought back by Russian adventurers, Buddhism and Kyakhta's role in World War II. Sadly, all explanations are in Russian, but an English speaking guide, we were assured, can be arranged if you phone ahead or organise your visit through a tour company in Ulan-Ude.

Other places of interest Kyakhta's all-important mid-19th-century **trading arches** are situated around 300m south of the museum on Lenin Street. They still serve the purpose for which they were built, containing a number of shops (though none sells bricks of tea). Kyakhta's erstwhile wealth and civic pride can best be seen in its **Troitsky Cathedral** which, despite its current derelict state, is still an impressive and quite unexpected sight in this corner of Asia. Built in 1817, it is a fine example of Russian Neoclassicism and boasts a large cupola. Closed in 1930, there are plans to renovate the building to its former splendour. Currently,

Eastern Baikal and Southern Buryatiya KYAKHTA

5

Kyakhta's only working place of worship is the **Uspenskaya Church** to the south of the centre, another Neoclassical structure but with a seemingly ancient interior and an incense-infused Orthodox atmosphere.

SELENGA DELTA (ДЕЛЬТА РЕКИ СЕЛЕНГИ)

The Selenga River winds its way from central Mongolia via Ulaanbaatar and Ulan-Ude to release its waters into Lake Baikal at a large delta, 85km to the northwest of the Buryat capital. Along with the Baikalsk paper plant, the Selenga River is one of Baikal's biggest polluters, washing sewage and heavy metals from Mongolia (and Ulan-Ude) to the lake's shores. Its currents also bring with them millions of tons of sand which have, over the millennia, created a delta measuring over 500km². Its channels, islands and reed beds are home to 200 species of bird, and the spring and autumn months see an amazing five million migrating feathered friends call a flapping halt here. Tranquil vistas across the flat marshlands and birdwatching are the main tourist baits.

GETTING THERE If you're putting together a DIY tour, the best way of reaching the delta is by *marshrutka* from in front of Ulan-Ude railway station to the district town of Kabansk. There you will have to find transport into the delta proper. However, it's much better to take a tour from Ulan-Ude as you won't be heading into the delta blind nor messing around with awkward or non-existent public transport.

WHAT TO SEE AND DO Birdwatching is by far the greatest attraction in the delta and almost every tour agency in Ulan-Ude can arrange a trip, even for just one day. The **Kabansk Protected Area** measuring 12,000ha is the place to go, especially in May and again in late autumn when millions of birds rest here on their long migrations north and south. When certain species are incubating their eggs, no motorboat traffic is allowed into the protected area. Very knowledgeable local guides know where to look for stork, duck, tern, gulls, heron, eagles, harrier and various species of wader, but you may have to brush up on your Latin bird names as their English is limited. Russian-speaking ornithologists (everybody knows one) may want to get hold of a Book called *Birds of the Selenga Delta* (Птицы Дельты Селенги) by I V Fefelov (2001), the definitive guide.

The Kabansk Protected Area is part of the wider Baikal Biosphere Reserve (see page 32) but, somewhat inconveniently, the headquarters are located in relatively faraway Tankhoy (see page 120). The staff there can arrange accommodation in the delta, and guides. Alternatively contact any tour company in Ulan-Ude who all run trips for groups and individuals. For those with a serious interest in Baikal's ornithology, contact PR-Naturetours (*www.pr-naturetours.de*) in Germany who run superb expeditions to the Selenga Delta and many other locations around Lake Baikal.

NORTH OF THE SELENGA DELTA A washboard road extends north of the delta through small lakeside villages to two well known centres of R&R. The first is **Novy Enkheluk** (Новый Энхэлук) where the local **Enkheluk Resort** (✆ 3102 222 245; *www.enkhaluk.ru*; $–$$$) is regarded as one of the best in Buryatiya. Accommodation is of a high standard and you can even stay in a yurt. Ten bone-shaking kilometres further on comes the straggling village of **Sukhaya** (Сухая), another holiday hotspot with several large *turbazy*, one a huge and less-than-attractive timber complex belonging to the Sagaan Morin tour company. Other more attractive guesthouses can be booked through Baikal Naran Tour in Ulan-Ude (see *Local tour companies and helpers* on page 39).

The road ends a little further up the shore at the picturesque, weather-worn fishing village of **Zarechye** (Заречье) where there are some pleasant forest walks. Don't amble too far into the taiga, however, as once lost in there, you're unlikely to find your way out again. North of Zarechye there is nothing – no road, village or track for the next 65km until Gremyachinsk, making it one of the most inaccessible parts of the Baikal shoreline. Even the locals are afraid of venturing far into this lonely landscape where, it's said, there are more bears than pine cones on the trees.

GREMYACHINSK TO UST-BARGUZIN

The 115km stretch of shoreline between Gremyachinsk, where the road from Ulan-Ude meets Baikal, and Ust-Barguzin (see below) is one of the most popular among Russian holidaymakers, with numerous *turbazy* in and around the lakeside villages. While heaving with berucksacked Moscow students and assorted travellers from across the old USSR in the baking summer season (July/August), things are considerably quieter the rest of the year, leaving you to engage in carefree exploration. The area's beaches, lakes and forests make this one of the most attractive bits of Baikal for just getting sand between your toes, grilling meat on the beach and having an authentic Russian *turbaza* experience.

The Russian authorities have earmarked the southern section of this route as a special economic zone. This could mean huge investment in five-star hotels, watersports centres and ski resorts in the coming years. However, the decision to develop the area was taken years ago, and so far zilch has happened, apart from the welcome appearance of smooth tarmac on some sections of the road.

GETTING AROUND Official and ad hoc *marshrutki* ply the washboard/virgin asphalt road in both directions, facilitating relatively easy if somewhat unpredictable travel from one village to the next. Very often *marshrutki* drivers can be contacted on their mobiles, but only some locals know the numbers. Stand at the roadside anywhere along the route below, thumb extended, and it won't be long before a vehicle of some description offers you a (paid) lift. From Ulan-Ude to Ust-Barguzin the fare is RUB300, from which you can guesstimate other fares along the route.

THE ROUTE From Ulan-Ude the most easily accessible Baikal beach can be found at **Gremyachinsk** (Гремячинск), just feasible as a day trip off the Trans-Siberian. A long expanse of sandy beach extending northeast from the mouth of the delightfully named River Kika makes this one of the most popular resorts on the lake's shores. There are plenty of homestays around as well as food shops, a bank and a baker's. Away from the golden strand, the main attraction lies 10km inland in the shape of large **Lake Kotokel** (Озеро Котокель) whose sandy shores are lined with holiday camps where there's always a free bed going. At only 8m deep, Kotokel is considerably warmer than Lake Baikal, and bathing here is rarely an in-out blue-legs experience. **Monastyrsky Island** at the northern end of the lake used to serve as lonely home to a hermitage and church.

Some 20km northeast along the shore comes **Turka** (Турка), another popular venue for Russian shashlyk and vodka hols. The only manmade object of interest here is the unusual church, which was financed by Presbyterian Koreans. The northern bays of Lake Kotokel can be reached from here, or there are pleasant walks to secluded Baikal bays in either direction along the coast. Separated from Baikal by a stretch of pine forest, nearby **Goryachinsk** (Горячинск) is eastern Siberia's oldest health resort, where guests have been taking the thermal waters since the mid 18th century. You can bed down at the spa even if you haven't come for the cure.

A long stint on the blacktop through uninhabited taiga eventually delivers you to **Maksimikha** (Максимиха) at the southern end of the Barguzin Bay. With its sandy beaches, warm water and magnificent views of the Svyatoy Nos Peninsula (see below), the small village is one of the most attractive holiday hotspots on the east coast. Attracting Russian sun-seekers in their droves, it offers plentiful accommodation, and the setting makes this a more attractive alternative than Ust-Barguzin up the coast, especially if you just want to sizzle on the sand under the Siberian sun.

UST-BARGUZIN (УСТЬ-БАРГУЗИН) *Telephone code: 30131*

Dominated by a huge whaleback of rock called the Svyatoy Nos Peninsula, Ust-Barguzin is by far the largest settlement on Baikal's eastern shore and a superb launch-pad to some of its greatest experiences. The town itself, with its sandy streets, weather-silvered houses and rusting car ferry across the River Barguzin, is little to write home about, but the range of day excursion options to the lofty Svyatoy Nos Peninsula, the almost impenetrable Zabaikalsky National Park, the widescreen Barguzin Valley and the seal kingdom of the Ushkanie Islands make this a gateway to adventure.

HISTORY If you think Ust-Barguzin looks a bit too recent to have been founded in 1666, the reason is that until 1952 the town was in fact situated on the opposite bank of the Barguzin River. It was relocated lock, stock and illegal vodka distillery across the river due to rising water levels in Baikal caused by the building of the Angara Dam in Irkutsk. In the intervening three centuries the locals had got on very well, thank you, fishing, hunting and keeping their timber houses in good nick, while most of the action went on in Barguzin up the road. However, with the arrival of tourists in the area, things have swung the other way with most preferring to bunk down here rather than in dilapidated Barguzin.

GETTING THERE The only way to reach the town from the south is by occasional *marshrutka* or bus from Ulan-Ude (*journey time: 7hrs; tickets: RUB300*). The journey is torturously long, though it may improve in coming years thanks to the new ribbon of tarmac currently being laid along the shore. Surprisingly there are few Baikal views from the bus window. In summer you may be able to wangle your way aboard a boat from Olkhon Island on the opposite shore of Lake Baikal, but it's very hit-and-miss and can cost a small fortune if you hire it yourself. No-one has, as yet, hit on the idea of launching a trans-Baikal ferry service. Transport connections improve slightly when the lake freezes over and a well frequented ice road runs from here to Severobaikalsk. The ice also opens up another adventurous route, a trek across the lake from the most northerly point of Olkhon Island to the most southerly point of the Svyatoy Nos Peninsula, a distance of around 80km. Ask Jack Sheremetoff in Irkutsk (see Baikaler under *Local tour companies and helpers* on page 39) for details.

 WHERE TO STAY

⌂ **Beketov homestay** Bolnichny pereulok 9; ☏ 91574; e baikalfamily@mail.ru. National park ranger Alexander Beketov & his wife have transformed their garden into a tourist haven with 4 very comfortable log cabins & a relaxing Russian *banya*. Rates inc delicious home-cooked b/fast & dinner eaten around the family kitchen table. The couple run day-long tours to the top of Svyatoy Nos, along the Barguzin Valley, & winter seal-spotting trips out on to the ice as well as many others. There's nothing better than returning from a long day's trek to their hot *banya* & some hearty Siberian grub. They're usually out accompanying tourists & difficult to get hold of, so book through

Baikal Naran Tour in Ulan-Ude (see page 40). $$–$$$

🏠 **Hotel Salyut** (5 rooms) ul Lenina 16; ✆ 606 336. Cheap & cheerful guesthouse adjoining the 24hr shop. Rooms are basic & décor is busy. Staff can arrange trips into the Barguzin Valley for groups of up to 7. $$

🏠 **Lyzhnaya baza Dyush** (4 rooms, 10 beds) ul Stroitelnaya 7; ✆ 91303. This ski hostel, clearly recognisable from the huge snowflake hoisted in front of the grand entrance, has basic rooms with shared facilities, a kitchen & a common room. Despite the name (*lyzhnaya baza* means 'ski base'), it's open all year round. $

🏕 **Svyatoy Nos** Not an official campsite by any means, but the sand flats between Ust-Barguzin & the Svyatoy Nos Peninsula are a popular place to camp in the summer months, especially for young cash-strapped Russians.

✗ WHERE TO EAT

✗ **Poznaya Shik** Next to ferry quay, ul Lenina; ⏰ 10.00–22.00. Ultra-basic but clean greasy spoon serving low-budget Russian stodge for less than RUB15 a shot. Handwritten menu. $

✗ **24hr shop** ul Lenina 16. There's (thankfully) one in every town & Ust-Barguzin's open-all-hours grocery store is next to the post office.

OTHER PRACTICALITIES

✉ **Post office** ul Lenina 16. There's a telephone box outside.

National Park office Bolnichny pereulok 11; ✆ 91578. Can arrange guides for trips into the Zabaikalsky National Park.

WHAT TO SEE AND DO Ust-Barguzin has very few attractions of its own and is used by most as a base for exploring the surrounding area.

Banya Museum (*Bolnichny pereulok 9;* ✆ *91574;* e *baikalfamily@mail.ru;* ⏰ *on request*) At the time of research Alexander Beketov was in the process of creating a banya museum behind his home, including a rare 'black banya' (see box *Full steam ahead – the Russian banya* on page 98). Ring ahead for Alexander to show you around (usually evenings only).

Svyatoy Nos (Святой Нос) The Svyatoy Nos (which translates as 'Holy Nose') is a huge chunk of mountain range which looks as though it's broken away from the shore and is gently floating across the lake. Connected by mud and sand flats to the mainland, it only just deserves the name 'peninsula' and is one Angara Dam-style project away from being demoted to an island. Some 53km long and around 20km wide, it is part of the Zabaikalsky National Park (see below) and consists entirely of soaring snow-capped mountains reaching as high as 1,877m. Bears vastly outnumber humans on the Holy Nose, though you'd be lucky to ever see one. Guided jeep-trek tours to the top of the Svyatoy Nos can be booked in Ust-Barguzin and are an all-day deal, but if you're going it alone, you'll probably end up overnighting on the mountainside. Sturdy walking boots are a must, and make sure you carry warm and waterproof clothing and emergency rations. Guides carry rifles due to the large bear population, but most have never fired a shot in anger. Snowmelt provides drinkable water along the route.

Having skirted the edge of the sand flats to the base of the peninsula, the trek begins at a trailhead in the tiny hamlet of Glinka, where a sign in Russian and English (!) plots out the route ahead. The first 20 minutes are on soft pine needles but the going gets progressively steeper until you are zigzagging across scree. Truly show-stopping views open up above the tree line where the path becomes boulder-strewn and some scrambling is needed. At the top, where snow remains even in summer, you'll be richly rewarded with absolutely awe-inspiring 360° views across

5

the lake, over to Olkhon Island and down to the Ushkanie Islands – some of the best vistas around Baikal. The up-down trek takes around seven to eight hours for fit walker-climbers, covering a distance of around 10km over a 1,400m gain in altitude.

Ushkanie Islands (Ушкание острова)
One of the best places around Lake Baikal to spot seals at play is the Ushkanie Islands, 7km off the northern flank of the Svyatoy Nos Peninsula. This archipelago of four small islands – called Bolshoy (Big), Tonky (Slender), Krugly (Round) and Dolgy (Long) – form part of the Zabaikalsky National Park and can only be accessed by boat from Ust-Barguzin. As these vessels disturb the seals, the park charges a RUB1,000 fee in an attempt to keep visitor numbers down, and a time limit of one hour is in force. The fee plus boat and guide hire make this a pricey outing, but it's worth it to see the loveable, doe-eyed seals lounging on the rocks. The trip is perhaps the only chance you'll get to observe these adorable creatures in their natural habitat, so ask at the National Park office about sailings or book through Baikal Naran Tour in Ulan-Ude. Prices start at a whopping RUB5,600 per person.

Zabaikalsky National Park (Забайкальский Национальный Природный Парк)
Covering over 267,000ha, this well-maintained park includes the Ushkanie Islands, the Svyatoy Nos Peninsula and a huge area of forested mountains to the north of Ust-Barguzin. Created in 1986, the mainland part of the park receives few visitors and is subject to relatively strict protection. Virtually the only way in is with a park ranger, so ask at the national park offices in Ust-Barguzin (see above).

BARGUZIN (БАРГУЗИН) Telephone code: 30131

Little remains in this fading town of a few thousand souls to hint at the proud mercantile tradition, once-lively Jewish life and Decembrist links which Barguzin was once known for around the region. Lying at the foot of the wide and eye-bogglingly beautiful Barguzin Valley, it would make a well positioned base for exploring were there anywhere decent to stay. Most plump for Ust-Barguzin and visit Barguzin *en route* to or from the valley.

HISTORY The year 1648 saw the first Cossacks make it this far up the Barguzin River and establish a timber fort roughly where Barguzin lies today. The name Barguzin comes from the Bargut tribe of Buryats who inhabited the area long before the Russian settlers arrived, and of whose stock the mighty Genghis Khan came (his mother was born here). Due to its location a long way from anywhere, Barguzin took the fancy of the imperial authorities who used it as a place of exile for political prisoners, including among others the Decembrist Küchelbecker brothers. Mikhail and Wilhelm's claim to fame is that they were schoolmates with Pushkin, and Mikhail in particular contributed to raising the cultural niveau of the town he took as his own. He's buried in the local cemetery, as are many Jews exiled here from Poland in the mid-19th century – the iron stars of David and Hebrew grave inscriptions are all that remain of their once-thriving community. Following seven decades of Soviet rule and subsequent economic meltdown, today's Barguzin is a drowsy backwater with a few scraps of architecture and a goat-infested cemetery.

GETTING THERE Infrequent buses and *marshrutki* operate from Ulan-Ude with at least one leaving around 08.00 (*tickets: RUB350*). Whichever way you travel, the journey via Ust-Barguzin takes a derrière-numbing and brain-rattling eight hours.

WHAT TO SEE AND DO Barguzin's handful of 'attractions' can be viewed on a ten-minute stroll through the town. From the bus stop, walk along ul Krasnoarmeyskaya to see the old **bank** with its Doric columns rising in stark contrast to the low timber dwellings which surround it. Further along comes the large **church**, the first to be built on this side of Lake Baikal but these days looking a bit worse for wear. The street eventually brings you to a culture centre sporting a fine socialist realist mosaic and nearby a silver **Lenin statue** (why *do* they paint him silver?). Keep heading northeast to find Barguzin's most interesting sight, the **old cemetery** where Orthodox Russians are buried to the right, Jews to the left. Goats crop the grass between the cracked and toppling headstones, many with Hebrew inscriptions still visible, and a raised mound of earth is sometimes the only indication you are looking at a grave. In the Russian sector you'll find the tomb of Mikhail Küchelbecker and that of Zenon Svatoš, Czech founder of the Barguzin Nature Reserve and its director for almost 30 years (see box on page 144).

BARGUZIN VALLEY (БАРГУЗИНСКАЯ ДОЛИНА)

Stretching almost 200km from Barguzin in the south to Alla in the north, the magnificently remote and incredibly beautiful Barguzin Valley is one of the most attractive places anywhere around Baikal's shores. Defined to the west by a procession of abrupt peaks belonging to the Barguzinsky Mountains and to the east by lower, greener hills, this even, broad vale of salt lakes, pastures and flower-filled meadows, punctuated by tiny timber villages, has a timeless appeal.

Of the 30,000 people who call the valley home, some are indigenous Evenks whose ancestors have lived here for thousands of years. They can be encountered mostly in the north, while Buryats dominate most villages throughout the valley. Cut off from the soothing meteorological influence of the lake's waters, the climate here is one of the most extreme in the region, with oven-hot summers and winter temperatures as low as –50°C.

Visiting this huge chunk of northern Buryatiya without a guide and car is not easy with next to no public transport available and large distances to travel. Two roads run the entire length of the valley; the eastern route passes through isolated villages and past petroglyphs and odd rock formations before hitting a huge empty landscape. The western route hugs the base of the mountain range all the way from Barguzin to Alla via Kurumkan. Buses from Ulan-Ude take the western road as far as Kurumkan.

HISTORY This fertile valley has been inhabited for millennia, evidence for which are the numerous petroglyphs and shamanic sites which dot the landscape. As locals will soon have you know, Genghis Khan's mother, Oulen, is said to have come from these parts, though this has only been deduced from her tribal allegiance. The first European to set eyes on the valley was Semyon Skorochod, who arrived at the head of a band of Cossacks in 1643. Settlers mostly stayed away from the valley – a long way from anywhere and with a harsh climate – except during a mini-gold rush in the 19th century. The once-nomadic Evenks of the valley were collectivised by the Soviets and have mostly lost their traditional way of life.

GETTING THERE AND AROUND Both Barguzin (*journey time: 8hrs; tickets: RUB350*) and Kurumkan (*journey time: 10hrs; tickets: RUB500*) are linked to Ulan-Ude by early morning bus or *marshrutka* with perhaps a couple of further *marshrutki* making the journey if there's sufficient demand. From the north a new road will link Kurumkan with Novy Uoyan on the BAM Railway, though whether buses will ply

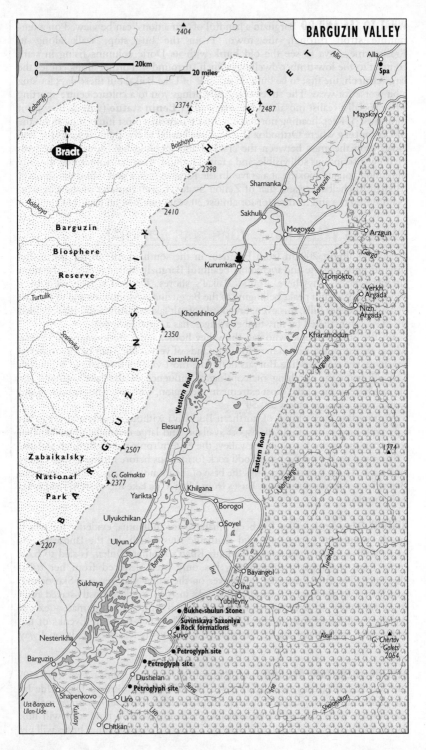

BARGUZIN VALLEY

0 [===] 20km
0 [===] 20 miles

N
Bradt

2404

Kabanya

2374
2487

Bolshaya

Mayskiy

Bolshaya

2398

K

Shamanka

H

Barguzin

R

Barguzin
Biosphere
Reserve

2410

Sakhuli

E

Mogoyto

Arzgun

Garga

S

Kurumkan

Turtulik

Tomokto

Verkh.
Argada
Nizh
Argada

I

Sosnovika

Khonkhino

Kharamodun

2350

N

Sarankhur

Argada

S

Western Road

K

Elesun

Eastern Road

1774

Zabaikalsky

2507

Ulan-Burga

National

G. Golmakta
2377

Khilgana

Park

Yarikta

Borogol

B

Ulyukchikan

Soyel

Turokch

Ulyun

Barguzin

2207

Bayangol

Ina

Iha

Sukhaya

Yubileyny

● Bukhe-shulun Stone
● Suvinskaya Saxoniya
● Rock formations

Akul

Nesterikha

Suvo

● Petroglyph site

G. Chertov
Golets
2064

Barguzin

● Petroglyph site

Dushelan

Suna

● Petroglyph site

Shapenkovo

Uro

Ina

Ust-Barguzin,
Ulan-Ude

Kulutay

Uro

Sholokokon

Chitkan

142

this route is not yet known. Once in the valley it's almost impossible to travel around by public transport unless you're willing to spend a day in every location; most visitors take day trips out of Ust-Barguzin or tours of the entire valley with an Ulan-Ude tour company. Expect to pay around RUB2,400 for an all-day excursion from Ust-Barguzin as far as the village of Suvo, meals included.

WHERE TO STAY There are very limited formal digs in the Barguzin Valley and you may have to ask around villages for a homestay if you've not arranged anything in advance. The **Tuyaa hotel** (*ul Budaina;* 🖰 *30149 41136*) in Kurumkan is a basic affair; otherwise it may be possible to get a bed at the Buddhist Temple. In Alla your best bet for a night between sheets is the tiny **spa** (🖰 *30149 42039*). Otherwise bringing a tent for a spot of wild camping makes good sense.

WHAT TO SEE AND DO

Eastern road Heading east out of Barguzin, the first village you come to is **Uro** (Уро), beyond which local guides can show you 3,000-year-old red-painted **petroglyphs**. Another 30km north lies the picture-perfect village of **Suvo** (Суво), set against the **Suvinskaya Saxoniya rock formations** (Сувинская Саксония, Suvo Saxony), so named for their vague similarity to an area on the Czech–Saxony border. Explore the oddly twisted and stacked boulders by climbing to the top of the hill above the village where show-stoppingly widescreen views of the valley's expanse, backed dramatically by snowy saw-tooth peaks, open up before you. A little further along the road look out for the **Bukhe-shulun** (Бухэ-шулун) or Ox Stone, so called for its shape, resembling a huge hoof. The tangle of blue and white rags tied to posts round about mark it out as an important shamanist site. From here a rough, unfrequented and utterly lonely road continues for another 110 desolate kilometres to **Maysky** (Майский) at the top of the valley, where hot springs bubble from the earth.

Western road Leaving Barguzin on the busier western route, you are accompanied for the entire journey by salt flats, lakes and twisting rivers on the right, and a wall of mountain on the left. The uneven road passes through tiny Buryat villages *en route* to **Kurumkan** (Курумкан), the largest settlement in the valley and an administrative centre with 5,000 inhabitants. The highlight here is the **Gandan She Duvlin Buddhist temple** which doubles up as an international meditation centre, attracting Buddhists from around Russia. Set against a picturesque alpine scene, it's little wonder many find this an ideal meditation retreat. There's also a small regional **museum** (*ul Shkolnaya*) in town and a couple of low-grade *pozy* joints. Some 50km north of Kurumkan lies the tiny town of **Alla** (Алла), 7km away from which hot springs rise from the earth and a small spa offers beds for the night. This is just one of 19 mini-spas in this part of the valley, though most are incredibly remote and known only to locals. Due to its Evenk minority, Alla also boasts an **Evenk Centre** (🖰 *30149 95371*) where local handicrafts can be purchased.

DAVSHA (ДАВША)

Tiny Davsha may win the prize for the most remote and difficult-to-reach settlement on the lake's shores. Conceived as a village for researchers, scientists and those tending to the **Barguzin Reserve**, it was deemed too expensive to maintain in 2005, and a year later most of the inhabitants were moved elsewhere. The only way here is by supply ship from Nizhneangarsk or by chartering a boat in Ust-Barguzin. Apart from (1) an opportunity to get as close as you ever might

ZENON SVATOŠ

Born to a Czech father and Russian mother in Novorossiysk in southern Russia, Zenon Svatoš was a colourful character and a devoted zoologist. Raised in Simferopol in Crimea, his education took him to St Petersburg where he worked in the Zoology Department of the Academy of Sciences. Having taken part in two 1912 expeditions to east Africa and to the island of Spitzbergen, the latter almost costing him his life, in 1913 Zenon said farewell to St Petersburg for the last time and joined a team of scientists on a trip to Lake Baikal. Their task was to assess sable numbers following the passing of a new imperial law protecting the animal. He never left, setting up the Barguzin Reserve in 1916 and managing it until 1945. Sable numbers in the reserve have increased over the last century from a mere 40 in total to over 40 per 1,000ha, thanks largely to the efforts of one devoted Czech.

wish to a hungry bear and (2) the settlement's tiny **museum**, the obvious attraction is the Barguzin Reserve, which extends in every direction away from the lake. There's a **guesthouse** for the odd tourist that does make it here.

6

Northern Baikal

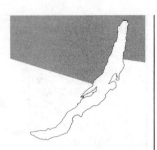

Bear-infested, frequently shaken by earthquakes and enduring winter temperatures of –40°C, you'd be excused for regarding the northern reaches of Lake Baikal as a place to avoid. But those who do venture to this remote, mountainous outpost are rewarded with some of the most breathtaking vistas, untouched places of natural beauty and unforgettable Baikal experiences. Although ever greater numbers of visitors are stepping off the train at Severobaikalsk or flying into Nizhneangarsk, the whole region remains a virtually undiscovered paradise for wilderness hikers, climbers and the odd spa fanatic, well away from any beaten track.

Although Russian settlement of Lake Baikal began in the north in the mid 17th century, the more accessible south naturally soon took over. Nizhneangarsk and Baikalskoe remained lonely communities almost cut off from the outside world for centuries, but this all changed in the 1970s when the Soviets decided to construct a railway line (the Baikalo-Amurskaya Magistral or BAM) from Tayshet on the Trans-Siberian to the Pacific coast (see box on page 150). The project brought thousands of engineers, labourers, technicians and their families from all corners of the USSR into the region. Severobaikalsk appeared almost overnight and has grown into the most important town on the northern shores, inhabited by a jumble of nationalities from just about every former republic of the Soviet Union. Despite recent settlement and the arrival of the railway, the landscapes and the lake itself have been less affected by human activity than the more industrialised and inhabited south.

For centuries before the arrival of the Russian Cossacks, the north was home to the Evenks, a nomadic people who lived peacefully in the taiga, hunting in winter, fishing in summer and breeding reindeer for meat and hides. Their traditional way of life, which some claim they had led for over three millennia, came to an abrupt end during the Stalinist collectivisations of the 1930s, and their tepees disappeared from the landscape, probably forever.

The region also includes the virtually uninhabited northeast coast, which can only be reached by boat in summer and ice road in winter. You'll need special permits to land there by boat (available from the information centre in Severobaikalsk) but these are waived when the lake is frozen over. Apart from the untouched natural beauty and stunningly deserted shores, the only two attractions here are the small spa at Khakusy and beautiful but hard-to-reach Lake Frolikha.

SEVEROBAIKALSK (СЕВЕРОБАЙКАЛЬСК) *Telephone code: 30130*

Had anyone travelled to Severobaikalsk's lakeside location a short 35 years ago, thick taiga, a few bears and Lake Baikal slapping at the shore is just about all they would have discovered. Established as recently as 1974 by workers building the BAM Railway, Severobaikalsk has grown into the largest town on the banks of Lake

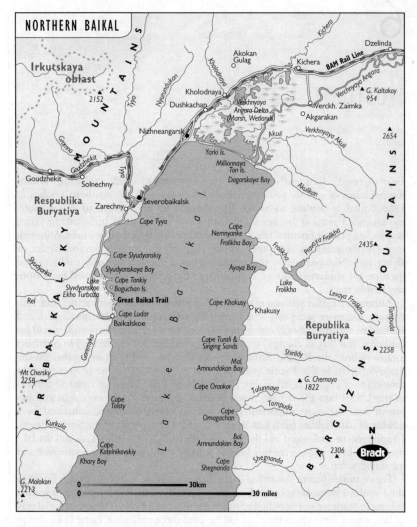

Baikal, Buryatiya's 'second city' and one of the newest settlements in Siberia. The town centre may be plagued by earthquake-proof Soviet-era blocks, but unattractive Severobaikalsk serves as the best base to explore the stunningly beautiful and uninhabited mountains and river valleys to the north and west, and is preferable to sprawling and less traveller-friendly Nizhneangarsk.

HISTORY If there was no BAM, there would be no Severobaikalsk, which started life as a site where building materials were stored for use on the new railway. In 1974 town planners from Leningrad (hence the name of the main thoroughfare – Leningradsky prospekt) were brought in to erect the streets of grey tremor-proofed blocks where most of the 30,000 locals dwell. Throughout the late 1970s and 1980s the population swelled as people arrived from all over the USSR and even Communist eastern Europe to do their bit on one of the greatest construction projects of the century – to push the railway 4,000km across inhospitable virgin wilderness to the Pacific. Severobaikalsk hit hard times in 1991 as the completion of the railway coincided with the collapse of the USSR. Still a railway town through and through, there's much nostalgia around for the pioneering spirit which brought many of the town's inhabitants to this remote outpost.

GETTING THERE AND AWAY Most travellers arrive in the north's main town by train from Irkutsk, Moscow or less often from points east along the BAM such as Komsomolsk-na-Amure and Tynda. The only other (and least likely) way to reach Severobaikalsk from Irkutsk by land is by combining road and rail travel via Bratsk. *Marshrutki* and the odd bus take at least 11 tortuous hours to reach Bratsk and it's another 17 hours by train to Severobaikalsk. You may also have to wait in Bratsk to get tickets, which lengthens the journey even further, though it's still shorter than the 36-hour trip by train.

By hydrofoil On Tuesdays and Fridays from mid-June until the end of August a hydrofoil runs all the way from Irkutsk to Severobaikalsk via Listvyanka and Olkhon Island (*journey time: 13hrs; tickets: RUB2,000*) with departures around 09.00 from the *Raketa* hydrofoil station near the Angara Dam. Boats return on Wednesdays and Saturdays at around 08.00.

By air By far the most comfortable way to make the trip north is to take a flight from either Irkutsk or Ulan-Ude to Nizhneangarsk. These operate around three to five times a week and tickets cost from RUB3,000. Flight times are around an hour for both flights; delays are frequent.

By train Nizhneangarsk can be reached by BAM train but the journey is hardly worth the hassle and most will take the hourly *marshrutka* 103 (*journey time: 30mins; tickets: RUB34*) which leaves from outside Severobaikalsk's futuristic railway station.

GETTING AROUND It's unlikely you will need to use the town's system of *marshrutki* unless you are particularly lazy and don't want to walk to the BAM Museum.

TOURIST INFORMATION Severobaikalsk has no less than two bona fide information centres, both operated by the enthusiastic Maryasov family. The first is a small blue and yellow kiosk just outside the railway station (⊕ *Jun–Aug 09.00–19.00 Mon–Sat*); the other, bearing the grand title of Baikal Hospitality Centre, is just off the main square (*Leningradsky prospekt 9,* ☎ *914 875 9818;* ⊕ *10.00–18.00 Mon–Fri, 10.00–15.00 Sat*) and is open all year round.

🏠 **WHERE TO STAY** Severobaikalsk has sufficient cheap accommodation to make hunting down a homestay unnecessary.

🏠 **Baikal Resort** (6 rooms, 8 cabins) pereulok Neptunsky 3; ☎ 23950, 22395; e kruiz@yandex.ru; www.baikal-kruiz.narod.ru. Those looking for a little comfort & privacy should try this grandly named guesthouse near the lake, where relatively well-furnished rooms have en-suite bathrooms but the row of snug timber cabins outside do not. There's a handy guest kitchen, communal area & billiards room on the premises. $$$

🏠 **Baikal Service** ul Promyschlennaya 18; ☎ 23912, 32473; f 22644. This resort set in an area of pine wood to the northeast of town has accommodation for every pocket & level of comfort requirement. Choose from a comfortable guesthouse, timber cabins, summer yurts, basic student hostel or even just a bit of grass where you can pitch a tent. A small café serving basic dishes means you won't have to keep traipsing into town to eat. $–$$$

🏠 **Zolotaya Rybka** (14 rooms) ul Sibirskaya 14; ☎ 21134; e golden_fish89@mail.ru; www.hotel-golden-fish.ru. Well signposted from the main road, the friendly 'Golden Fish' is excellent value for money, with well-appointed rooms, a fully equipped kitchen & friendly owners. $$

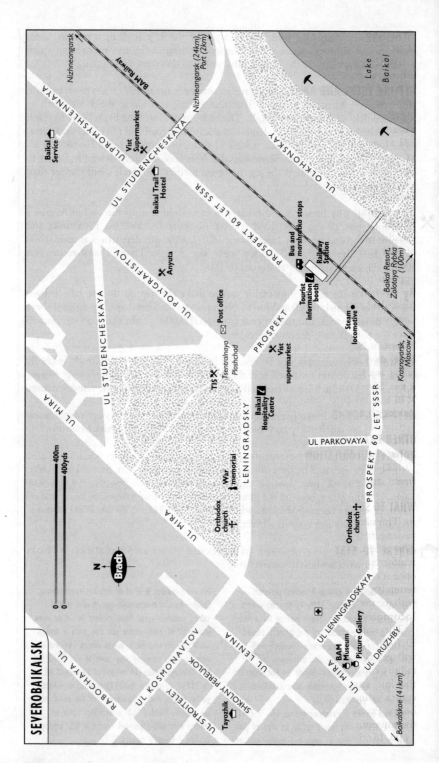

SEVEROBAIKALSK

Nizhneangarsk

BAM Railway

Nizhneangarsk (24km), Port (2km)

UL PROMYSHLENNAYA

Baikal Service

Vist Supermarket

UL STUDENCHESKAYA

Baikal Trail Hostel

PROSPEKT 60 LET SSSR

UL POLYGRAFISTOV

Anyuta

Post office

UL STUDENCHESKAYA

UL MIRA

Tentralnaya Ploshchad

Tis

War memorial

Orthodox church

LENINGRADSKY

Bus and marshrutka stops

Railway Station

Baikal Resort, Zolotaya Rybka (100m)

Tourist information booth

Steam locomotive

PROSPEKT

Vist supermarket

Baikal Hospitality Centre

UL PARKOVAYA

Krasnoyarsk, Moscow

PROSPEKT 60 LET SSSR

UL OLKHONSKAY

Lake Baikal

Orthodox church

UL LENINGRADSKAYA

Picture Gallery

BAM Museum

UL MIRA

UL DRUZHBY

Baikalskoe (4 km)

UL LENINA

SHKOLNY PERREULOK

UL KOSMONAVTOV

UL STROITELEY

Tayozhik

RABOCHAYA UL

Bracht

N

0 400m
0 400yds

148

🏠 **Baikal Trail Hostel** (3 dorms) ul Studentcheskaya 12, apt 16; 📞 23860 or 9148 759818; e kolonok2004@y&ex.ru; www.baikaltrailhostel.com. Severobaikalsk's 1st & only hostel is situated on the 1st floor of an apt block opposite the Vist Supermarket to the north of the town centre. It was originally set up as informal accommodation for volunteers building the Great Baikal Trail, but in 2008 the owners opened it up to travellers. Rooms are large & bunks are not packed in like sardines. There's a fully equipped kitchen & a bathroom with a washing machine. Price inc b/fast. Book early through Hostelworld as this place is, understandably,

a summer hotspot. 💲

🏠 **Tayozhik** (3 dorms) pereulok Shkolny 11; 📞 20323; e davan2001@mail.ru. This dorm used by students on ecology field trips, volunteers working on the Great Baikal Trail & wilderness trekkers exploring the surrounding mountains is housed in a part of the School for Tourism & Ecological Education. Dorms are basic but cozy, & guests can use a communal kitchen & the school's internet & library facilities. The headmaster of the school, Mr Maryasov, is one of the most knowledgeable guides in the area. 💲

WHERE TO EAT Most visitors to Severobaikalsk self-cater or rely on their hotel or guesthouse to provide sustenance. If you are cooking your own, the town's chain of **Vist supermarkets** (*Leningradsky prospect;* ⊕ *08.30–21.00*) is the best place to source supplies. There's another handy store (*Studentcheskaya ul;* ⊕ *08.30–20.00*) opposite the Baikal Trail Hostel. Self-catering can be a better option than visiting the town's eateries as these tend to fill with bored, staring youths in flat caps (described by one traveller as a surreal Siberian mutation of *The Jocks and the Geordies*).

✗ **Anyuta** ul Poligrafistov 3A; ⊕ 18.00–02.00. Evening dinner spot housed in a new red brick building amid high-rise blocks at the northern end of town. **$$**
✗ **TIS** Inside the Railway Culture Centre, Tsentralny ploshchad; ⊕ 12.00–15.00 & 18.00–02.00. A

sound option for some appetising grub by day (including some veggie dishes) or a few late beers. Provides at least a bit of nightlife for Severobaikalsk's jaded youth. **$$**

OTHER PRACTICALITIES
✉ **Post office** Leningradsky prospekt 6;
⊕ 10.00–19.00 Mon–Fri, 10.00–17.00 Sat.
Provides cheap internet access.

WHAT TO SEE AND DO Far and away the architectural highlight of Severobaikalsk is its Thunderbirds-style 1970s **railway station** which welcomes arriving BAM passengers with its confident lines. Severobaikalsk's pride and joy and virtual *raison d'être* is best viewed from Leningradsky prospekt from where its majestic sweep of reinforced concrete, Russia's favourite building material, reminds outsiders of the once self-assured days of the USSR. It's no coincidence that the building's form reminds people of a ski jump; the architect was attempting to ingratiate himself with the then mayor, a keen ski jumper. Next to the station stands a restored **steam locomotive**.

The railway theme continues at the **BAM Museum** (*ul Mira 2;* 📞 *21663;* ⊕ *10.00–13.00 & 14.00–17.00 Tue–Sat; adult RUB50*) containing exhibitions that will get BAM buffs hot under the anorak. Exhibits include workers' medals, railway construction tools, a ticket for the first service on the Buryatiya stretch of the line and grainy black and white photos illustrating the happy days of comradeship the BAM workers enjoyed. The rest is an eclectic mix of mammoth bones, Evenk skis and the ubiquitous mineral samples. Around the corner from the museum, drop by at the **Picture Gallery** (*ul Druzhby 40;* ⊕ *10.00–13.00 & 14.00–16.00*) where local artists display and sell their work.

Anyone with a passion for travel knows the Trans-Siberian Railway. But very few will have heard of its mega-branch line, the BAM (Baikalo-Amurskaya Magistral) which leaves the main route at Tayshet, 600km northwest of Irkutsk. From here it rattles across the mighty Angara River at Bratsk, then flirts with the northern shores of Lake Baikal before embarking on an incredible journey across empty mountain country to the Pacific Ocean. The BAM's tunnels, embankments and bridges are regarded as one of the greatest feats of Soviet track-laying engineering, but the route is virtually unknown in the West.

The railway was begun in the 1930s, but the tracks were ripped up to help with the Soviet Union's war effort. Driven by a fear of China, to whose borders the Trans-Siberian passed uncomfortably close, it wasn't until the 1970s and 1980s that Young Communist brigades began slashing their way through the taiga to re-lay the tracks and forge a new route through incredibly inhospitable back country. Looking at the map, the BAM really goes from nowhere to nowhere, passing through nowhere on the way. You may think it was built to link up the towns it serves, but these were established by workers from all the Soviet republics who had come to build the railway! The project cost billions of roubles and was one of the contributing factors in the economic collapse of the USSR. The downfall of Soviet rule coincided with the launch of the first services, and the region's economic meltdown turned the entire project into a 4,300km-long white elephant almost overnight.

Only a handful of passenger trains a day now ply the BAM, but a journey along its tracks is a truly unforgettable travel experience. The nostalgic 1970s towns along its route are real throwbacks to Soviet days and have changed little over the past 20 years. The best stop by far is Severobaikalsk, though Tynda and Komsomolsk-na-Amure further down the line are also interesting places to get off and explore. On board, lonely snow-flecked mountain vistas open up in your carriage window as the locomotive fights its way across nameless landscapes. Westerners are thin on the ground, the off-the-beaten-track towns unprepared for tourists and the conditions in every season harsh.

Severobaikalsk's two **Orthodox churches** are worth a look if you're passing. The new church on Leningradsky prospect had yet to be consecrated when we visited but already sported two impressive gilt onion domes. The older timber church on ul Truda is a humbler, temporary-looking affair surrounded by a tall fence, presumably so that no-one carts it off for firewood. It's only open during services (⊕ *18.00 Sat, 09.00 Sun, 18.00 Tue*). Cross the railway line and pick your way through a wooded area to reach the shore of Lake Baikal where a sandy **beach** arches northwards.

NIZHNEANGARSK (НИЖНЕАНГАРСК) Telephone code: 30130

The most northerly settlement on Baikal's shores, 24km northeast of Severobaikalsk, Nizhneangarsk is a sprawling, untidy place with no real central focus. From the airport to where the road leaves the village for Severobaikalsk, several parallel thoroughfares extend for almost 6km. Though more attractive than Severobaikalsk, there are few places to stay and visitor infrastructure is lacking. Even the village's BAM station cannot be compared with the architectural innovation of its newer upstart neighbour. Despite the recent growth of Severobaikalsk, Nizhneangarsk is still the administrative centre of the North Baikal District.

Nearby attractions include Yarki Island, a spit of land dividing Lake Baikal from the delta of the Verkhnaya Angara River, the Evenk village of Kholodnaya and the remains of Akokan Gulag.

HISTORY Now upstaged in every respect by Severobaikalsk, Nizhneangarsk once had this entire end of Lake Baikal to itself. In fact, from the appearance of the first wooden *ostrog* (established by Cossack explorers Semyon Skorokhod and Vasily Kolesnik in the 1640s) until the arrival of the first BAM workers, Nizhneangarsk enjoyed over three centuries of fishing, sable hunting and utter isolation. Only the clank and thump of the BAM navvies woke the town from its slumber, though for some reason this never became the railway centre it could have been. The decision was taken sometime in the 1970s to build a brave new world in concrete further down the tracks, a fact many in Nizhneangarsk still resent.

GETTING THERE
By *marshrutka* There are many ways of reaching Nizhneangarsk but most arrive on the local *marshrutka* 103 (*departs: hourly; journey time: 30mins; tickets: RUB34*) from outside Severobaikalsk railway station.

By hydrofoil Twice weekly summer hydrofoils (*departs: Tue & Fri*) from Irkutsk via Listvyanka and Olkhon Island terminate here (*journey time: 13hrs; tickets: RUB2,000*) with boats returning on Wednesday and Sunday. If you're arriving by rail, the Moscow–Tynda service No 076 stops here three to four times a week, as do local *elektrichki* from Severobaikalsk, Olongdo and Taksimo.

By air Nizhneangarsk, to the surprise of many, has its very own airport! Flights from Irkutsk and Ulan-Ude land and take off around five times a week with fares starting at around RUB3,000. Expect long delays, cancellations and general confusion.

LOCAL TOUR COMPANY
109 Meridian ul Rabochaya 143 (airport); ✆ 30130 47700; e baikalmeridian@mail.ru; www.109meridian.ru; ⏰ 10.00–19.00 Sun–Fri. Based next to the snack bar at Nizhneangarsk's tiny airport, this professionally run tour company offers boat trips on Lake Baikal & up the Verkhnaya Angara River, as well as excursions to Kholodnaya, Baikalskoe, Dzelinda & Akokan. Prices start at around RUB600 pp & normally inc a simple packed lunch. No English is spoken in the office, but English-speaking guides can be hired for trips.

🏠 **WHERE TO STAY** The overwhelming majority stay in Severobaikalsk and visit Nizhneangarsk on day trips. Due to the size of the village, homestays are difficult to track down. If you're really stuck, try asking at 109 Meridian (see page 40) at the airport, or at the regional administration building (*ul Rabochaya*).

🏠 **Gostinny Dom** (11 rooms) ul Rabochaya 10; ✆ 22206. A stone's throw from Lake Baikal, the town's only bona fide guesthouse has comfortable, cosy en-suite rooms, some with TV & bathroom. For RUB1,600 for a dbl, this is a pretty good deal. $$$

✖ **WHERE TO EAT** Nizhneangarsk has precious few places to eat, though when we visited grand plans were afoot to open a restaurant in the town. This may or may not have happened by the time you get there.

✖ **Airport snack bar** ul Rabochaya 143 (airport); ⏰ 09.00–17.00. The small cafeteria within the airport building does a good line in *chebureki* & fizzy drinks. Open even when no flights are due. $

✗ **Baikalsky Bereg** ul Pobedy 53. This place could be one of hundreds across the region – scuffed lino floor, Formica tables & chairs, a hand-written menu of glutinous Siberian *pelmeni, plov* & *pozy,* plastic plates, cups & cutlery & net curtains at the windows. But the food is honestly prepared & inexpensive, & the location on the shore of Lake Baikal is pretty enough. Marshrutki stop outside. **$**

WHAT TO SEE AND DO

Museum (*Pereulok Shkolny 3; ⊕ on request; adults RUB50*) Nizhneangarsk's only tourist attraction is a quirky little museum housed in classrooms 8, 11 and 12 of the art block at the local brick-built school. The colourful 'curator' is an eccentric former headmistress who must be summoned on her mobile to let you in. Whether you understand Russian or not, you will be subjected to her rather OTT and somewhat scary Stalinist-era lecture/performance on the village's history, before being allowed to view the displays under your own steam. Exhibits include mock-ups of Evenk tepees (called *chums*), tens of Russian-language folders on all aspects of Nizhneangarsk's history (individual families, BAM, Cossacks) and a whole room dedicated to the 'Great Patriotic War'. But by far the most telling exhibit is kept obscured by the overseer of this private fiefdom – a portrait of Stalin, lovingly concealed behind a curtain.

Banya (*ul Rabochaya 127; RUB500 per hour*) After all that hiking in the taiga why not take a well-earned steam and scrub at this quite unexpectedly modern sauna complex near the airport.

Yarki Island and most northerly point of Lake Baikal Nizhneangarsk lies just a couple of kilometres shy of Lake Baikal's most northerly point. From the town, a large artificial spit of land leads to Yarki Island, linking it with the shore and protecting natural habitats around the mouth of the Verkhnyaya Angara River from big waves and storms. At the end of this dike a monument is planned to mark the lake's most northerly point (though squabbles continue about exactly what form this should take).

Getting there The only way to reach it is to walk along the dyke from Nizhneangarsk, a distance of around 5km. Many consider the views of the lake, the wooded hills lining its shores and the saw-toothed mountains rearing up behind the most beautiful in the entire Lake Baikal region.

Akokan Gulag Many speak of Siberia as the Land of the Gulag, but despite this reputation, visitors rarely see any hard evidence that these places really existed. Communities would very often prefer to forget this chapter of Russian history and certainly don't want foreign visitors poking around and asking awkward questions. As yet no tour company has come up with a 'Gulag Tour'.

One exception is Akokan, around 20km northeast of Nizhneangarsk, which Colin Thubron visited and described in his book *In Siberia*. Mica had been mined here in the early 19th century, but it wasn't until it began to be used in radios that the mine shafts were opened up fully. Between 1929 and 1932 around 200 prisoners laboured here in inhumane conditions, though they still managed to launch a rebellion in 1930, which saw many escape into the taiga. Mica mining lost its economic value in 1932, the mineshafts were flooded and the Gulag left to rot. Enough remains today to make the trip worthwhile, usually in combination with a visit to the nearby village of Kholodnaya. It's just possible that you might find the mine yourself, but going with a guide from Nizhneangarsk or Severobaikalsk will save you a whole lot of trouble.

Kholodnaya This ramshackle village some 15km northeast of Nizhneangarsk is one of the few places around Lake Baikal where you are likely to encounter Evenk culture in a formal, organised setting. The community was created when semi-nomadic Evenks from the surrounding taiga were forcibly concentrated in one place by the Soviets and made to live in houses, work in collectives and renounce their nomadic way of life, which the authorities regarded as backwards and out of kilter with the new workers' paradise.

Turn up unannounced in Kholodnaya (whose name fittingly means 'cold') and you'll see very little. Tour companies from the two big towns can arrange visits to the school museum, tours of the handicrafts centre and trips out to see reindeer herds.

BAIKALSKOE (БАЙКАЛЬСКОЕ)

Some 45km south of Severobaikalsk lies the picture-perfect fishing village of Baikalskoe, a collection of typical Siberian timber houses gathered around the mouth of the River Rel. The village enjoys a dramatic location, fronted by the watery expanse of the lake and backed by snow-covered peaks (perfect *feng shui*, some would say). High cliffs to the north provide incredible views of the whole scene (see *Hiking from Baikalskoe* page 154). The mainstay of village life here today is *omul* fishing, while some villagers commute into Severobaikalsk to work. The cultural epicentre is the large school, which also contains a single-room museum.

The inhabitants of Baikalskoe are many years from realising the full potential of their humble settlement as a tourist attraction, and visitor infrastructure is virtually non-existent – surely one of the village's most endearing features.

HISTORY Established by Cossacks in 1643 on meadowland used by the native Evenks for summer grazing, Baikalskoe predates now-dominant Severobaikalsk by over three centuries. As the curator of the school museum will tell you, the village has chopped and changed names over the centuries, going from Letniki to Goremyka and ending up as Baikalskoe in 1939. The gory, blood-soaked *nerpovka* (seal cull) played, and still occasionally plays, a critical role in Baikalskoe's existence, as it once represented a vital source of meat, skins and fat. Thankfully the practice is severely restricted in these times of environmental protection, and it's been many years since the village folk were unleashed on a bloodthirsty bludgeoning spree.

In the early 20th century Baikalskoe was also a thriving fish processing centre, attracting workers from across the region, but prosperity was short-lived. Today it's little more than a drowsy backwater at the end of the road, though the village did see a mini-revival during the short period of construction on the BAM railway, when it supplied the workers and new towns with sustenance.

GETTING THERE

By *marshrutka* *Marshrutki* depart from Severobaikalsk railway station daily at 08.00 and 17.00, returning from Baikalskoe at 09.00 and 18.00, thus making a day trip simple to plan.

By guided tour Tour companies and helpers in Severobaikalsk and Nizhneangarsk are only too willing to arrange private transfers and guides. Prices start at around RUB2,000. A taxi costs a minimum of RUB500 each way plus waiting time.

WHERE TO STAY Ask at the school about homestays or enquire around the village if the school is closed, but do be careful with whom you bed down for the night as numerous Baikalskoe families have a drink problem. The headmaster of the school has been known to let groups sleep at the school itself, but this cannot be relied upon.

✖ WHERE TO EAT While Baikalskoe has no café, several grocery stores keep the village in basic foodstuffs, meaning you won't go hungry. The easiest shop to find is probably Berezka near the church.

WHAT TO SEE AND DO Baikalskoe's informal **School Museum** (*pereulok Shkolny;* ⊕ *10.00–16.00; adult RUB100*) displays a fascinating collection of artefacts and themed folders, but if your Russian's not up to much, you'll need a translator. On arrival at the school, find the secretary's office or any teacher, who will arrange for you to visit. The curator is a teacher and you may have to wait until she finishes her class before you can enter. The most intriguing part of the 'tour' is handling Stone Age tools belonging to hunter-gatherers who inhabited the region 25,000 years ago; the Russian-only folder on the *nerpovka* is also an eye-opener.

Apart from its dirt lanes of wooden houses with their carved, blue-painted picture windows, the only other 'attraction' here is the timber **Church of St Inokent** down by the shore. As you'll learn at the museum, during the decades of Communist rule the building was used as a school and a cultural centre, but reverted to its intended purpose two decades ago. Some of the original pre-Revolution icons can also be viewed at the museum.

HIKING FROM BAIKALSKOE An 18km hike along the Great Baikal Trail (see box on page 105) from Baikalskoe to the Ekho Turbaza by cold Lake Slyudyanskoe is feasible without a guide as the route traces the shoreline for most of the way and is relatively well marked (follow the blue spots). However, without a knowledgeable local you'll be lucky to find the faint petroglyphs tucked away in awkward places along the cliff faces. The route heads uphill out of Baikalskoe towards the TV antenna, following the cliff edge. Look back as you ascend for amazing views of the village huddling against a backdrop of snowy mountains. The path skirts the tops of the cliffs sporting the above-mentioned petroglyphs, then passes through woodlands of larch and pine, occasionally dipping down to secluded beaches or following the waterline itself. Look out for the black heads of seals bobbing in the water. Tiny Boguchan Island is one of the high points of the hike, as is a picnic stop high up on the cliffs or down by the gently lapping lake. Having arrived at the cosy **Ekho Turbaza** (✆ *30130 20323; RUB500 per bed*), stay for the night and a spot of very chilly swimming in the lake, or push 4km further along a dirt track to the road, from where you can hitch a lift (or catch the daily *marshrutka* from Baikalskoe if you time things right) back into Severobaikalsk. Pocket maps of the route produced by GBT volunteers and giving an idea of flora and fauna you might spot along the way are available from Tayozhik or the Baikal Trail Hostel (see *Where to stay* on page 149) and tourist information points in Severobaikalsk.

Southwards there are many other adventurous trip options from Baikalskoe such as to the top of Mt Chersky or to Cape Kotelnikovskiy. However, this is serious hiking through virtually uninhabited, bear-infested and swampy forest, and the services of a very experienced guide are essential. South of Baikalskoe there isn't another settlement on Lake Baikal until the hamlet of Kocherikova around 270km away, just short of the Maloe More. A rough track of some description which hugs the shoreline almost all the way presents the tempting possibility of some genuine wilderness trekking between the two settlements, carrying all your supplies with you, camping on the shore and bathing in Lake Baikal as you go. Magic.

Hot springs, a lonely BAM station and impressively high mountains await you at Goudzhekit, around 30km west of Severobaikalsk. This tiny spa just off the washboard dirt road to Bratsk is surrounded by forest and bald peaks and makes for a superb day trip from Lake Baikal or even an adventurous overnight stop.

GETTING THERE

By train You can reach Goudzhekit by westbound BAM train (*journey time: 30–60mins*); between one and three services (depending on whether the date is an even or odd number) stop there *en route* to Moscow, Irkutsk and Lena. Tickets for the return journey are bought on board, or book ahead in Severobaikalsk. The unmanned railway station is around 300m from the spa on the main dirt road and there are some spectacular views from the platform, down the line towards the menacing summits of the Baikalsky Mountains.

By *marshrutka* None of the trains is timed to make a day trip feasible, and it's much simpler to squeeze yourself into a *marshrutka* from outside Severobaikalsk railway station (*departs: 3 times daily; tickets: RUB35*). These return an hour after arriving.

WHERE TO STAY

Goudzhekit (19 rooms) ☎ 21276. The larger Goudzhekit has en-suite dbls with TV & cheaper rooms with shared facilities. There's a summer swimming pool filled with hot spring water, & a café. $$

Vstrecha (5 rooms) ☎ 26610; e baikal06@ mail.ru. The small Vstrecha has 5 rooms with en-suite facilities & TV. Book ahead. $$

✗ WHERE TO EAT The café at the Goudzhekit Hotel and the **Kafe Pogrebok** (⏰ *09.00–01.00*) beneath the spa house both do a good line in refreshments such as salads, sandwiches and a couple of more substantial meals.

WHAT TO SEE AND DO

Hot springs (⏰ *07:00–03:00; adult RUB70 for 90mins*) The hot springs were discovered here during construction work on the nearby railway, and over the last three decades a low-rise spa complex has grown up where once there was just taiga. The water in several indoor and outdoor pools has a naturally maintained temperature of 40–50°C, toasty enough even on the coldest of days. Having wallowed in the mineral-packed aqua mineralis, retreat downstairs for a beer or coffee before heading off into the surrounding country for a walk on the wild side.

DZELINDA (ДЗЕЛИНДА)

If you are the type of person constantly on the lookout for ever more remote and undiscovered places to be pummelled, pampered and bathed in relaxing spring water, Dzelinda is the end of the line. Some 92km along the BAM Railway from Nizhneangarsk, this tiny and wildly far-flung mini-spa built around thermal springs which rise in the valley of the Verkhnyaya Angara River has a pool where the water temperature remains at a constant 44°C and is surrounded by thick taiga. Guests stay in timber huts (*around RUB700 per night*) and all meals are provided. Alternatively you could come here on a day trip from Nizhneangarsk or Severobaikalsk, but you'd need your own transport. The water is rich in radon and other microelements with almost miraculous curative properties, but the pool is also just great for a wallow. Walk for a short distance along the stream through the forest to another (sadly derelict) bathing spot where you won't have to pay for a dip in the tepid water. Locals say it's better to come to Dzelinda in the winter as mosquitoes are a pest in summer, and there is something about lounging in a warm pool while the snow lays thick all around and the temperature plummets to a jaw-stiffening –35°C.

GETTING THERE Two trains a day ply the BAM between Severobaikalsk and Dzelinda. Service 950 (to Olongdo) departs at 9.11, arriving at the Dzelinda halt at 11.30. Train 656 (to Taksimo) leaves Severobaikalsk at 18.15, arriving at 19.58. If you're travelling late in the day, warn whoever is on duty at the spa (through agencies in Severobaikalsk or Nizhneangarsk) of your arrival time and ask them to come to meet you at the station as the spa may prove impossible to find in the dark.

A far easier option is to arrange a transfer through 109 Meridian in Nizhneangarsk.

NORTHEAST SHORE

Few foreigners travel to the isolated and virtually uninhabited northeast and it takes real determination to make the trip across the lake. Those who do are rewarded with some of Baikal's most remote shoreline, off-the-map wilderness trekking and a general feeling of being a very long way from anywhere.

Easy-to-obtain permits are needed to land here, though these are waived when Baikal freezes over. The winter is the easiest and cheapest time to come, when ice roads are opened up. Move inland from the shoreline and you're into serious wild trekking country with all that entails.

Thanks to the absence of man, the hinterland teems with animals such as bears, roe deer, hares and even the illusive sable. No roads slice the forests and mountains, no villages dot its expanse, and only barely passable hiking trails lead inland. This is Baikal at its wildest, an unforgettable experience for all who make it this far.

PRACTICALITIES Permits for the northeast coast can be arranged through 109 Meridian and the regional authority offices in Nizhneangarsk, or the Baikal Hospitality Centre in Severobaikalsk.

If all you want to do is satisfy your curiosity, take a dip in the spa waters at Khakusy and lounge on the beach, travelling here independently is safe enough, though the boat ride could cost you a small fortune. Bring a tent or somehow warn the spa of your arrival through tour companies and helpers across the lake. Stocking up on food may also be a good idea. Heading inland, however, is a completely different matter, and you're strongly advised not to wander off into the taiga without experience of wilderness trekking.

GETTING THERE In the peak summer months various boats make the 40km crossing (*journey time: 4hrs; tickets: RUB800–4,000*) from Severobaikalsk and Nizhneangarsk to Khakusy fairly regularly, depending on demand. At other times of the year you have no choice but to hire a boat privately, a costly proposition indeed. Things improve considerably when the ice becomes thick enough for roads to be etched out across the lake. Permits are waived at this time of year, and it's usually fairly easy to hitch a lift from the opposite shore for around RUB400.

WHAT TO SEE AND DO
Khakusy (Хакусы) This remote mini-spa on Baikal's shore is where you will take your first steps on the northeast coast, as boats from across the lake anchor here.

As you approach the rickety plank quay you'll see just how remote this place is, with just a few timber structures lining the beach, behind which rise thickly wooded hills. The 140-bed **spa complex** (⊕ *Jun–Sep*) around a kilometre into the forest was commissioned in the early 1950s, but the thermal springs which rise here had been familiar to the native Evenks for millennia. It's still possible to bathe in the 46°C water even outside of the season as the pools, connected by duckboard walkways, are out in the open. Other than the spa, the main attraction is the long sandy beach which stretches in both directions.

The only place to stay is the spa (*RUB900 pp per night*), so bring a tent when it's closed. There's a small and overpriced shop on the shore selling basics.

Cape Turali and the Singing Sands Some 12km south of Khakusy lies Cape Turali, on the southern side of which you'll discover the Singing Sands. These are dunes, 200m long and around 20m high, which once gave out an odd sound when the wind was blowing in the right direction. The Angara Dam project in Irkutsk silenced the phenomenon when it raised the water level in Lake Baikal. Theoretically, the sands can be reached on foot, but this would probably involve camping overnight nearby. Boat trips leave sporadically from Khakusy.

Ayaya Bay and Lake Frolikha (Губа Аяя and Озеро Фролиха) Wonderfully named **Ayaya Bay**, 12km north of Khakusy as the crow flies, is one of Baikal's most sheltered bays, and a place fishing boats seek refuge in when one of the lake's unpredictable storms ruffle its waters. From here a rough but fairly popular hiking trail heads 8km inland to alpine **Lake Frolikha** where the water is pleasantly warm in late summer. You can make the trek there and back in a long day, but take extra rations just in case. Camping by Lake Frolikha overnight means you can attempt to reach the other side and hike southeast along the valley of the River Levaya Frolikha. This will take you into some incredibly remote back country with nothing but mountains and the fast flowing river for company. This should only be attempted by hikers with experience of this sort of terrain.

Appendix I

LANGUAGE

RUSSIAN The main reason the Russian language seems so daunting to many is the fact that it employs the Cyrillic alphabet. But learning your Russian ABC will make any trip a lot less painful and solve numerous problems on the road. Information in Siberia such as bus and train timetables, menus, street signs and place names are never transcribed into English, and just buying a bus ticket or ordering a meal requires at least some knowledge of the alphabet. Russian words may seem like a series of backward 'Rs' and 'Ns' but the characters are simple to master and can be learnt in an hour or two. Some letters are even the same as their Latin counterparts used in English (eg: a, e, k, m, o, t). Because of the alphabet issue, many would consider other Slavic languages 'easier' to learn than Russian but this is not so. Russian grammar is slightly simpler than Czech or Polish and uses many more loan words from French, English and German. Russian is also a very economical language, and very often a whole English sentence can be expressed with just one Russian word.

Pronunciation It may be oversimplifying matters considerably, but Russian has almost phonetic pronunciation, meaning you say what you see. However, this doesn't always work, and as it is claimed of almost all Slavic languages (which all sound completely different) it is of limited help to learners. It may be better to say that Russian pronunciation is relatively consistent across the language (an 'i' is usually an 'i', no matter where it falls in a word) and consistency in your pronunciation will aid you in making yourself understood.

Stress is vital in Russian and getting it wrong can change the meaning of what you intended to say, with sometimes hilarious consequences. For example *pisat'*, with the emphasis on the last syllable, means 'to write', while *pisat'* means 'to piss' – hence an Englishman's dismay when informed that every time he had promised his Russian sweetheart he would write to her... you get the picture. Stress can fall anywhere in a word, but once you've heard it several times, you won't get it wrong (unless it moves according to number and case!).

Two of the mysteries of the Russian language for beginners are the so-called hard and soft signs (ъ and ь). These are letters unpronounceable on their own but which affect the letter immediately preceding. For example, 'н' (n) on its own is pronounced as the 'n' in 'not'. The combination 'нь' is like the 'ny' in the word 'canyon'. No other letter gives beginners a greater headache than 'ъ', as very often it's almost impossible to hear it's there at all.

REST ON BAIKAL

'Have a rest on Baikal' you might hear while in the region, or read on various English-language websites and in brochures. 'Rest' corresponds to the Russian word *'otdykh'* which can also mean 'holiday'. *'Na Baikalye'* means 'in the Baikal area' or 'by Baikal', though 'na' also translates as 'on'.

The alphabet

Letters		Pronunciation
А	а	as the 'a' in 'almond'
Б	б	as the 'b' in 'bed'
В	в	as the 'v' in 'vet'
Г	г	as the 'g' in 'got'
Д	д	as the 'd' in 'dog'
Е	е	as the 'ye' in 'yes'
Ё	ё	as the 'yo' in 'yo-yo'
Ж	ж	as the 's' in 'pleasure'
З	з	as the 'z' in 'zoo'
И	и	as the 'ee' in 'meet'
Й	й	as the 'y' in 'yell'
К	к	as the 'k' in 'kill'
Л	л	as the 'l' in lemon
М	м	as the 'm' in man
Н	н	as the 'n' in 'never'
О	о	as the 'o' in 'oh'
П	п	as the 'p' in 'pen'
Р	р	rolled 'r', no matter where it falls in a word
С	с	as the 's' in 'sin'
Т	т	as the 't' in 'tell'
У	у	as the 'oo' in 'moon'
Ф	ф	as the 'f' in 'fan'
Х	х	as the 'ch' in 'loch'
Ц	ц	as the 'ts' in 'cats'
Ч	ч	as the 'ch' in 'chat'
Ш	ш	as the 'sh' in 'shell'
Щ	щ	as the 'sh ch' in 'fresh cheese'
Ъ	ъ	hard sign; causes an audible break in the word
Ы	ы	as the 'y' in 'myth'
Ь	ь	soft sign; 'softens' the consonant before (see above)
Э	э	as the 'e' in 'set'
Ю	ю	as the 'you' in 'youth'
Я	я	as the 'ya' in 'yahoo'

Grammar Although not as complicated as some other Slavic languages (Czech being the most difficult), mastering Russian still demands an understanding of classical grammar systems, unless you expressly want to speak in the infinitive and nominative case all the time (as some foreigners we've heard pull off with amusing effect). Russian is a highly inflected language, meaning words change or add endings according to gender, number and case (the relationship between words). With three genders and six cases, mastering the myriad combinations which result, as well as verb forms and tenses, is the key to speaking passable Russian. Some beginners think they have gone a long way towards learning Russian once they have learnt the 33 letters of the alphabet, but that's just the first tiny step.

Essentials

Good morning	Доброе утро	*dobroye utra*
Good afternoon	Добрый день	*dobry dyen*
Good evening	Добрый вечер	*dobry vecher*
Hello	Здравствуйте	*zdrastvuytye*
Goodbye	До свидания	*da svidaniya*
My name is…	Меня зовут…	*menya zavut…*

I am from Britain/America/ Australia	Я из Британии/Америки/ Австралии	ya iz britanii/ameriki/avstralii
How are you?	Как ваши дела?	kak vasheh dyela?
Pleased to meet you	Очен приятно	ochen priyatna
Thank you	Спасибо	spasiba
Don't mention it	Не за что	nye za shto
Cheers!	На здоровье	na zdaroviye
yes/no	да/нет	da/nyet
I don't understand	не понимаю	nye panimayu
Please speak more slowly	Говорите медленее, пожалуйста	gavaritye myedlenyeye, pazhaluysta
Do you understand?	Понимаете?	panimayetye?

Questions

How?	Как?	kak?
What?	Что?	shto?
Where?	Где?	gdye?
What is it?	Что это?	shto eta?
Which?	Какой? (M), Какая? (F), Какое? (N)	kakoy? (M), kakaya? (F), kakoye? (N)
When?	Когда?	kagda?
Why?	Почему?	pachemu?
Who?	Кто?	kto?
How much?	Сколько?	skolka?

Numbers

1	один	adin
2	два	dva
3	три	tri
4	четыре	chetyri
5	пять	pyat
6	шесть	shest
7	семь	syem
8	восемь	vosyem
9	девять	dyevyat
10	десять	dyesyat
11	одиннадцать	adinatsat
12	двенадцать	dvyenatsat
13	тринадцать	trinatsat
14	четырнадцать	chetyrnatsat
15	пятнадцать	pyatnatsat
16	шестнадцать	shestnatsat
17	семнадцать	syemnatsat
18	восемнадцать	vosyemnatsat
19	девятнадцать	dyevyatnatsat
20	двадцать	dvatsat
21	двадцать один	dvatsat adin
30	тридцать	tritsat
40	сорок	sorak
50	пятьдесять	pyatdesyat
60	шестьдесят	shestdesyat
70	семьдесят	syemdesyat

80	восемьдесят	*vosyemdesyat*
90	девяносто	*dyevyanosta*
100	сто	*sto*
1,000	тысяча	*tysyacha*

Time

What time is it?	Который час?	*katory chas?*
It's 3 o'clock, it's 8 o'clock	Три часа, пять часов	*tri chasa, pyat chasov*
today	сегодня	*sivodnya*
tonight	сегодня вечером	*sivodnya vecherom*
tomorrow	завтра	*zaftra*
yesterday	вчера	*fchera*
morning	утро	*utra*
evening	вечер	*vyecher*

Days

Monday	понедельник	*panyedyelnik*
Tuesday	вторник	*ftornik*
Wednesday	среда	*sreda*
Thursday	четверг	*chetverk*
Friday	пятница	*pyatnitsa*
Saturday	суббота	*subota*
Sunday	воскресенье	*vaskreseniye*

Months

January	январь	*yanvar*
February	февраль	*fevral*
March	март	*mart*
April	апрель	*aprel*
May	май	*mai*
June	июнь	*iyun*
July	июль	*iyul*
August	август	*avgust*
September	сентябрь	*sentyabr*
October	октябрь	*aktyabr*
November	ноябрь	*nayabr*
December	декабрь	*dyekabr*

Getting around
Public transport

I'd like…	Дайте пожалуйста…	*daytye pazhaluysta…*
…a one-way ticket	…билет в одну сторону	*…bilyet fadnu storanu*
…a return ticket	…билет туда и обратно	*…bilyet tuda i abratna*
How much is it?	Сколько стоит?	*skolka stoyit*
What time does it leave?	Во сколько он отправляется?	*va skolka on atpravlyayetsa?*
What time is it now?	Который час?	*katory chas?*
The train has been…	Поезд…	*poyezd…*
…delayed	…задерживается	*…zadyerzhivayetsa*
…cancelled	…отменили	*…atmenili*
first class	СВ	*SV (es-veh)*
coupe class	купе	*kupeh*
hard class	плацкарт	*platskart*

platform	платформа	*platforma*
ticket office	касса	*kasa*
timetable	расписание	*raspisaniye*
from	с	*s*
to	до	*do*
bus station	автовокзал	*aftavagzal*
railway station	вокзал	*vagzal*
airport	аэропорт	*eraport*
port	порт	*port*
bus	автобус	*aftobus*
train	поезд	*poyezd*
plane	самолёт	*samalyot*
boat	катер	*katyer*
ferry	паром	*parom*
car	машина	*mashina*
4x4	джип	*dzhip*
taxi	такси	*taksi*
minibus	маршрутка	*marshrutka*
motorbike/moped	мотоцикл/мопед	*matatsikl/moped*
bicycle	велосипед	*velociped*
arrival	прибытие	*pribitiye*
departure	отправление	*atpravlyeniye*
here	здесь	*zdyes*
there	там	*tam*
Bon voyage!	Счастливого пути	*schastlivava puti*

Private transport

Is this the road to...?	Это дорога на...?	*eta daroga na...*
Where is the petrol station?	Где находится бензозаправка?	*gdye nakhoditsa benzazapravka?*
Please fill it up	Полный бак, пожалуйста	*polny bak, pazhaluysta*
I'd like...litres	Налейте пожалуйста... литров	*naleytye pazhaluysta... litrov*
diesel	дизель	*disel*
petrol	бензин	*benzin*
I have broken down	У меня поламалась машина	*u menya palamalas mashina*

Directions

Where is it?	Где это?	*gdye eta?*
Go straight ahead	Едьте прямо	*yedtye pryama*
Turn left	Поверните налево	*pavyernitye nalyeva*
Turn right	Поверните направо	*pavyernitye naprava*
...at the traffic lights	...на светофоре	*...na svyetaforye*
...at the roundabout	...на ротунде	*...na ratundye*
north	север	*syever*
south	юг	*yug*
east	восток	*vastok*
west	запад	*zapad*
behind	за	*za*
in front of	перед	*pered*
near	возле	*vozlye*
opposite	напротив	*naprotiv*

Street signs

entrance/exit	вход/выход	*fkhod/vykhad*
open/closed	открыто/закрыто	*atkrita/zakrita*
toilets – men/women	туалет –мужской/дамский	*tualyet – muzhskoy/damsky*
information	информация	*infarmatsiya*

Accommodation

Where is a cheap/good hotel?	Где находится недорогая/ хорошая гостиница?	*gdye nakhoditsa nyedaragaya/ kharoshaya gastinitsa?*
Could you please write the address?	Напишите пожалуйста адрес	*napishitye pazhaluysta adres*
Do you have any rooms available?	У вас есть свободные номера?	*u vas yest svabodniye nomera?*
I'd like…	Мне нужен...	*mnye nuzhen...*
…a single room	…одноместный номер	*…adnamyestny nomer*
…a double room	…двухместный номер	*…dvukhmyestny nomer*
…a room with two beds	…номер с двумя кроватями	*…nomer s dvumya kravatyami*
…a room with a bathroom	…номер с ванной	*…nomer s vanoy*
How much is it per person/night?	Сколько стоит за человека/за ночь?	*skolka stoyit za chelavyeka/za noch?*
Where is the toilet?	Где туалет?	*gdye tualyet?*
Where is the bathroom?	Где ванная?	*gdye vanaya?*
Is there hot water?	У вас есть горячая вода?	*u vas yest garyachaya vada?*
Is there electricity?	У вас есть электричество?	*u vas yest elektrichestva?*
Is breakfast included?	Завтрак включён в цене?	*zaftrak vklyuchon ftsenye?*
I am leaving today	Я уезжаю сегодня	*ya uyezhayu sivodnya*

Food

Do you have a table for … people?	У вас есть столик на ... человек?	*u vas yest stolik na ... chelavyek?*
Do you have a children's menu?	У вас есть детское меню?	*u vas yest dyetskaye menyu?*
I am a vegetarian	Я вегетарианец (M), вегетарианка (F)	*ya vegetarianyets vegetarianka*
Do you have any vegetarian dishes?	У вас есть вегетарианские блюда?	*u vas yest vegetarianskiye blyuda?*
Please bring me…	Принесите мне, пожалуйста...	*prinesitye mnye pazhaluysta…*
…a fork/knife/spoon	…вилку/нож/ложку	*…vilku/nozh/lozhku*
Please may I have the bill?	Счёт пожалуйста	*schyot pazhaluysta*

EMERGENCIES

Help!	Помогите!	*pamagitye!*
Call a doctor!	Вызовите врача!	*vyzavitye vracha!*
There's been an accident	Случилась авария	*sluchilas avariya*
I'm lost	Я потерялся	*ya patyeralsa*
Go away!	Оставьте меня в покое!	*astavtye menya fpakoye!*
police	милиция	*militsiya*
fire	пожарная помощь	*pazharnaya pomashch*
ambulance	скорая помощь	*skoraya pomashch*
thief	кража	*krazha*
hospital	больница	*balnitsa*
I am ill	Я болен	*ya bolen*

Basics

bread	хлеб	*khlyeb*
butter	масло	*masla*
cheese	сыр	*syr*
oil	масло	*masla*
pepper	перец	*perets*
salt	соль	*sol*
sugar	сахар	*sakhar*

Fruit

apples	яблоки	*yablaki*
bananas	бананы	*banany*
grapes	виноград	*vinagrad*
oranges	апельсины	*apelsiny*
pears	груши	*grushi*

Vegetables

carrots	морковка	*markovka*
garlic	чеснок	*chesnok*
onion	лук	*luk*
peppers	болгарский перец	*balgarsky perets*
potatoes	картофель	*kartofel*

Fish

omul	омуль	*omul*
salmon	лосось	*losas*
tuna	тунец	*tunyets*
caviar	икра	*ikra*

Meat

beef	говядина	*gavyadina*
chicken	курица	*kuritsa*
goat	козлятина	*kazlyatina*
pork	свинина	*svinina*
lamb	баранина	*baranina*
sausage	сосиска	*sasiska*

Drinks

beer	пиво	*piva*
coffee	кофе	*kofye*
juice	сок	*sok*
milk	молоко	*malako*
tea	чай	*chay*
vodka	водка	*vodka*
water	вода	*vada*
wine	вино	*vino*

Shopping

I'd like to buy…	Я хочу купить…	*ya khachu kupit…*
How much is it?	Сколько это стоит?	*skolka eta stoyit?*
I don't like it	Мне это не нравится	*mnye eta nye nravitsa*
I'm just looking	Я просто смотрю	*ya prosta smatryu*
It's too expensive	Это слишком дорого	*eta slishkom doraga*

I'll take it	Я это возьму	*ya eta vazmu*
Please may I have…	Дайте пожалуйста	*daytye pazhaluysta*
Do you accept credit cards?	Вы принимаете кредитные карточки?	*vy prinimayetye kreditniye kartachki?*
more, bigger	больше	*bolshe*
less, smaller	меньше	*menshe*

Communications

I am looking for…	Ищу…	*ishchu…*
…bank	…банк	*bank*
…post office	…почту	*pochtu*
…church	…церковь	*tserkav*
…embassy	…посольство	*pasolstva*
…exchange office	…пункт обмена валют	*punkt abmyena valyut*
…telephone centre	…переговорный пункт	*peregavorny punkt*
…tourist office	…информационный центр	*informatsyony tsentr*

Health

diarrhoea	понос	*panos*
nausea	тошнота	*tashnata*
doctor	врач	*vrach*
prescription	рецепт	*retsept*
pharmacy	аптека	*aptyeka*
paracetamol	парацетамол	*paratsetamol*
antibiotics	антибиотики	*antibiotiki*
antiseptic	антисептики	*antiseptiki*
tampons	тампоны	*tampony*
condoms	презервативы	*prezervativy*
contraceptive	противозачаточные	*prativazatochniye*
sun block	солнцезащитный крем	*sontsezashchitny krem*
I have…	У меня…	*u menya…*
…asthma	…астма	*…astma*
…epilepsy	…эпилепсия	*…epilepsiya*
…diabetes	…диабет	*…diabet*
I'm allergic to…	У меня аллергия на…	*u menya alergiya na…*
…penicillin	…пеницилин	*…penitsilin*
…nuts	…орехи	*…arekhi*
…bee sting	…пчелиный укус	*…pchelny ukus*

Travel with children

Is/Are there…	У вас есть…	*u vas yest…*
…baby changing room?	…комната для пеленания ребёнка?	*…komnata dlya pelenaniya rebyonka?*
…infant milk formula?	…смесь для кормления детей	*…smyes dlya kormlyeniya dyetyey?*
…nappies?	…подгузники?	*…padguzniki?*
…potty?	…горшок?	*…garshok?*
…babysitter?	…няня?	*…nyanya?*
…highchair?	…высокий стульчик?	*…vysoky stulchik*
Are children allowed?	Детям вход разрешён?	*dyetyam fkhod razreshon?*

Other

and/but	и/а	*i/a*
this/that	этот/тот	*etat/tot*
expensive/cheap	дорогой/дешёвый	*daragoy/dyeshovy*
beautiful/ugly	красивый/уродливый	*krasivy/urodlivy*
old/new	старый/новый	*stary/novy*
good/bad	хороший/плохой	*kharoshy/plakhoy*
early/late	рано/поздно	*rana/pozdna*
hot/cold	горячий/холодный	*garyachy/khalodny*
difficult/easy	сложный/лёгкий	*slozhny/lyohky*
boring/interesting	скучный/интересный	*skuchny/intyeresny*

BURYAT Of course Russian is not the only language you'll hear around Lake Baikal. Buryat, the native language of the Buryat people, belongs to a completely different linguistic family and is very close to Mongolian. It is, however, written in the Cyrillic alphabet like Russian, giving you yet another reason to learn the Russian characters before you leave. All Buryats, with perhaps the exception of very old people in the remotest of villages in rural areas, speak Russian, though amongst themselves they may speak Buryat or an odd mixture of the two languages. For Russian speakers it is amusing to hear villagers speaking Buryat interspersed with Russian words for which the Buryat language has no equivalent, or young people inflicting Buryat grammar on Russian phrases. Unlike in Ukraine or the Baltic states, there is no language issue in Buryatiya, and the vast majority of Buryats accept Russian as the tongue of everyday discourse.

Appendix 2

BOOKS

Not a huge amount has been written about Lake Baikal, the Irkutsk oblast or Buryatiya, with all three mentioned in various works of fiction and non-fiction but with few volumes dedicated solely to the region. If you read just one book before you leave, it should be Colin Thubron's superb travelogue, *In Siberia*, which gives an entertaining insight into many aspects of the region.

Travel

Bull, Bartle *Around the Sacred Sea: Mongolia and Lake Baikal on Horseback* Canongate Books, 1999. The clue's in the title.

McGregor, Ewan & Boorman, Charlie *The Long Way Round* Sphere, 2005. These celebrities were sadly wholly unimpressed by the east coast of Lake Baikal and a shamaness they meet there.

Theroux, Paul *Great Railway Bazaar* and *Riding the Red Rooster* Penguin Classics, 2008. Both of these fascinating travelogues, by one of the world's best travel writers, include a trip on the Trans-Siberian.

Thomson, Peter *Sacred Sea: A Journey to Lake Baikal* OUP USA, 2007. An eminently readable account of a journey to Baikal.

Thubron, Colin *In Siberia* Penguin, 2007. The definitive travelogue on the places and people of Siberia, with a large section dealing with many of the places in this guide. Now ever so slightly dated but still an essential read.

Natural history

Fefelov, IV *Birds of the Selenga Delta* East Siberian Publishing Company, 2001. Obviously a must for anyone heading out to the Selenga Delta for a birdwatching break.

History

Andrew, Jack *Inside Putin's Russia* Publisher unknown, 2005. An account of President Putin's first term in office.

Avery, Martha *The Tea Road: China and Russia Meet Across the Steppe* China Intercontinental Press, 2004. The definitive English-language work on the Tea Road.

Bawden, CR *Shamans, Lamas and Evangelicals* Routledge & Kegan Paul PLC, 1985. A detailed and fascinating account of the English missionaries sent to convert the Buryats in what was then Selenginsk (now Novoselenginsk).

Bobrick, Benson *East of the Sun* Poseidon Press, 1992. A commendably readable general history of Siberia.

Man, John *Ghengis Khan: Life, Death and Resurrection* Bantam Books, 2005. Though little mention is made of Lake Baikal itself, this is by far the most readable account of the life of a man whose influence can still be felt across the region.

Sutherland, Christine *Princess of Siberia* Quartet Books, 2001. An historical biography which tells the story of Decembrist wife Maria Volkonskaya.

Literature

Bouis, Valentin & Rasputin, Antonina *Farewell to Matyora* Northwestern University Press US, 2006. An English translation, relating the nostalgic tale of a doomed Siberian village destined to be submerged under the waters of the Bratsk reservoir.

Health

Wilson-Howarth, Dr Jane & Ellis, Dr Matthew *Your Child Abroad: A Travel Health Guide* Bradt Travel Guides, 2005

Wilson-Howarth, Dr Jane *Bugs, Bites & Bowels* Cadogan, 2006

WEBSITES
Lake Baikal

www.baikalinfo.com An online guide to Lake Baikal.

www.baikalplan.de Website of a Dresden-based association heavily involved with various projects around Baikal, including the GBT.

www.greatbaikaltrail.ru Internet portal of the GBT, providing information on every aspect of this superb organisation, including details on how to volunteer.

www.tahoebaikal.org Website of Baikal's twin lake in California/Nevada.

www.crossbaikal.de A fascinating site on what is thought to be the first ice trek along the entire length of Lake Baikal, undertaken by a German expedition in 2003.

Transport

www.poezda.net Useful online Russian railway timetable (just remember that trains run on Moscow time!).

www.rzd.ru Official Russian Railways site, featuring detailed online timetable, but slow-loading and jumpy.

www.transib.ru Site dedicated solely to the longest rail journey on the planet.

http://bam.railways.ru/eng/ Incredibly detailed site on the BAM Railway, maintained by amateur enthusiasts.

Irkutsk

www.irkutskout.ru Sounds like a site dedicated to Irkutsk's gay community… but it isn't. Comprehensive listings of all Irkutsk's businesses (in Russian only).

www.vibirai.ru Listings for most large cities in Russia (in Russian).

www.irk.ru A comprehensive site dedicated to the city which the locals swear by.

Buryatiya

http://egov-buryatia.ru/eng/ Buryat government portal.

www.sbaikal.ru Everything you ever wanted to know about Baikal's north but were afraid to ask.

www.baikaltravel.ru Buryatiya tourism portal (mostly in Russian).

www.buryatia.ru Gateway to everything Buryat (in Russian).

http://tunki.baikal.ru A website dedicated to travel in the Tunka Valley, with detailed maps, images from the Eastern Sayan Mountains and heaps of information on the area.

News

www.ruvr.ru The Voice of Russia website – the official Kremlin line in English but also featuring fascinating articles on many topics including obscure Baikal-related info.

www.itar-tass.com/eng/ Russia's official state news agency – as impartial and nonpartisan as it ever was.

www.bgtrk.ru Literally up-to-the-minute news from Buryatiya (in Russian).

Natural history

http://oopt.info/ A detailed database of all Russia's national parks and nature reserves, but only in Russian.

http://home.worldonline.dk/mccons/Birds/Baikal.html Lists of birds and mammals spotted by a Danish nature-lover during a 1993 expedition.

www.baikal.ru Scientific information relating to the lake in English, from the Slavic boffins of Irkutsk State University.

Miscellaneous

www.eki.ee/books/redbook/ A fascinating English-language overview of all the indigenous peoples living within the Russian Federation.

www.unclepasha.com If you're routing through Moscow, let Uncle Pasha take care of you. The 'misery tourism' section of the website is hilarious for anyone who knows a bit about Russia.

www.semeyskie.narod.ru A website dedicated to the Old Believers of the region, unfortunately only in Russian.

www.waytorussia.net A free and independent online guide to Russia but with a lot of out-of-date information cluttering what could be an excellent site.

WIN £100 CASH!
READER QUESTIONNAIRE

Send in your completed questionnaire for the chance to win £100 cash in our regular draw

All respondents may order a Bradt guide at half the UK retail price – please complete the order form overleaf.

(Entries may be posted or faxed to us, or scanned and emailed.)

We are interested in getting feedback from our readers to help us plan future Bradt guides. Please answer ALL the questions below and return the form to us in order to qualify for an entry in our regular draw.

Have you used any other Bradt guides? If so, which titles? . . . .
. . . .

What other publishers' travel guides do you use regularly? . . . .
. . . .

Where did you buy this guidebook? . . . .

What was the main purpose of your trip to Lake Baikal (or for what other reason did you read our guide)? eg: holiday/business/charity etc. . . . .
. . . .

What other destinations would you like to see covered by a Bradt guide? . . . .
. . . .

Would you like to receive our catalogue/newsletters?

YES / NO (If yes, please complete details on reverse)

If yes – by post or email? . . . .

Age (circle relevant category) 16–25   26–45   46–60   60+

Male/Female (delete as appropriate)

Home country . . . .

Please send us any comments about our guide to Lake Baikal or other Bradt Travel Guides. . . . .
. . . .
. . . .
. . . .

Bradt Travel Guides
23 High Street, Chalfont St Peter, Bucks SL9 9QE, UK
✆ +44 (0)1753 893444 **f** +44 (0)1753 892333
e info@bradtguides.com
www.bradtguides.com

CLAIM YOUR HALF-PRICE BRADT GUIDE!

Order Form

To order your half-price copy of a Bradt guide, and to enter our prize draw to win £100 (see overleaf), please fill in the order form below, complete the questionnaire overleaf, and send it to Bradt Travel Guides by post, fax or email.

Please send me one copy of the following guide at half the UK retail price

Title	Retail price	Half price
. . .	. . . .	. . . .	. . . .

Please send the following additional guides at full UK retail price

No	Title	Retail price	Total
. . .	. . . .	. . . .	. . . .
. . .	. . . .	. . . .	. . . .
. . .	. . . .	. . . .	. . . .

	Sub total	. . . .
	Post & packing	. . . .
(£2 per book UK; £4 per book Europe; £6 per book rest of world)		
	Total	. . . .

Name . . . .

Address. . . . .

Tel . . . .   Email . . . .

☐ I enclose a cheque for £. . . . . made payable to Bradt Travel Guides Ltd

☐ I would like to pay by credit card. Number: . . . .

   Expiry date: . . . / . . .   3-digit security code (on reverse of card) . . . . .

   Issue no (debit cards only) . . . . .

☐ Please add my name to your catalogue mailing list.

☐ I would be happy for you to use my name and comments in Bradt marketing material.

Send your order on this form, with the completed questionnaire, to:

Bradt Travel Guides LB1
23 High Street, Chalfont St Peter, Bucks SL9 9QE
✆ +44 (0)1753 893444   f +44 (0)1753 892333
e info@bradtguides.com   www.bradtguides.com

Bradt Travel Guides

www.bradtguides.com

Africa

Access Africa: Safaris for People with Limited Mobility	£16.99
Africa Overland	£16.99
Algeria	£15.99
Botswana: Okavango, Chobe, Northern Kalahari	£15.99
Burkina Faso	£14.99
Cameroon	£15.99
Cape Verde Islands	£14.99
Congo	£15.99
Eritrea	£15.99
Ethiopia	£16.99
Gambia, The	£13.99
Ghana	£15.99
Johannesburg	£6.99
Madagascar	£15.99
Malawi	£13.99
Mali	£14.99
Mauritius, Rodrigues & Réunion	£15.99
Mozambique	£13.99
Namibia	£15.99
Niger	£14.99
Nigeria	£17.99
North Africa: Roman Coast	£15.99
Rwanda	£14.99
São Tomé & Principe	£14.99
Seychelles	£14.99
Sierra Leone	£16.99
Sudan	£15.99
Tanzania, Northern	£14.99
Tanzania	£17.99
Uganda	£15.99
Zambia	£17.99
Zanzibar	£14.99

Britain and Europe

Albania	£15.99
Armenia, Nagorno Karabagh	£14.99
Azores	£13.99
Baltic Cities	£14.99
Belarus	£14.99
Bosnia & Herzegovina	£13.99
Bratislava	£9.99
Britain from the Rails	£17.99
Budapest	£9.99
Bulgaria	£13.99
Cork	£6.99
Croatia	£13.99
Cyprus see North Cyprus	

Czech Republic	£13.99
Dresden	£7.99
Dubrovnik	£6.99
Estonia	£13.99
Faroe Islands	£15.99
Georgia	£14.99
Hungary	£14.99
Iceland	£14.99
Kosovo	£14.99
Lapland	£13.99
Latvia	£13.99
Lille	£9.99
Lithuania	£14.99
Ljubljana	£7.99
Luxembourg	£13.99
Macedonia	£14.99
Montenegro	£14.99
North Cyprus	£12.99
Riga	£6.99
Serbia	£14.99
Slovakia	£14.99
Slovenia	£13.99
Spitsbergen	£16.99
Switzerland Without a Car	£14.99
Tallinn	£6.99
Transylvania	£14.99
Ukraine	£14.99
Vilnius	£6.99
Zagreb	£6.99

Middle East, Asia and Australasia

Bangladesh	£15.99
Borneo	£17.99
China: Yunnan Province	£13.99
Great Wall of China	£13.99
Iran	£15.99
Iraq: Then & Now	£15.99
Israel	£15.99
Kazakhstan	£15.99
Kyrgyzstan	£15.99
Maldives	£15.99
Mongolia	£16.99
North Korea	£14.99
Oman	£13.99
Shangri-La: A Travel Guide to the Himalayan Dream	£14.99
Sri Lanka	£15.99
Syria	£14.99
Tibet	£13.99
Turkmenistan	£14.99
Yemen	£14.99

The Americas and the Caribbean

Amazon, The	£14.99
Argentina	£15.99
Bolivia	£14.99
Cayman Islands	£14.99
Chile	£16.95
Colombia	£16.99
Costa Rica	£13.99
Dominica	£14.99
Grenada, Carriacou & Petite Martinique	£14.99
Guyana	£14.99
Panama	£14.99
St Helena	£14.99
Turks & Caicos Islands	£14.99
USA by Rail	£14.99

Wildlife

100 Animals to See Before They Die	£16.99
Antarctica: Guide to the Wildlife	£15.99
Arctic: Guide to the Wildlife	£15.99
Central & Eastern European Wildlife	£15.99
Chinese Wildlife	£16.99
East African Wildlife	£19.99
Galápagos Wildlife	£15.99
Madagascar Wildlife	£16.99
New Zealand Wildlife	£14.99
North Atlantic Wildlife	£16.99
Peruvian Wildlife	£15.99
Southern African Wildlife	£18.95
Sri Lankan Wildlife	£15.99
Wildlife and Conservation Volunteering: The Complete Guide	£13.99

Eccentric Guides

Eccentric Australia	£12.99
Eccentric Britain	£13.99
Eccentric California	£13.99
Eccentric Cambridge	£6.99
Eccentric Edinburgh	£5.95
Eccentric France	£12.95
Eccentric London	£13.99

Others

Something Different for the Weekend	£9.99
Weird World	£14.99
Your Child Abroad: A Travel Health Guide	£10.95

NOTES

174

Index

Entries in **bold** indicate main entries; those in *italics* indicate maps